CATALOGUE OF
STANDARD
ORDNANCE
ITEMS

Volume 1: Tanks, Armored Cars, Motor Carriages, Trucks and Automotive Equipment

★

By Office of the Chief of Ordnance Technical Division

WASHINGTON, D. C.

1944

LIGHT TANK M3 SERIES

LIGHT TANK, M3, standardized in July, 1940, and produced in quantity beginning in March, 1941, was supplied to our Allies, under Lend-Lease, as well as to our own Army through 1941 and 1942. Nicknamed the "General Stuart" by British troops, these tanks won high praise during the Libyan campaign, and are now considered obsolete only because of the great improvements in later vehicles.

Based on Light Tank, M2A4, but using heavier armor and incorporating other improvements, Light Tank, M3, for its day, was heavily armed and armored and provided a high standard of mechanical reliability.

Through the production period, numerous improvements were made, so that the final M3s were vastly different from the first. First models were entirely riveted, with a seven-sided turret. Later a welded, seven-sided turret was used, and still later, a rounded, welded, homogeneous turret. The final models were entirely welded.

The volute spring suspension is used, with the rear idler "trailing" on ground level, rather than "mounted" above the ground as on Light Tank, M2A4. This lengthens the ground contact of the track, thus decreasing the pressure per square inch, and gives additional support to the rear of the tank.

Power is supplied by a 7-cylinder Continental W670–9A gasoline engine. Some models of Light Tanks, M3 and M3A1, were powered by a Guiberson T1020-4 Diesel engine. A synchromesh transmission provides five forward speeds and one reverse.

The driver and assistant driver occupy seats in the hull, with vision ahead through hatches equipped with windshields. In combat areas, the armored hatch cover may be closed, whereupon vision is possible through a protectoscope, a form of periscope.

The gunner and commander-loader occupy seats in the turret, which may be traversed through 360° by a hand-operated mechanism. Entrance to the turret is through the cupola hatch, which also provides an observation post for the commander. In noncombat areas, the commander may operate with his head and

LIGHT TANK, M3, WITH SEVEN-SIDED, WELDED TURRET, RIVETED HULL

PISTOL PORT DOOR AND PROTECTOSCOPE

TOP OF ROUNDED, HOMOGENEOUS TURRET

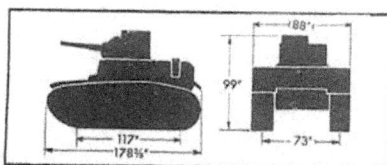

LIGHT TANK, M3, WITH ROUNDED, HOMOGENEOUS, WELDED TURRET

LIGHT TANK, M3A1, HAS POWER-TRAVERSED TURRET WITHOUT CUPOLA

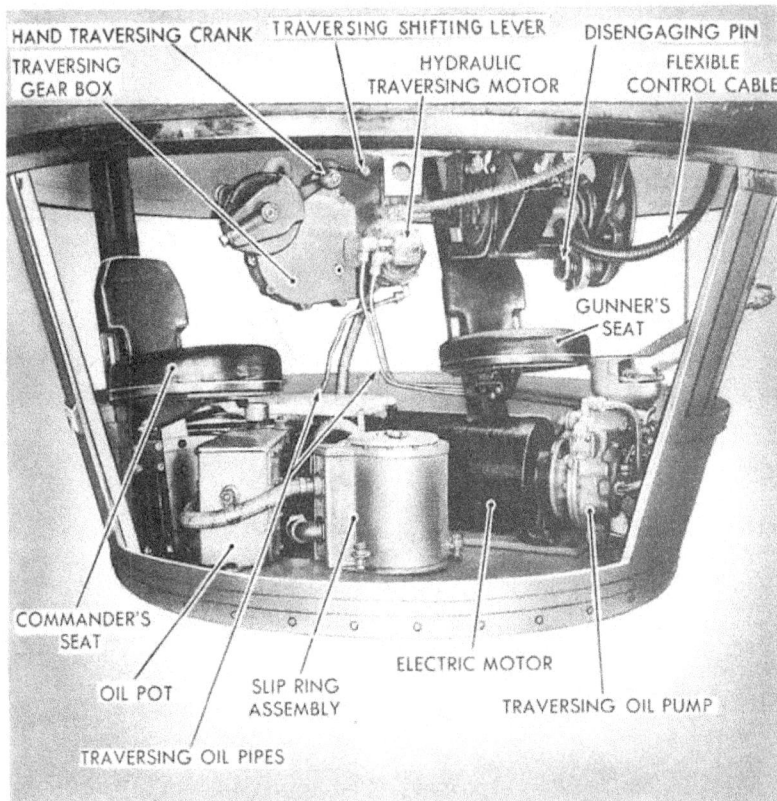

HAND TRAVERSING CRANK · TRAVERSING SHIFTING LEVER · DISENGAGING PIN
TRAVERSING GEAR BOX · HYDRAULIC TRAVERSING MOTOR · FLEXIBLE CONTROL CABLE
GUNNER'S SEAT
COMMANDER'S SEAT
OIL POT · SLIP RING ASSEMBLY · ELECTRIC MOTOR · TRAVERSING OIL PUMP
TRAVERSING OIL PIPES

LIGHT TANK, M3A1, TURRET BASKET SHOWING TRAVERSING MECHANISM

shoulders above the cupola. In danger zones, vision from the cupola is through pistol ports equipped with protectoscopes. (Early models used direct vision "peepholes" instead.)

Principal armament is a 37 mm gun, M5 or M6, mounted with a cal. .30 machine gun in a combination mount in the turret. The turret guns have elevations from $-10°$ to $+20°$. An A.P.C. projectile, fired from the 37 mm gun, has a muzzle velocity of 2,900 feet per second. It has a maximum range of 12,850 yards, and will penetrate 1.8-inch face-hardened armor plate at 1,000 yards.

Late models are provided with a gyro-stabilizer to increase the accuracy of aiming and firing the turret guns when the vehicle is in motion.

Other armament includes a cal. .30 machine gun, in the bow, one on the turret for antiaircraft use, and one in each sponson.

Normal fuel capacity of 56 gallons may be increased when necessary by the use of two 25-gallon jettison fuel tanks. These can be abandoned upon entering a combat zone. The vehicle is equipped with a two-way radio.

Light Tanks, M3 and M3 (Diesel), were declared obsolete by Ordnance Committee action in July, 1943. These and later vehicles of the Light Tank, M3, Series, were built by the American Car and Foundry Co.

REFERENCES—TM 9-726; OCM 15920, 15932, 16135, 16258, 16370, 16531, 16583, 16603, 16610, 16611, 17200, 17107, 17201, 17235, 17578, 17949, 17984, 20076, 20317, 20852, 21015.

LIGHT TANK, M3A1, was standardized in August, 1941, as a modification of Light Tank, M3. It was declared obsolete in July 1944.

The turret is similar to that used in the final version of Light Tank, M3, but omits the cupola. A fighting compartment is integrated with the turret and is rotated with it, either by a hydraulic mechanism or by hand. This compartment contains seats for the gunner and commander-loader as well as the traversing and gyro-stabilizer mechanisms and ammunition.

An improved Combination Gun Mount, M23, for the turret guns has a periscopic sight. An additional periscope, with 360° traverse, is provided in the turret roof. Other armament is the same as on Light Tank, M3, except that the sponson guns are omitted.

The vehicle is equipped with an improved radio and with an interphone

Diagram labels: 99", 90½", 117", 178⅜", 198", 73"

LIGHT TANK, M3A3, HAS IMPROVED TURRET WITH RADIO BULGE. FRONT PLATE IS STRENGTHENED AND SPONSONS ARE EXTENDED FORWARD

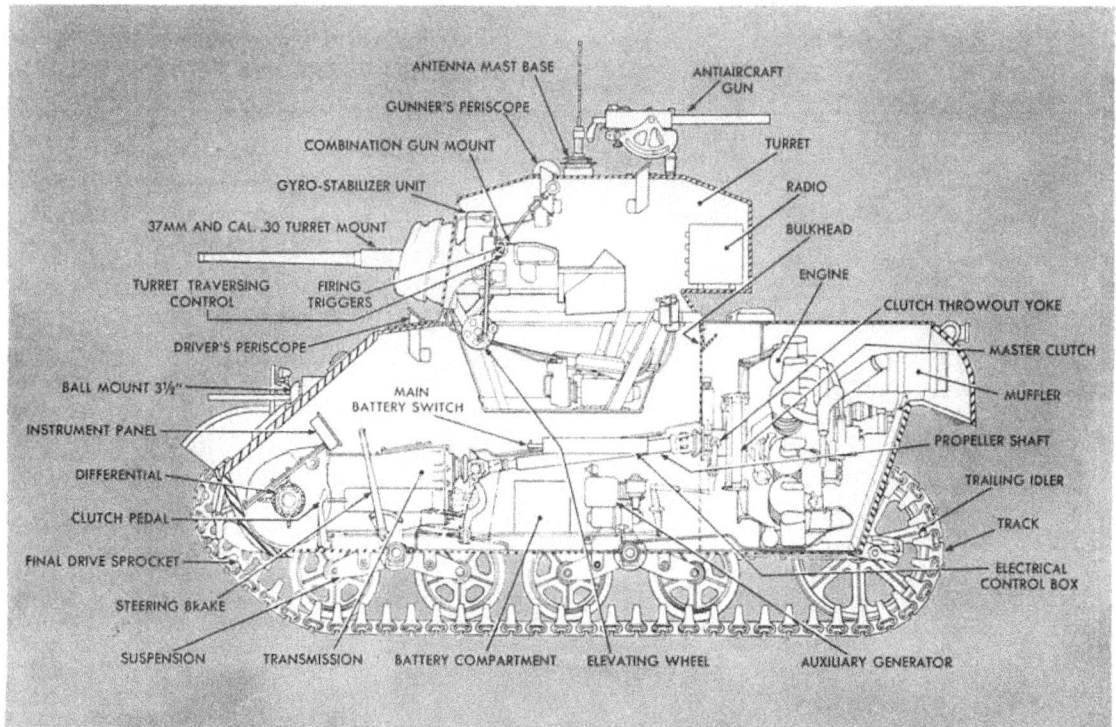

Labels: ANTENNA MAST BASE · GUNNER'S PERISCOPE · COMBINATION GUN MOUNT · GYRO-STABILIZER UNIT · 37MM AND CAL. .30 TURRET MOUNT · TURRET TRAVERSING CONTROL · FIRING TRIGGERS · DRIVER'S PERISCOPE · BALL MOUNT 3½" · INSTRUMENT PANEL · DIFFERENTIAL · CLUTCH PEDAL · FINAL DRIVE SPROCKET · STEERING BRAKE · SUSPENSION · TRANSMISSION · MAIN BATTERY SWITCH · BATTERY COMPARTMENT · ELEVATING WHEEL · AUXILIARY GENERATOR · ANTIAIRCRAFT GUN · TURRET · RADIO · BULKHEAD · ENGINE · CLUTCH THROWOUT YOKE · MASTER CLUTCH · MUFFLER · PROPELLER SHAFT · TRAILING IDLER · TRACK · ELECTRICAL CONTROL BOX

CROSS SECTION OF LIGHT TANK, M3A3, SHOWING INTERIOR ARRANGEMENT. CHARACTERISTICS ARE GIVEN ON PAGE 4

system, with connections for each crew member.

Light Tank, M3A1 (Diesel), was declared obsolete in July, 1943.

REFERENCES—TM 9-727; OCM 17235, 17330, 17578, 17680, 17906, 17952, 17984, 18639, 19396, 20076, 20317, 20852, 21015, 21037, 24120; SNL G-103, Vol. 5.

The nomenclature, Light Tank, M3A2, was authorized in March, 1942, for a tank to be similar to Light Tank, M3A1, but with a welded hull. This model was never put into production.

REFERENCES — OCM 17984, 18639, 20076.

LIGHT TANK, M3A3, was standardized in August, 1942, as a modification of Light Tank, M3A1. It was reclassified as Limited Standard in April, 1943.

An improved turret, with a radio bulge at the rear, provides greater space in the fighting compartment. The hull is welded and streamlined in design. The front plate is extended forward and reinforced, providing more space and greater safety for the driver and assistant. The drivers' hatches, formerly in the front plate, are relocated in the top plate and equipped with periscopes to provide indirect vision in combat zones. Three additional periscopes are provided in the turret.

Sponsons are lengthened to the rear of the vehicle and contain additional gasoline tanks as well as additional ammunition storage. Sand shields are provided over the suspensions. A storage box is located at the rear.

Other improvements include easier steering, improved fire protection and ventilation, relocation of battery, switch and instruments and provision of detachable head lamps and a detachable windshield and weather cover.

The redesigned Combination Gun Mount, M44, includes a telescope which may be used through all degrees of gun elevation.

REFERENCES — TM 9-726C; OCM 18639, 19119, 19182, 19396, 20076, 20153, 20317; SNL G-103, Vol. 7.

COMBINATION GUN MOUNT, M44

TYPICAL CHARACTERISTICS

LIGHT TANK, M3

Crew	4

Physical Characteristics

Weight (gross)	27,400 lb.
Length (hull)	14 ft., 10⅜ ins.
Width	7 ft., 4 ins.
Height	8 ft., 3 ins.
Turret ring diameter	46¾ ins.
Ground clearance	16½ ins.
Tread (center to center of tracks)	73 ins.
Ground contact length	117 ins.
Ground pressure	10.47 lb./sq. in.

Armor

	Actual	Basis
Hull, Front, Upper	1½ ins.	1¾ ins.
Lower	⅝-1¾ ins.	1¾-3 ins.
Sides and rear	1 in.	1 in.
Top	⅜ in.	
Bottom	⅜-½ in.	
Turret, Front	1½ ins.	1¾ ins.
Sides and rear	1¼ ins.	1¼ ins.
Top	½ in.	

Performance

Maximum speed on level	36 m.p.h.
Maximum grade ability	60%
Trench crossing ability	6 ft.
Vertical obstacle ability	24 ins.
Fording depth (slowest forward speed)	36 ins.
Turning radius	21 ft.
Fuel capacity—without jettison tanks	56 gal.
with jettison tanks	106 gal.
Maximum drawbar pull	14,800 lb.
Cruising range (approx.)	70 miles

Engine,

	Continental	Guiberson
Make		
Model	W670-9A	T1020-4
Type	Radial A.C.	Radial A.C.
Cylinders	7	9
Fuel	Gasoline (80 octane)	Diesel (50 cetane)
Max. governed speed	2,400 r.p.m.	2,200 r.p.m.

Rated hp.	250 at 2,400 r.p.m.
	220 at 2,200 r.p.m.
Max. torque	584 lb.-ft. at 1,800 r.p.m. / 580 lb.-ft. at 1,400 r.p.m.

(See additional engine characteristics on page 27)

Vision and Fire Control

Protectoscopes	2
Direct vision slots	2

Communications — Radio	SCR-245
Battery, Voltage, Total	12

Fire Protection and Decontamination

Fire Extinguisher, CO_2-10 lb. (fixed)	1
CO_2-4 lb. (hand)	1
Decontaminating Apparatus, M2, 1½ qts.	1

Transmission, Type . . . Manual shift

Gear ratios

First speed	5.37:1
Second speed	2.82:1
Third speed	1.72:1
Fourth speed	1.09:1
Fifth speed	.738:1
Reverse speed	6.19:1

Differential, Controlled, Gear Ratio . . 2.62:1

Steering Ratio . . . 1.845:1

Final Drive, Type . . . Herringbone

Gear Ratio	2.41:1
Sprocket, no. of Teeth	14
Pitch diameter	24.56

Suspension, Type . . . Volute spring

Wheel or tire size	20x6
Wheel construction	Welded

Idler, Trailing, Type . . . Ind. vol. spring

Wheel or tire size	30x6
Wheel construction	Welded

Track, Type . . . Rubber block

Width	11⅝ ins.
Pitch	5½ ins.
No. of shoes per vehicle	132 or 134

LIGHT TANK, M3A1

Characteristics same as for Light Tank, M3, except as noted:

Physical Characteristics

Weight	28,500 lb.
Height	7 ft., 6½ ins.
Ground pressure	10.56 lb./sq. in.

Vision—Protectoscopes . . . 5

Periscopes	2
Direct vision slots	2

Communications—Radio . . . SCR-508

Interphone stations . . . 4

LIGHT TANK, M3A3

Characteristics same as for Light Tank, M3A1, except as noted:

Physical Characteristics

Weight (gross) (with Track, T16)	31,752 lb.
Length (with bustle box)	16 ft., 6 ins.
Width	8 ft., 3 ins.
Height	7 ft., 6½ ins.

Fuel Capacity . . . 102 gals.

Vision and Fire Control

Periscopes	5
Protectoscopes	Omitted
Direct vision slots	Omitted
Telescope, M54	1

Armament—Light Tanks, M3, M3A1, M3A3

37 mm Gun, M5 or M6, and . . . } In Combination Mount, M22, M23 or M44, in turret
1 cal. .30 Browning machine gun . . .

1 cal. .30 Browning machine gun . . . In ball mount in bow
1 cal. .30 Browning machine gun . . . On turret, antiaircraft
2 cal. .30 Browning machine guns . . . Sponsons: on M3 only
1 Tripod Mount, cal. .30, M2
Provision for 1 cal. .45 submachine gun

Ammunition Stowage

	M3	M3A1	M3A3
37 mm (A.P.C., M51B1; A.P.C., M51B2; H.E., M63; Can., M2)	103 rds.	116 rds.	174 rds.
Cal. .30	8,270 rds.	6,400 rds.	7,500 rds.
Cal. .45	500 rds.	510 rds.	540 rds.
Grenades, Hand (Fragmentation, Mk. II, 4; Offensive, Mk. IIIA2, w/Fuze, Detonating, M6, 2; Smoke, W.P., M15, 4; Thermite, Incendiary, 2)	12	12	12

LIGHT TANKS M5 LIMITED STANDARD—M5A1 SUBSTITUTE STANDARD

LIGHT TANK, M5, WITH PISTOL PORTS AND HATCHES CLOSED; HULL AND TURRET PERISCOPES UP; GROUSERS ON SIDE OF TURRET

LIGHT TANK, M5, standardized in February, 1942, was designed as a modification of Light Tank, M3A1, to use twin Cadillac engines and Hydra-Matic transmissions, providing automatic gear shifting. It was reclassified as Limited Standard in April, 1943.

The hull is fabricated of welded, homogeneous armor plate with the reinforced front plate, extended sponsons, and streamlined effect subsequently adopted for Light Tank, M3A3. Elimination of bolts and rivets reduced the danger of having these parts driven inside the tank by the impact of projectiles on the exterior.

The welded, power-operated turret and integrated turret basket are similar to those used on Light Tank, M3A1. However, because of the lower driveshaft tunnel required by the use of the Cadillac engines and Hydra-Matic transmissions, it was possible to relocate the turret-traversing mechanism and portions of the gun stabilizer under the turret basket, thus providing more space in the fighting compartment.

The turret, of welded, curved-plate armor plate, is covered on the front by a

LEFT SIDE OF COMBINATION GUN MOUNT, INCLUDING 37 mm GUN, M6

TRAVERSING MECHANISM BENEATH TURRET BASKET

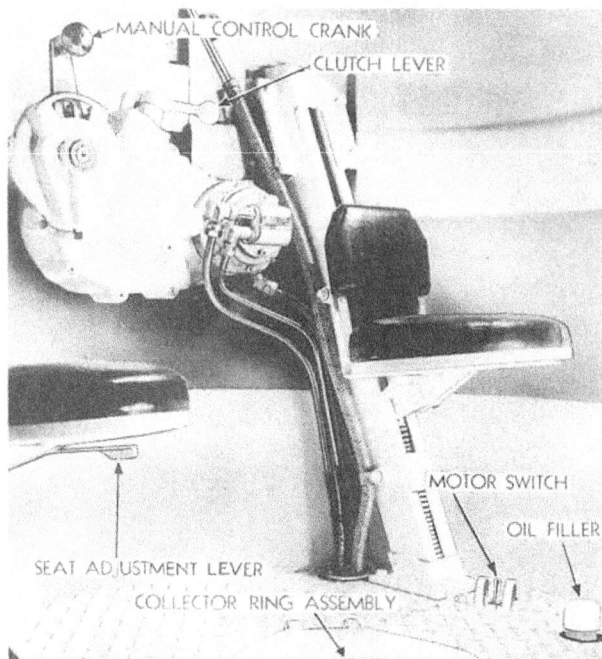

ADJUSTABLE SEATS AND CONTROLS IN TURRET BASKET

heavy armor-plate casting which serves as a base for the combination gun mount. The turret can be rotated through a traverse of 360° either by a hydraulic mechanism or by hand.

Principal armament is a 37 mm Gun, M6, mounted with a cal. .30 Browning machine gun, in the turret. Elevation is from −10° to +20°. An A.P.C. projectile, when fired from the 37 mm gun, has a muzzle velocity of 2,900 feet per second. It has a maximum range of 12,850 yards, and will penetrate 1.8 inches of face-hardened armor plate at 1,000 yards.

A gyrostabilizer is provided to keep the turret gun sufficiently close to a fixed elevation while the tank is in motion over normal terrain so that the gunner can accurately aim and fire the gun.

The two 8-cylinder, 90°, V-type, liquid-cooled Cadillac engines are located in the rear of the hull. The flywheel end of each engine is connected to a Hydra-Matic transmission. These transmissions, plus a two-speed stepdown in the transfer unit, provide six forward speeds and one reverse speed.

An auxiliary power plant consisting of a generating set powered by a single-cylinder gasoline engine supplements the engine generators for charging the battery.

Seats for the driver and assistant driver are adjustable horizontally or vertically. Seats go up under spring pressure and

down under body weight and can be locked in any position.

The vehicle is provided with dual controls and has four escape hatches, one for each member of the crew. It is equipped with 360° periscopes for the driver, assistant driver, and commander and a periscopic gun sight, as well as with three protectoscopes in the turret ports. Two knockout plugs cover ports in the front armor plate. The tank is wired for radio and for an interphone system.

REFERENCES—TM 9–732, 9–1732A; OCM 15959, 16135, 17428, 17451, 17471, 17578, 17680, 17827, 17906, 17952, 17984, 18544, 18639, 19119, 20076, 20317; SNL E–103, Vol. II.

LIGHT TANK, M5A1, was standardized in September, 1942, and replaced Light Tank, M5, in production. It was reclassified as Substitute Standard in July, 1944.

Principal change was in the use of an improved turret with a radio bulge at the rear, similar to the turret of Light Tank, M3A3. The improved turret provides more room for turret crew members and permits desirable rearrangements in stowage. A radio antenna bracket is mounted above the bulge. A removable plate in the rear of the bulge permits removal of the 37 mm gun.

The antiaircraft gun mount is improved

and repositioned to the right side of the turret. Dual traverse is incorporated, permitting the commander to traverse the turret while firing the antiaircraft gun.

Larger escape hatches, with improved positive water-sealing door latches, are provided, and there is an additional escape hatch for emergency use in the floor of the hull.

The improved Combination Gun Mount, M44, for the turret guns, incorporates a direct-sighting 3-power telescope. The breech guard permits hinging upward, facilitating travel from one seat to another by personnel. A new mount for the commander's periscope permits 360° traverse. An additional periscope in the turret facilitates rear vision for the commander.

Pistol port doors are redesigned and relocated, and equipped with locking devices. A direction finder fastened to the turret roof ahead of the commander's periscope indicates the straight ahead position. A spotlight is provided.

Sand shields, which extend down from the sponsons and cover the top portion of the track, are supplied when required.

Pilot models for Light Tanks, M5 and M5A1, were manufactured by the Cadillac Motor Car Division, General Motors Corp.

REFERENCES—TM 9–732; OCM 17471, 17827, 18639, 18925, 19182, 19396, 20153, 24175; SNL G–103, Vol. VIII.

LIGHT TANK, M5A1, SHOWING REDESIGNED TURRET WITH SHIELD FOR ANTIAIRCRAFT GUN MOUNT; SAND SHIELDS OVER SUSPENSIONS

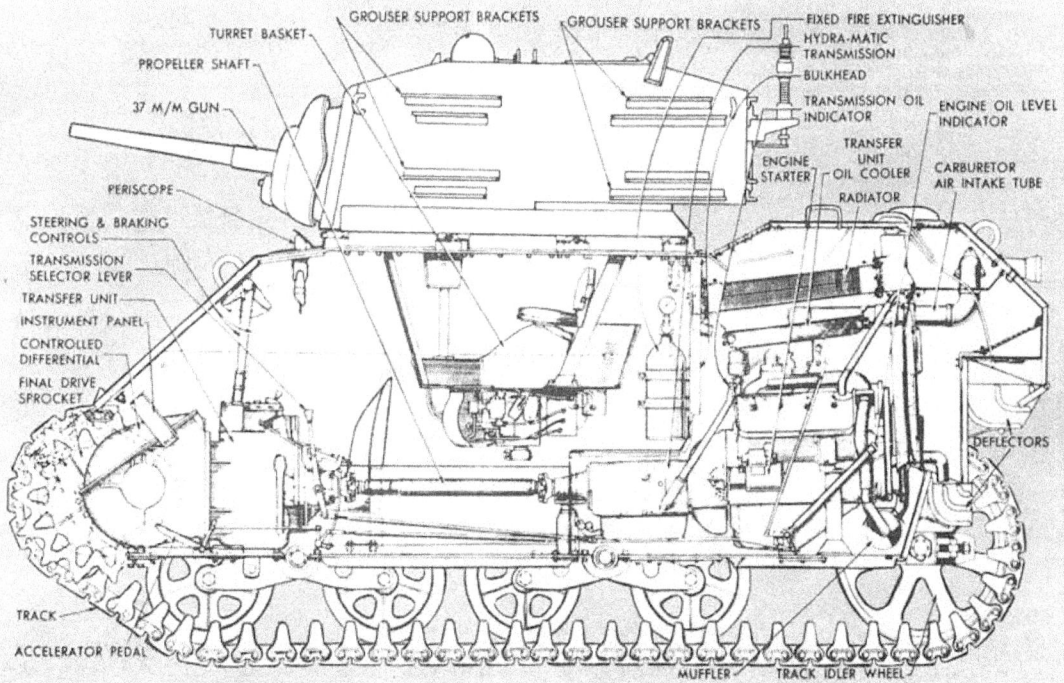

CROSS SECTION DIAGRAM OF LIGHT TANK, M5A1, SHOWING INTERIOR ARRANGEMENT. CHARACTERISTICS ARE GIVEN ON PAGE 8

LIGHT TANKS **M5, M5A1** (Continued)

LIGHT TANK, M5A1, REAR VIEW SHOWING EXTERIOR STOWAGE

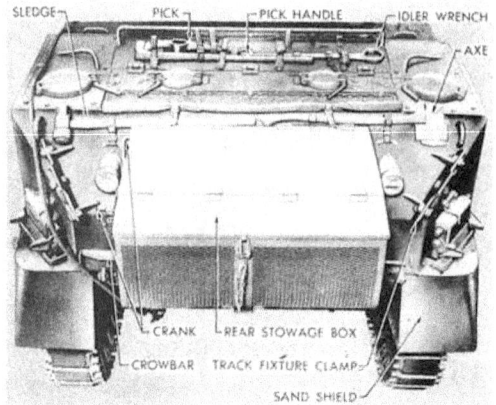

REAR VIEW SHOWING USE OF STOWAGE BOX

TYPICAL CHARACTERISTICS

LIGHT TANK, M5

Crew. 4

Physical Characteristics

Weight (gross).	33,000 lb.
Length.	14 ft., 2¾ ins.
Width.	7 ft., 4¼ ins.
Height.	7 ft., 6½ ins.
Height—to center line of bore . .	6 ft., 5⅜ ins.
Turret ring diameter.	46¾ ins.
Ground clearance.	13¾ ins.
Center of gravity—above ground	33½ ins.
rear of sprocket.	79½ ins.
Tread (center to center of tracks). .	73½ ins.
Ground contact length.	117 ins.
Ground pressure.	12.4 lb./sq. in.

Armor

	Actual	Basis
Hull, Front, Upper. . .	1⅛ ins.	2½ ins.
Lower. . . .	2–2½ ins.	2–2½ ins.
Sides and rear.	1–1⅛ ins.	1–1⅛ ins.
Top.	½ in.	
Bottom.	⅜–½ in.	
Turret, Front.	1¾ ins.	2 ins.
Sides and rear.	1¼ ins.	1¼ ins.
Top.	½ in.	

Performance

Maximum speed on level.	36 m.p.h.
Maximum grade ability.	60%
Trench crossing ability.	5 ft., 4 ins.
Vertical obstacle ability.	18 ins.
Fording depth (slowest forward speed). .	36 ins.
Fuel capacity.	89 gals.
Cruising range.	100 miles
Turning radius.	21 ft.

Vision and Fire Control

Periscopes (M6, 3; M4, 1).	4
Protectoscopes (in pistol ports).	3

Communications

Radio.	SCR–508, 528 or 538
Command tank.	SCR–506
Interphone stations.	4
Flag Set, M238.	1

Battery, Voltage. 12

Fire Protection and Decontamination

Fire Extinguisher, CO₂–10 lb. (fixed). . . .	1
CO₂–4 lb. (hand).	1
Decontaminating Apparatus, M2, 1½ qts. .	1

Engine, Make and Model. . . Cadillac, Series 42
Type.	Dual, V–8, L.C.
No. of cylinders.	16
Displacement.	346 cu. ins.
Fuel (gasoline).	70 and 80 octane
Max. governed speed.	4,000 r.p.m.
Net h.p..	220 at 4,000 r.p.m.
Max. torque.	488 lb.-ft. at 1,200 r.p.m.*

(Additional engine characteristics on page 27)

Transmission, Type. . . . . Hydra-Matic
Gear ratios
First speed.	3.26:1
Second speed.	2.26:1
Third speed.	1.44:1
Fourth speed.	1.00:1
Reverse.	3.81:1

Transfer Case, Type. . . . . Hydraulic
No. of speeds.	2
Gear ratios.	2.37:1; 1.00:1

Differential, Controlled, Gear Ratio. . 2.62:1
Steering ratio. 1.845:1

Final Drive, Type. . . . . Herringbone
Sprocket, No. of teeth.	13
Pitch diameter.	22.8
Gear ratio.	2.57:1

Suspension, Type . . . . . Vertical volute spring
Wheel or tire size. . . . . 20x6 ins.

No. of wheels per vehicle.	8
Wheel construction Rubber tired, spoked or disk
Idler, Type.	Trailing
Wheel or tire size.	30x6 ins.
Track, Type.	T16, T55E1, or T36E6
Width.	11⅝ ins.
Pitch.	5½ ins.
No. of shoes per vehicle.	132

*Transmission output in direct drive.

LIGHT TANK, M5A1

Characteristics same as for Light Tank, M5, except as noted.

Physical Characteristics

Weight (gross) (with T16 tracks). . .	33,907 lb.
Length—over stowage box. .	15 ft., 10½ ins.
Width—with sand shields.	90 ins.
Height—over gun mount. . . .	7 ft., 10½ ins.
Ground clearance.	13¾ ins.
Ground pressure.	12.5 lb./sq. in.

Vision and Fire Control

Periscope, M4, w/Telescope, M40,
or Periscope, M4A1, with Telescope,
M40, and Instrument Light, M30. 1
Periscopes, M6.	4
Protectoscopes.	Omitted
Telescope, M70D, with Instrument Light, M39C.	1

Armament—Light Tanks, M5 and M5A1

1 37 mm Gun, M6, and. . . . . } In Combination Mount, M23, in turret
1 cal. .30 Browning Machine Gun, M1919A5 (fixed). . . . . } (Mount, M44, in Light Tank, M5A1)
1 cal. .30 Browning Machine Gun, M1919A4 (flexible). . . . . In bow
1 cal. .30 Browning Machine Gun, M1919A4 (flexible). . . . . On turret, antiaircraft
1 Tripod Mount, cal. .30, M2
Provision for:
1 cal. .45 submachine gun. . . . . Equipment of crew

Ammunition, Stowage

	M5	M5A1
37 mm (A.P.C., M51B1; A.P.C., M51B2; H.E., M63; Can., M2).	123 rounds	147 rounds
Cal. .30.	6,250 rounds	6,500 rounds
Cal. .45.	420 rounds	540 rounds
Grenades, Hand (Fragmentation, Mk. II, 4; Offensive, Mk. III (w/Fuze, M6), 2; Smoke, H.C., M8, 4; Thermite, Incendiary, 2). .	12	12

LIGHT TANK M22—LIMITED STANDARD

LIGHT TANK, M22, IS BUILT SMALL AND LIGHT TO PERMIT CARRYING BY AIRPLANE. NOTE BRACKETS AT SIDES

Light Tank, M22, is designed to provide light tank firepower in a vehicle light enough to be carried by airplane. It weighs approximately 16,000 pounds, completely stowed and with a crew of three, or approximately half the weight of Light Tank, M5A1. Size and silhouette also are much less. To achieve the weight saving, armor thickness was reduced and all but the most essential stowage was eliminated.

Four brackets, located above and to the rear of the bogie suspension are provided for attaching the vehicle to an airplane. The fighting compartment and turret are readily removable for transport purposes.

Armament consists of one 37 mm Gun, M6, and one cal. .30 machine gun mounted in a Combination Gun Mount, M53, in the turret. The guns can be elevated from −10° to +30°, and can be traversed 360° in the hand-operated turret. The A.P.C. projectile fired from the 37 mm gun has a muzzle velocity of 2,900 feet per second. It has a range at 30° elevation of 12,000 yards and will penetrate 1.8-in. of 20° obliquity face-hardened armor plate at 1,000 yards.

Provision is made for carrying a cal. .45 submachine gun.

Because of weight limitations, no power traverse or gyrostabilizer are provided. Maximum armor thickness is 1 inch. The crew consists of the commander-loader and gunner, seated in the turret,

LIGHT TANK, M22, WITHOUT TURRET, SUSPENDED BENEATH AIRPLANE

LIGHT TANK, M22, TURRET BASKET WITH TURRET REMOVED

and the driver, seated in the hull. There is no assistant driver.

A volute spring suspension with a trailing idler is used. Tracks are of steel.

Power is supplied by a 6-cylinder, horizontally opposed, air-cooled Lycoming O-435-T gasoline aircraft engine located at the right rear. The power train, located at the front of the vehicle, consists of a fixed-ratio transfer case, a 4-speed transmission, and controlled differential.

The vehicle has a fuel capacity of 55 gallons and a cruising range of approximately 135 miles.

The driver's hatch in the front plate can be fastened upward for direct vision in non-combat zones. A detachable windshield with weather cover is provided. There are two hatches in the turret and an emergency escape hatch in the floor of the hull.

The tank is equipped with a two-way radio and an interphone system. It has three periscopes for vision and a gunner's periscope.

Development of Light Tank, T9, was approved by Ordnance Committee action in May, 1941. Action in May, 1941, authorized limited procurement of Light Tank, T9E1, which has an improved front hull and improved turret. In September, 1944, the vehicle was redesignated Light Tank, M22, and reclassified as Limited Standard.

REFERENCES — OCM 16747, 17087, 17953, 19545, 19726, 20680, 21002, 23958, 24935, 25333; SNL G-148.

TYPICAL CHARACTERISTICS

Crew 3

Physical Characteristics
Weight (gross w/o crew) . . . . 16,000 lb.
Length . . . . 12 ft., 11 in.
Width . . . . 7 ft., 3¾ in.
Height . . . . 5 ft., 8½ in.
Turret ring diameter . . . . 47½ in.
Ground clearance . . . . 10 in.
Tread (center to center of tracks) . 70½ in.
Ground contact length . . . . 104 in.
Ground pressure at 0 penetration . 7.03 lb./sq. in.

Armament
1 37 mm Gun, M6, and
1 cal. .30 Machine Gun, M1919A4 (flexible)
    In Combination Mount, M53, in turret
    Elevation . . . . −10° to +30°
    Traverse . . . . 360°
1 Tripod Mount, cal. .30, M2
Provision for:
    3 cal. .45 Submachine Guns, M3, or
    1 cal. .30 Carbine and
    2 Submachine Guns, M3

Ammunition, Stowage
37 mm (A.P.C., M51B1 or M51B2;
    A.P., M74; H.E., M63;
    and Can., M2) . . . . 50 rounds
Cal. .30 (in belts and boxes) . . 2,500 rounds*
*2,250 rounds in command tank.

Cal. .45 . . . . 450 rounds
Grenades, Hand (Fragmentation, Mk. II,
    4; Smoke, M8, 4; Thermite, Incendiary,
    2; Offensive, Mk. III, 2) 12

Armor	Actual	Basis
Hull, Front, Upper		1 in.
Lower		1 in.
Sides, Upper		¾ in.
Lower		½ in.
Rear		½ in.
Top	⅜ in.	
Bottom	½ in.	
Turret, Front		1 in.
Sides		1 in.
Rear	¾ in.	1 in.
Top	¾ in.	

Performance
Maximum speed on level . . . . 35 m.p.h.
Maximum grade ability 50%
Trench crossing ability . . . . . . 5 ft., 5 in.
Vertical obstacle ability . . . . 16 in.
Fording depth . . . . 36 in.
Fuel capacity . . . . 55 gal.
Cruising range . . . . 110 miles
Turning radius . . . . 20 ft.

Vision and Fire Control
Direct vision for driver
Periscopes, M6 3

Periscope, M8 or M8A1
    (w/Telescope, M46) 1

Communications
Radio SCR-510
Interphone stations 3
Flag Set, M238 1

Battery, Voltage, total 12

Fire Protection and Decontamination
Fire Extinguisher, CO₂–10 lb. (fixed) 1
    CO₂–4 lb. (hand) 1
Decontaminating Apparatus, M2, 1½ qts. . . 1

Engine, Make and Model . . Lycoming O-435-T
Type . . . . Opposed, A.C.
Number of cylinders 6
Fuel (gasoline) . . . . 80 octane
Maximum governed speed . . . . . 2,800 r.p.m.
Net hp. . . . . 162 at 2,800 r.p.m.
Maximum torque . . 332 lb.-ft. at 2,100 r.p.m.
(See additional characteristics on page 27.)

Transmission, Type . . . . Manual shift
Gear ratios
    First speed 1.857:1
    Second speed 1:1
    Third speed 463:1
    Fourth speed 304:1
    Reverse 1.666:1

Transfer Case, Type . . . . 3-gear, Fixed ratio
Gear ratio 2:1

Differential, Controlled, Gear ratio . . . 3.05:1
Steering ratio 2:1

Final Drive, Type . . . . Spur gear
Sprocket, Number of teeth 22
Pitch diameter 21:08
Gear ratio 2.23:1

Suspension, Type . . . . . . Vertical volute spring
Wheel or tire size 15x6

Idler, Trailing, Type . . . . Volute spring
Wheel or tire size 28x6

Track, Type . . . . T78, Steel
Width . . . . 11¼ in.
Pitch . . . . 3 in.
Number of shoes per vehicle 212

Brakes, Type . . . . Mechanical

OVERHEAD VIEW SHOWING ENTRANCE HATCHES AND COMBINATION GUN MOUNT

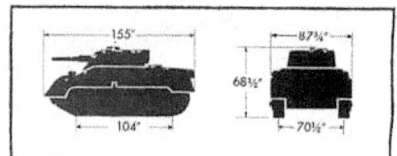

LIGHT TANK M24—STANDARD

LIGHT TANK, M24, HAS LOW SILHOUETTE AND TORSION BAR SUSPENSION. IT MOUNTS 75 MM AIRCRAFT GUN IN TURRET

TYPICAL CHARACTERISTICS

Crew 4

Physical Characteristics
Weight (gross, approx.) . . . . .38,750 lb.
Length—hull . . . . .16 ft., 3 ins.
  overall, with armament . . . . 18 ft.
Width . . . . .9 ft., 4 ins.
Height—top of cupola . . . . .8 ft., 1 in.
  top of A.A. mount . . . . .8 ft., 4 ins.
Turret ring diameter (inside) . . . . .60 ins.
Ground clearance . . . . .17 ins.
Tread (center to center of tracks) . . . .96 ins.
Ground contact length . . . . .112 ins.
Ground pressure . . . . .10.7 lb./sq. in.

Armament
1 75 mm Gun, M6, and
1 cal. .30 Machine Gun, M1919A4 (flexible)
  In Combination Gun Mount, M64, in turret
  Elevation . . . . −10° to +15°
  Traverse .360°
1 cal. .50 Machine Gun, M2, HB
  (flexible) . . . . .On turret, antiaircraft
1 cal. .30 Machine Gun, M1919A4
  (flexible) . . . . .In bow mount
1 2-Inch Mortar, M3 . . . . .In turret
1 cal. .30 Tripod Mount, M2
Provision for:
4 cal. .45 Submachine Guns, M3, or
3 cal. .45 Submachine Guns, M3, and
1 cal. .30 Carbine, M1, with Grenade
  Launcher, M8

Ammunition, Stowage
75 mm . . . . .48 rounds
Cal. .50 .440 rounds
Cal. .30 . . . . .3,750 rounds
Cal. .45 . . . . .720 rounds
2-Inch Smoke Bombs, Mk. I/L (British) 14 rounds
Grenades (Smoke, 2; Fragmentation, 6) 8

Armor

	Actual	Basis
Hull, Front, Upper	1 in.	2½ ins.
Lower	1 in.	1½ ins.
Sides, Forward	1 in.	1 in.
Rear	¾ in.	¾ in.
Rear, Upper	¾ in.	¾ in.
Lower	¾ in.	1¼ ins.

Top	½ in.	
Bottom (first 36 ins.)	½ in.	
(remainder)	⅜ in.	
Turret, Front and sides	1 in.	1¼ ins.
Rear	1 in.	1 in.
Roof	½ in.	
Gun shield, Upper	1½ ins.	2 ins.
Lower	1½ ins.	2¼ ins.

Performance
Maximum speed on level . . . . .35 m.p.h.
  3% grade . . . . .17 m.p.h.
  10% grade . . . . .11 m.p.h.
Maximum grade ability 60%
Trench crossing ability . . . . .6½ ft.
Vertical obstacle ability . . . . .36 ins.
Fording depth (slowest forward speed) . .40 ins.
Turning radius . . . . .40 ft.
Fuel capacity . . . . .110 gals.
Cruising range (approx.) Highway . .175 miles
  Cross country . . . . .100 miles
Maximum drawbar pull . . . . .22,000 lb.

Vision and Fire Control
Periscope, M6 3
Telescope, M71G, with Instrument Light,
  M33 (or Telescope, M70N, with Instru-
  ment Light, M39C) in Telescope Mount,
  M65, with Headrest 1
Periscope, M10C, in Periscope Mount, M66
  (or Periscope, M4A1) 2
Azimuth Indicator, M21 1
Elevation Quadrant, M9, with Instrument
  Light, M30 1
Gunner's Quadrant, M1 1
Vision Blocks (in cupola) 6

Communications
Radio . .SCR–508, 528, 538, or British No. 19
  Command tank SCR–506
Interphone stations 5
Flag Set, M238 .1

Battery, Voltage, total 24

Fire Protection and Decontamination
Fire Extinguisher, CO₂–10 lb. (fixed) 1
  CO₂–4 lb. (hand) 1
Decontaminating Apparatus, M2, 1½ qts. . . .2

Engine, Make and Model . .Cadillac, Series 42
Type . . . . .Dual, V–8, L.C.
No. of cylinders 16
Fuel (gasoline) . . . . .80 octane
Max. governed speed . . . . .4,000 r.p.m.
Net hp. . . . . .220 at 3,400 r.p.m.
Max. torque . . . . . . .488 lb.-ft. at 1,200 r.p.m.
(Additional engine characteristics on page 27.)

Transmission, Type . .Hydra-Matic, with transfer
                  unit and synchronizer
Gear ratios (with transfer unit)
  Forward—First speed 9.19:1
    Second speed 5.96:1
    Third speed 3.62:1
    Fourth speed 2.34:1
    Fifth speed 4.05:1
    Sixth speed 2.62:1
    Seventh speed 1.59:1
    Eighth speed 1.03:1
  Reverse—First speed 9.57:1
    Second speed 6.17:1
    Third speed 3.78:1
    Fourth speed 2.44:1

Transfer Case, Type . . . . .Synchromesh
Gear ratios—Forward 2.34:1; 1.03:1
  Reverse 2.44:1

Differential, Controlled, Gear ratio . . .2.625:1
Steering ratio 1.55:1

Final Drive, Type . . . . .Herringbone
Gear ratio 2.571:1
Sprocket, No. of teeth 13
Pitch diameter 23.108

Suspension, Type . . . . .Torsion bar
No. of wheels . . . . .10, dual
Wheel or tire size 25½x4½
Wheel construction . . . . .Stamped disk

Idler, Type .Fixed
Wheel or tire size . . . . . . .22½x4½, dual
Wheel construction . . . . .Stamped disk

Track, Type . . . . .Steel block, single pin,
           rubber bushed, with center guide
Width . . . . .16 ins.
Pitch . . . . .5½ ins.
No. of shoes per vehicle 150

Light Tank, M24, was designed to provide an improved light tank mounting a 75 mm gun, and having increased flotation and mobility and greater accessibility of all components. It was standardized in July, 1944.

The crew consists of four men.

Principal armament consists of a 75 mm Gun, M6, in a concentric recoil mechanism, mounted with a cal. .30 machine gun in Combination Gun Mount, M64. A gyrostabilizer is provided. The combination mount has an elevation from −10° to +15°, and can be traversed 360° in the power-operated turret.

A cal. .50 machine gun is pintle mounted at the rear of the turret for antiaircraft protection. A cal. .30 machine gun is in the bow, and a 2-inch mortar in the right front turret. Provision is made for carrying four cal. .45 submachine guns.

There is no turret basket. Seats for the turret crew members are suspended from the base ring. The 75 mm ammunition is stowed on the floor of the vehicle in water-protected containers.

Power is supplied by two 8-cylinder, 90°, V-type, liquid-cooled Cadillac engines, through two Hydra-Matic transmissions. Right and left engines are interchangeable. A manual shift transfer unit with two speeds forward and one reverse is incorporated in the gear train used to couple the two engines together.

A controlled differential for steering and braking is located in the front of the hull.

A synchronizer incorporated in the transfer unit permits a speedy shift from the low to high range or vice versa, and allows a total of eight speeds forward with an overlap of third and fourth speeds in the low range with the first and second speeds in the high range. In addition, four speeds can be obtained in reverse, making possible reverse speeds up to 18 miles per hour.

As compared with Light Tank, M5A1, the vehicle has a 22% increase in overall low gear ratio, with correspondingly increased grade ability and pulling capacity.

An individually sprung, compensated torsion bar suspension, together with a single pin, rubber-bushed, center guide track, 16 inches wide, provides better riding qualities, a more stable gun platform, and reduced ground pressures, allowing better cross-country mobility than could be obtained with Light Tank, M5A1.

Radiators are of larger capacity, and are so placed that they can be readily cleaned from openings in the fighting compartment bulkhead. Fans are directly in the rear of the radiators.

Doors for the driver and assistant driver are larger and can be opened and closed without interference irrespective of turret position. The turret doors are also larger. An escape hatch is provided in the floor of the hull.

Wherever possible, unit assemblies have been made so that they can be easily removed and rapidly replaced in the field. Interchangeability of components and assemblies has been applied throughout the design.

Three periscopes for vision, a commander's vision block cupola, a sighting periscope, and other sighting equipment are provided. The vehicle is equipped with a two-way radio and an interphone system. A quick release pintle of 69,000 pounds capacity is provided.

Development of this vehicle as Light Tank, T24, was authorized by Ordnance Committee action in March, 1943. Limited Procurement of the vehicles was authorized in September, 1943.

The pilot vehicle was manufactured by the Cadillac Motor Car Division, General Motors Corporation.

REFERENCES—TM 9-729; OCM 19674, 20078, 20316, 21038, 21446, 21699, 22642, 22870, 23446, 24175, 24395, 25324.

LIGHT TANK, M24, LEFT REAR VIEW, WITH CAL. .50 GUN ON TURRET

ENTRANCE HATCHES ARE LARGER THAN ON EARLIER LIGHT TANKS

MEDIUM TANK M3 SERIES

These were the first American medium tanks produced in quantity under the defense program prior to the entry of the United States into World War II. Supplied to the British and Russians as Lend-Lease materiel, they compared favorably with other medium tanks at that time.

They were the first of our tanks to employ 75-mm guns, gyrostabilizers, and power-traversed turrets with integral fighting compartments. Their armor was thicker than that of our earlier tanks.

Battle experience in Africa and Russia suggested improvements, some of which were introduced as production continued. Most of the improvements, however, were incorporated in the design of Medium Tank M4. When the latter was standardized in October 1941, tanks of the M3 series were designated Substitute Standard. In April 1943 they were reclassified as Limited Standard, and in April 1944 they were declared obsolete.

MEDIUM TANK M3—This was the original vehicle of the series. It had a riveted hull and was powered by a Continental (Wright) R-975-EC2 or R-975-C1 gasoline engine.

MEDIUM TANK M3A1—This was similar to Medium Tank M3 but had a cast hull.

MEDIUM TANK M3A2—This was similar to Medium Tank M3 but had a welded hull.

MEDIUM TANK M3A3—This was similar to Medium Tank M3A2, with a welded hull, but was powered by twin General Motors 6-71 Diesel engines.

MEDIUM TANK M3A4—This was similar to Medium Tank M3, with a riveted hull, but was powered by a Chrysler multibank engine.

MEDIUM TANK M3A5—This was similar to Medium Tank M3, with a riveted hull, but was powered by twin General Motors 6-71 Diesel engines.

Principal armament was a 75-mm Gun M3, in a rotor mount in the right front of the crew compartment. This gun had an elevation from $-9°$ to $+20°$ and could be traversed 15° in each direction. The gun could be fired manually or electrically. The A.P.C. projectile M61, fired from this gun with a muzzle velocity of 1,920 feet per second, has a maximum range of 13,090 yards and will penetrate 2.9 inches of face-hardened armor plate at 1,000 yards.

A 37-mm Gun M6 and a Cal. .30 Machine Gun M1919A4 were mounted in a Combination Gun Mount M24, in the turret, which had a traverse of 360°. The turret guns were fired electrically and had elevations from $-7°$ to $+60°$. The

MEDIUM TANK M3 HAD RIVETED HULL AND CAST TURRET WITH 360° TRAVERSE

MEDIUM TANK M3A1 HAD CAST HULL AND CAST TURRET, GIVING STREAMLINED EFFECT

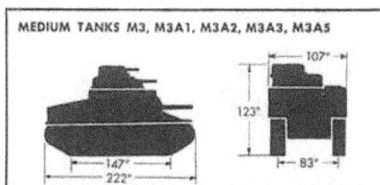

MEDIUM TANKS M3, M3A1, M3A2, M3A3, M3A5

107"
123"
147"
222"
83"

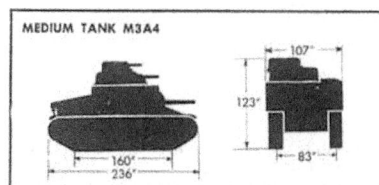

MEDIUM TANK M3A4

107"
123"
160"
236"
83"

A. P. C. projectile, fired from the 37-mm gun with a muzzle velocity of 2,900 feet per second, has a maximum range of 12,850 yards and will penetrate 1.8 inches of face-hardened armor plate at 1,000 yards.

A cal. .30 machine gun for antiaircraft use was mounted on the cupola, and two cal. .30 machine guns were in the bow. Provision was made for carrying one cal. .45 submachine gun.

The turret and integrated fighting compartment could be traversed by a hydraulic mechanism or by hand. The cupola normally rotated with the turret but could be rotated by hand.

The crew consisted of six men. The driver and radio operator occupied seats forward in the hull. The 75-mm gunner sat on the left side of the gun mount. The 37-mm gunner and gun loader and the commander were seated in the turret.

Both the 75-mm gun and the 37-mm gun were provided with gyrostabilizers, which aided in keeping the guns aimed at their targets while the tank was in motion.

Periscopic sights were provided for the 75-mm and 37-mm guns. The driver's door and the pistol port doors were provided with protectoscopes for indirect vision.

The armor of the front upper section, cupola, and turret sides was 2 inches thick, and that on the sides of the hull and the front lower section was 1½ inches thick.

The tank was wired for radio installation and for an interphone system.

An auxiliary generating set provided additional electric power when required.

The vehicle had five forward speeds and one reverse.

REFERENCES—TM 9-750; OCM 16052, 16111, 16258, 16610, 16728, 16935, 16699, 16911, 16860, 17090, 17159, 17293, 17201, 17301, 17316, 17503, 17440, 17503, 17578, 17591, 17613, 17677, 17722, 17723, 17799, 17800, 17906, 23185, 23495; SNL G-104, Vols. 1, 3, 5, 10, 12.

TYPICAL CHARACTERISTICS

	M3 (riveted)	M3A1 (cast)	M3A2 (welded)	M3A3 (welded)	M3A4 (riveted)	M3A5 (riveted)
Crew	6	6	6	6	6	6
Physical Characteristics						
Weight (gross)	60,000 lb.	60,000 lb.	60,000 lb.	63,000 lb.	64,000 lb.	64,000 lb.
Length	18 ft., 6 in.	18 ft., 6 in.	18 ft., 6 in.	18 ft., 6 in.	19 ft., 8 in.	18 ft., 6 in.
Width	8 ft., 11 in.	8 ft., 11 in.	8 ft., 11 in.	8 ft., 11 in.	8 ft., 11 in.	8 ft., 11 in.
Height	10 ft., 3 in.	10 ft., 3 in.	10 ft., 3 in.	10 ft., 3 in.	10 ft., 3 in.	10 ft., 3 in.
Turret ring diameter (inside)	57 in.	57 in.	57 in.	57 in.	57 in.	57 in.
Ground clearance	17⅛ in.	17⅛ in.	17⅛ in.	17⅛ in.	17⅛ in.	17⅛ in.
Tread (center to center of track)	83 in.	83 in.	83 in.	83 in.	83 in.	83 in.
Ground contact length at 0 penetration	147 in.	147 in.	147 in.	147 in.	160 in.	147 in.
Ground pressure per sq. in.	13.36 lb.	13.36 lb.	13.36 lb.	13.36 lb.	12.9 lb.	13.36 lb.
Performance						
Maximum speed	26 m.p.h.	26 m.p.h.	26 m.p.h.	29 m.p.h.	26 m.p.h.	29 m.p.h.
Maximum grade ability	60%	60%	60%	60%	60%	60%
Trench crossing ability	6.2 ft.	6.2 ft.	6.2 ft.	6.2 ft.	6.2 ft.	6.2 ft.
Vertical obstacle ability	24 in.	24 in.	24 in.	24 in.	24 in.	24 in.
Fording depth (slowest forward speed)	40 in.	40 in.	40 in.	36 in.	40 in.	40 in.
Fuel capacity	175 gal.	175 gal.	175 gal.	150 gal.	160 gal.	175 gal.
Cruising range	120 miles	120 miles	120 miles	160 miles	120 miles	160 miles
Turning radius	37 ft.	37 ft.	37 ft.	37 ft.	39 ft.	37 ft.
Engine, Make	Continental	Continental	Continental	G.M. 6-71	Chrysler	G.M. 6-71
Model	R-975-EC2 or C1	R-975-EC2 or C1	R-975-EC2 or C1	6046	A-57	6046
Type	Radial A.C.	Radial A.C.	Radial A.C.	Twin, In-Line, L.C.	Multibank, L.C.	Twin, In-Line, L.C.
No. of cylinders	9	9	9	12	30	12
Fuel, Octane or cetane	92 or 80	92 or 80	92 or 80	50	80	50
Type	Gasoline	Gasoline	Gasoline	Diesel	Gasoline	Diesel
Max. governed speed	2,400 r.p.m.	2,400 r.p.m.	2,400 r.p.m.	2,100 r.p.m.	2,400 r.p.m.	2,100 r.p.m.
Net hp. at r.p.m.	340 at 2,400	340 at 2,400	340 at 2,400	375 at 2,100	370 at 2,400	375 at 2,100
Max. torque, lb.-ft. at r.p.m.	800 at 1,800	800 at 1,800	800 at 1,800	1,000 at 1,400	1,020 at 1,200	1,000 at 1,400

(See additional engine characteristics on page 28.)

Armament
1 75-mm Gun M2 or M3 . . . . . . In Mount M1
1 37-mm Gun M5 or M6 and ⎫ In Combination
1 Cal. .30 Browning Machine ⎬ Mount M24
Gun M1919A4 (flexible) ⎭ in turret
1 Cal. .30 Browning Machine Gun M1919A4 (flexible) . On cupola, antiaircraft
1 Cal. .30 Browning Machine Gun M1919A4 . . . . . . In bow
Provision for:
1 Cal. .45 submachine gun . Equipment of crew

Ammunition, Stowage
75-mm . . . . 46 rounds
37-mm . . . . 178 rounds
Cal. .45 . . . . 1,200 rounds
Cal. .30 . . . . 9,200 rounds
Hand Grenades 12

Armor	Actual	Basis
Hull, Front, Upper	2 in.	4⅜ in.
Lower	1½ in.	2¾ in.
Sides	1½ in.	1½ in.
Rear	1½ in.	1⅝ in.
Top	½ in.	
Bottom	½ in.–1 in.	
Turret, Front	2¼ in.	6½ in.
Sides and rear	2¼ in.	2 in.
Top	⅞ in.	

Vision and Fire Control
Periscope M1 1
Periscope M3 1
Protectoscopes 7

Communications
Radio (with interphone) SCR-508
Command tank SCR-506

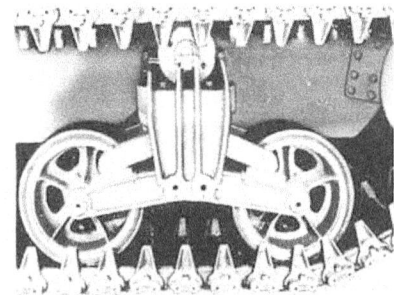

DETAIL OF SUSPENSION BOGIE AND TRACKS

Battery, Voltage, total 24

Fire Protection
Fire Extinguisher, CO₂-10 lb. (fixed) 2
CO₂-4 lb. (hand) 2

Transmission, Type . . . . Synchromesh
Gear ratios
First speed 7.56:1
Second speed 3.11:1
Third speed 1.78:1
Fourth speed 1.11:1
Fifth speed 0.73:1
Reverse 5.65:1

Differential, Controlled, Gear ratio 3.53:1
Steering ratio 1.515:1

Final Drive, Type . . . . Herringbone
Gear ratio 2.84:1
Sprocket, No. of teeth 13
Pitch diameter 25.038

Suspension, Type . . . . Volute spring
Wheel or tire size 20x9

Idler, Type . . . . Adjustable eccentric
Wheel or tire size 22x9

Track, Type . . . . Rubber block
Width . . . . 16⁹⁄₁₆ in.
Pitch . . . . 6 in.
No. of shoes per tank . . 158 (166 on M3A4)

MEDIUM TANK, M3A3, HAS WELDED HULL, CAST TURRET. M3 SERIES MEDIUM TANKS MOUNT 75 mm GUN IN RIGHT ROTOR, 37 mm GUN IN TURRET

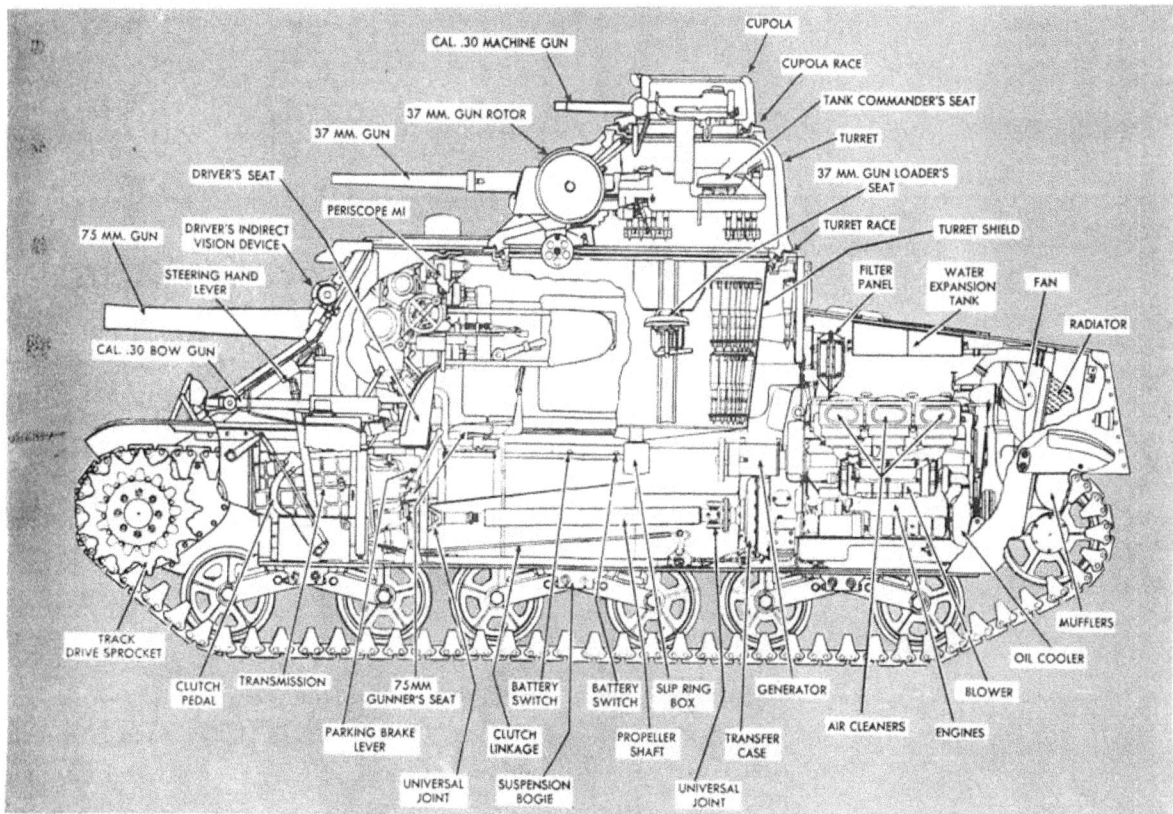

DIAGRAM OF MEDIUM TANK, M3A3, SHOWING INTERIOR ARRANGEMENT. ARRANGEMENT OF OTHER M3 SERIES MEDIUM TANKS IS GENERALLY SIMILAR

MEDIUM TANK M4* SERIES—STANDARD

MEDIUM TANK, M4, WITH WELDED HULL AND SAND SHIELDS. 75 MM AND CAL. .30 GUNS ARE IN COMBINATION GUN MOUNT, M34A1

These medium tanks, nicknamed "General Shermans" by British troops, have played an important part in Allied victories in Africa, Sicily and Russia ever since they first helped rout Marshal Rommel's troops at El Alamein.

Standardized in October, 1941, they introduced a number of improvements over the Medium Tank, M3, Series, which they replaced in production.

The 75 mm gun was relocated in the turret, providing 360° traverse and greater elevation and depression than was possible in Medium Tank, M3. The silhouette was lowered by the elimination of the cupola, thus making the tank a less conspicuous target and also resulting in a lowered center of gravity, making the tank more stable. The 37 mm gun was eliminated. The crew was decreased to five, including an assistant driver.

The 75 mm gun breech was turned 90° from the vertical, allowing for easy right-hand loading. The radio was relocated in a turret "bulge." Greater comfort and safety were provided for all crew members.

Produced simultaneously by different manufacturers, the various models differ from each other principally in their engines. A further difference is that the M4A1 has a cast hull, whereas the others have welded hulls. In addition, the M4A5, produced in Canada, embodies differences requested by the Canadian government. All have cast turrets.

Principal armament (except for the M4A5) is a 75 mm Gun, M3, mounted with a cal. .30 machine gun in a combination gun mount in the turret. The turret guns may be elevated from −10° to +25°. They are fired electrically by means of foot and hand switches. A gyro-stabilizer is provided.

An A.P.C. projectile, fired from the 75 mm gun, has a muzzle velocity of 2,030 feet per second, and will penetrate 3.1 inches of face-hardened armor plate at 1,000 yards.

Other armament includes a cal. .30 machine gun in the bow, operated by the assistant driver; a cal. .50 machine gun, mounted at the top of the turret, operated by the commander for antiaircraft use, and a 2-inch smoke mortar. A clip is

OVERHEAD VIEW OF MEDIUM TANK, M4A1, SHOWING ENTRANCE HATCHES

*See also Medium Tanks, M4 (105 mm), and M4A3 (105 mm), page 21, and Medium Tanks, M4 (76 mm), Series, page 22.

mounted in the turret to carry a cal. .45 submachine gun, which can be used through the pistol port in the side of the turret.

The turret is a one-piece casting of armor which rotates on a ball bearing race recessed and protected against direct hits and lead splash from enemy fire. The turret basket is rigidly fastened to the turret by means of a ring of bolts around its circumference. The turret hatch ring acts as antiaircraft gun mount.

The driver sits at the left bow of the tank. The assistant driver sits at the right bow. The loader sits in the turret, to the left of the 75 mm gun, and the gunner to its right. The tank commander sits in the rear of the turret, behind the gunner. Adjustable seats, allowing 12 inches of movement up and down and 5 inches fore and aft, are provided for the gunner, driver and assistant driver.

Access to the tank is through two hatches in the bow and a revolving hatch in the turret. An emergency escape hatch is located in the tank floor, behind the assistant driver.

Indirect vision is provided for each member of the crew by means of periscopes. The gunner's periscope is synchronized with the gun, contains a telescopic sight, and changes its line of sight only if the gun is elevated or depressed or the turret rotated. All other periscopes are mounted so that they can be tilted up or down and rotated through 360°. Early models had direct vision slots, protected by thick glass plates and hinged covers, for the driver and assistant driver. Because of their vulnerability to bullet splash, these were eliminated in later production, and additional periscopes were provided.

The transmission has five forward speeds and one reverse speed. A parking brake is built into the transmission. The

MEDIUM TANK, M4A1, HAS CAST HULL. PHOTO SHOWS EARLY PRODUCTION GUN MOUNT, M34

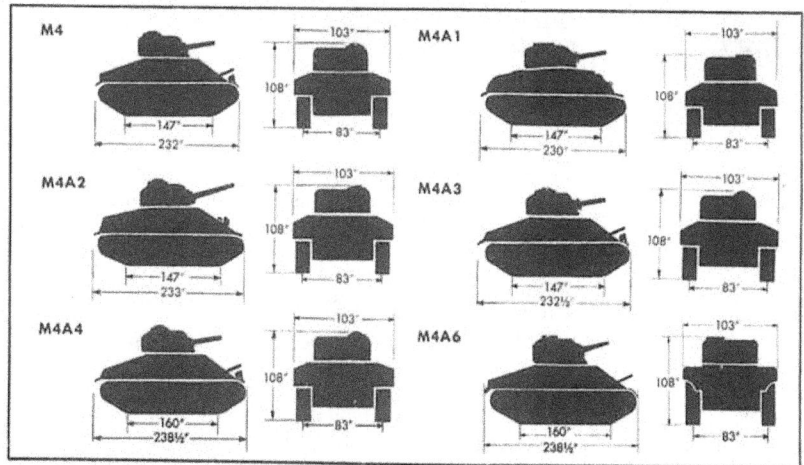

MEDIUM TANK, M4A3, WELDED, WITH CAST LOWER FRONT HULL

MEDIUM TANK, M4A4, WELDED, WITH THREE-PIECE LOWER FRONT HULL

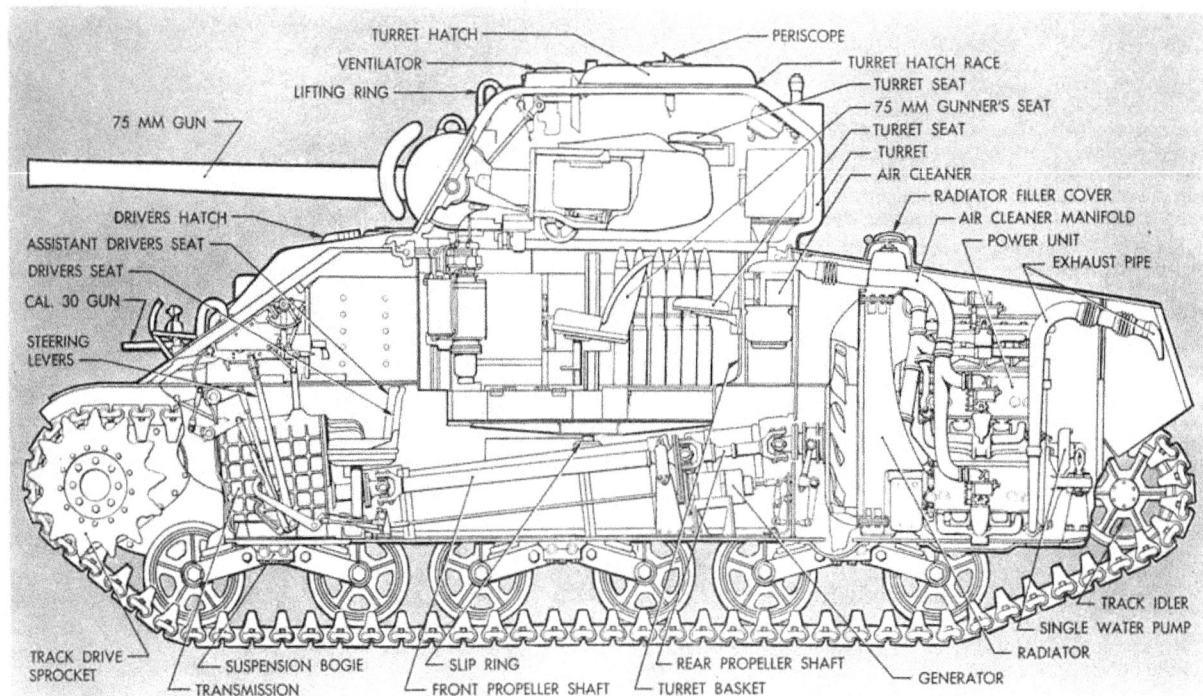

Labels in figure (clockwise from top): TURRET HATCH — PERISCOPE — TURRET HATCH RACE — TURRET SEAT — 75 MM GUNNER'S SEAT — TURRET SEAT — TURRET — AIR CLEANER — RADIATOR FILLER COVER — AIR CLEANER MANIFOLD — POWER UNIT — EXHAUST PIPE — TRACK IDLER — SINGLE WATER PUMP — RADIATOR — GENERATOR — REAR PROPELLER SHAFT — TURRET BASKET — FRONT PROPELLER SHAFT — SLIP RING — TRANSMISSION — SUSPENSION BOGIE — TRACK DRIVE SPROCKET — STEERING LEVERS — CAL. 30 GUN — DRIVERS SEAT — ASSISTANT DRIVERS SEAT — DRIVERS HATCH — 75 MM GUN — LIFTING RING — VENTILATOR

CROSS SECTION OF MEDIUM TANK, M4A4 SHOWING TYPICAL INTERIOR ARRANGEMENT. CHARACTERISTICS APPEAR ON PAGE 20

controlled differential transmits engine power to the final drive unit, and contains a brake system for steering and stopping the vehicle. The final drive units transmit power from the controlled differential to the hub of the driving sprockets through a set of reduction gears. The entire power train can be removed from the vehicle when necessary.

Six 2-wheeled, rubber-tired bogies or suspensions, bolted to the hull, support the vehicle on volute springs. The tracks are driven by sprockets on the front of the vehicle. Two idlers are mounted on eccentric shafts at the rear end of the hull, and provide for adjustment of the track tension. The weight of the upper portion of the track is carried by track-supporting rollers. (Some vehicles have the track-support roller directly over the suspension bracket. A second type has the roller offset to the rear of the bracket and is fitted with a track skid on top of the bracket.)

Two fixed 10-lb. fire extinguishers are provided in the engine compartment, and may be operated from the driver's seat or from outside the tank. Portable 4-lb. fire extinguishers are provided in the driver's compartment and in the turret.

The tank is equipped with a two-way radio and an interphone system. An auxiliary generator provides additional current at times of unusual drain, and may also be used in preheating the engine compartment in cold weather.

The pilot tank, designated Medium Tank, T6, was built at Aberdeen Proving Ground, and had a cast hull. The vehicle had an entrance hatch at the side and had two additional machine guns in the bow, which were eliminated from the production tanks.

A number of changes were made during production, with the result that newer vehicles differ somewhat from those produced earlier.

The original Combination Gun Mount, M34, had a front shield which protected the 75 mm gun only. Ordnance Committee action in October, 1942, standardized Combination Gun Mount, M34A1, a modification which incorporated a direct sighting telescope. This mount may be recognized by its front shield which protects the Cal. .30 machine gun and the direct sighting telescope, as well as the 75 mm gun. It has two "ears" projecting a few inches over the 75 mm gun.

The lower front plate of the hull on early models consisted of three pieces, bolted together. Later production vehicles used a one-piece plate.

Introduction of sand shields over the suspensions, and of water-protected ammunition chests, were among other changes on later vehicles.

MEDIUM TANK, M4, standardized in October, 1941, is built with a welded hull and a cast turret.

Power is supplied by a Continental R975, 9-cylinder, radial, aircraft-type engine.

The turret may be traversed manually or by a hydraulic mechanism. In the past, some models used an electric power traverse.

These tanks are built by the Baldwin Locomotive Works, American Locomotive Co., Detroit Tank Arsenal (Chrysler); Pressed Steel Car Co., and Pullman Standard Car Mfg. Co.

REFERENCES — TM 9-731A; OCM 16052, 16111, 16556, 16744, 16861, 17202, 17316, 17387, 17570, 17578, 17800, 17906, 17952, 17981, 18391, 18518, 18661, 18843, 18874, 18961, 20155, 20518, 20531, 20680, 20719, 20724, 20798, 20848, 21002, 21111, 21286, 21462.

MEDIUM TANK, M4A1, standardized in December, 1941, is similar to Medium Tank, M4, but has a cast hull which is curved to present less opportunity for a direct hit on a flat surface from any angle. It is powered by a Continental R975 engine. These tanks are built by the Lima Locomotive Works, Inc., Pacific Car and Foundry Co. and Pressed Steel Car Co.

REFERENCES — TM 9-731A; OCM 17578, 19277, 19279, 19983, 19984, 20518, 20984, 21414, 22199.

MEDIUM TANK, M4A2, standardized in December, 1941, has a welded hull and a cast turret and is generally similar to Medium Tank, M4, except that it is powered by twin General Motors 6-71 Diesel engines, which are assembled as a single unit known as the G.M. 6046 power unit. Either engine may be operated independently of the other, if necessary.

These vehicles are manufactured by the Fisher Tank Division, General Motors Corp.; Pullman Standard Car Mfg. Co., and the Federal Machine and Welding Co.

REFERENCES — TM 9-731B; OCM 17578, 19456, 19724, 19725, 19983.

MEDIUM TANK, M4A3, standardized in January, 1942, has a welded hull and a cast turret and is generally similar to Medium Tank, M4, except that it is powered by a 500 hp. Ford tank engine. This is an 8-cylinder, liquid-cooled "V" type engine designed for tanks.

These tanks are built by the Ford Motor Co.

REFERENCES—TM 9-759; OCM 17678, 19982, 19983, 20205, 20518, 21053.

MEDIUM TANK, M4A4, standardized in February, 1942, has a welded hull and a cast turret, and is generally similar to Medium Tank, M4, except that it is powered by a Chrysler tank engine power unit, consisting of five banks of cylinders, each of which is in itself a conventional "L" head, water-cooled engine. The five units are geared together and operate as a single unit.

These tanks were built by the Detroit Tank Arsenal (Chrysler).

MEDIUM TANK, M4A5, THE CANADIAN RAM, MOUNTS 57 MM AND CAL. .30 GUNS

REFERENCES—TM 9-754; OCM 17855, 19280, 19983, 20205.

MEDIUM TANK, M4A5, was given this designation for record purposes by OCM 17856. It is produced in Canada under the designation, RAM II. It is generally similar to the Medium Tank, M4, but has variations requested by the Canadian Government.

Principal armament is a 57 mm gun in a combination mount with a cal. .30 machine gun in the British type cast turret. A small cupola is added on the left front of the hull roof and mounts a cal. .30 machine gun. A smoke projector is mounted on the right side of the turret front plate.

The tank is powered by a Wright R975 engine.

The pilot tank was manufactured by the American Locomotive Co.

REFERENCE—OCM 17856.

MEDIUM TANK, M4A6, is similar to Medium Tank, M4A4, but is powered by an RD-1820 Ordnance engine manufactured by the Caterpillar Tractor Co. This is a radial Diesel-type engine with a displacement of 1,820 cubic inches. This tank is manufactured by the Detroit Tank Arsenal (Chrysler).

REFERENCES — OCM 19200, 19439, 19630, 19631, 20716.

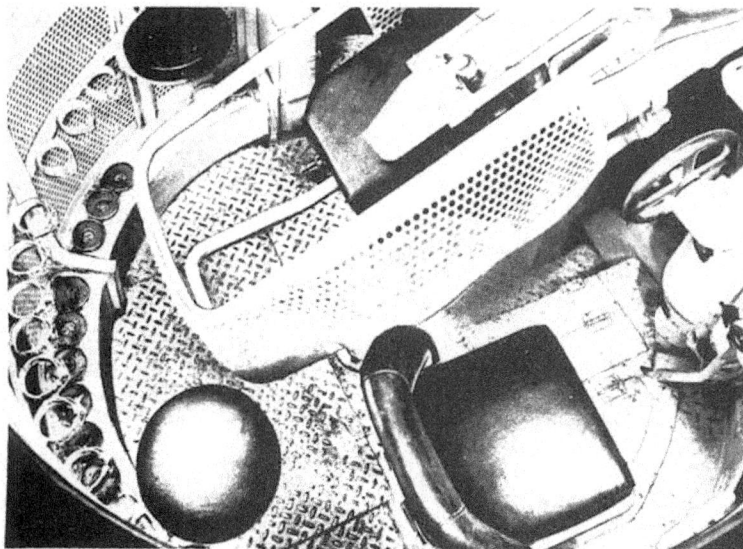

GUN MOUNT AND GUARD AND TURRET SEATS IN MEDIUM TANK, M4A1

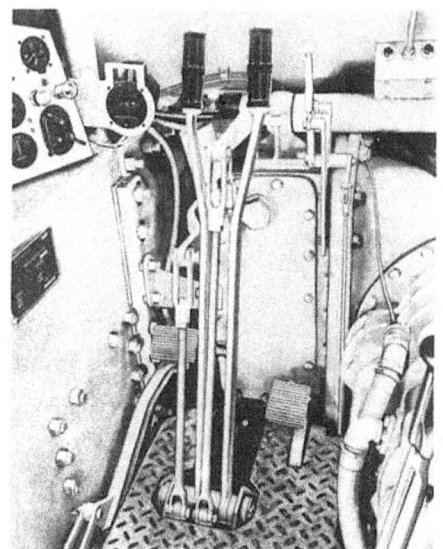

STEERING LEVERS AND OTHER DRIVING CONTROLS

TYPICAL CHARACTERISTICS

	M4	M4A1	M4A2	M4A3	M4A4	M4A6
Crew	5	5	5	5	5	5

Physical Characteristics

	M4	M4A1	M4A2	M4A3	M4A4	M4A6
Weight (gross)	66,500 lb.	66,500 lb.	69,000 lb.	68,500 lb.	71,000 lb.	71,000 lb.
Length	19 ft., 4 ins.	19 ft., 2 ins.	19 ft., 5 ins.	19 ft., 4½ ins.	19 ft., 10½ ins.	19 ft., 10½ ins.
Width	8 ft., 7 ins.	8 ft., 7 ins.	8 ft., 7 ins.	8 ft., 7 ins.	8 ft., 7 ins.	8 ft., 7 ins.
Height	9 ft.	9 ft.	9 ft.	9 ft.	9 ft.	9 ft.
Ground clearance	17⅛ ins.	17⅛ ins.	17⅛ ins.	17⅛ ins.	15¾ ins.	15¾ ins.
Tread (center to center of tracks)	83 ins.	83 ins.	83 ins.	83 ins.	83 ins.	83 ins.
Ground pressure, per sq. in.	13.7 lb.	13.7 lb.	14.2 lb.	14.1 lb.	13.4 lb.	13.4 lb.
Ground contact length at 0° penetration	147 ins.	147 ins.	147 ins.	147 ins.	160 ins.	160 ins.

Performance

	M4	M4A1	M4A2	M4A3	M4A4	M4A6
Sustained speed on level	24 m.p.h.	24 m.p.h.	29 m.p.h.	26 m.p.h.	25 m.p.h.	25 m.p.h.
Maximum grade ability	60%	60%	60%	60%	60%	60%
Trench crossing ability	7 ft., 5 ins.	7 ft., 5 ins.	7 ft., 5 ins.	7 ft., 5 ins.	8 ft.	8 ft.
Vertical obstacle ability	24 ins.	24 ins.	24 ins.	24 ins.	24 ins.	24 ins.
Fording depth (slowest forward speed)	36 ins.	36 ins.	40 ins.	36 ins.	42 ins.	42 ins.
Fuel capacity	175 gals.	175 gals.	148 gals.	174 gals.	150 gals.	150 gals.
Cruising range	120 miles	120 miles	150 miles	130 miles	100 miles	100 miles
Maximum drawbar pull	42,350 lb.	42,350 lb.	44,800 lb.	43,050 lb.	47,600 lb.	47,600 lb.
Engine, Make	Continental	Continental	G.M. 6-71	GAA-III	Chrysler	Caterpillar
Model	R975-C1	R975-C1	6046	V-W.C.	5-line W.C.	RD-1820
Fuel (gasoline)	80	80		80	80	
(Diesel)	—	—	50	—	—	45
Max. governed speed	2,400 r.p.m.	2,400 r.p.m.	2,100 r.p.m.	2,600 r.p.m.	2,400 r.p.m.	2,000 r.p.m.
Net hp. at r.p.m.	353 at 2,400	353 at 2,400	375 at 2,100	450 at 2,600	370 at 2,850	450 at 2,000
Max. torque (lb.-ft. at r.p.m.)	800 at 1,800	800 at 1,800	1,000 at 1,400	950 at 2,100	1,025 at 1,200	1,470 at 1,200

(See additional engine characteristics on pages 28 and 29.)

ASSISTANT DRIVER'S STATION IN RIGHT BOW

Armament and Ammunition

75 mm Gun, M3, and
1 cal. .30 Browning Machine Gun, M1919A4 (flexible) . . In Combination Gun Mount, M34A1, in turret
1 cal. .30 Browning Machine Gun, M1919A4 (flexible) . . . . In bow
1 cal. .50 Machine Gun, M2, H.B. (flexible) . . . . On turret (antiaircraft)
1 Mortar, 2-Inch, M3
1 Tripod Mount, M2, Cal. .30
Provision for:
1 cal. .45 Submachine Gun . . . . Equipment of crew

Ammunition, Stowage

	M4, M4A2, M4A3, M4A4, M4A5	M4A1
75 mm (H.E., M48, A.P., M72; A.P.C., M61)	97	90
Cal. .30 (A.P. and tracer)	4,750	4,750
Cal. .45	600	600
Cal. .50 (A.P. and tracer)	300	300
Grenades, Hand (Fragmentation, Mk. III, 4; Smoke, H.C., M8, 4; Offensive, Mk. III, w/fuze, Detonating, M2; Thermite, incendiary, 2)	12	12
Smoke Ammunition (minimum)	12	12

Armor

	Actual	Basis
Hull, Front, Upper	2 ins.	2-4 ins.
Lower	1½-2 ins.	2-2½ ins.
Sides	1½-2 ins.	1½-2 ins.
Rear	1½ ins.	
Top	1 in.	
Bottom	½-1 in.	
Turret, Front	3 ins.	3¾ ins.
Sides	2 ins.	2 ins.
Top	1 in.	

Vision and Fire Control

Periscope, M4 (w/Telescope, M38)	1
Periscope, M6	6
Gunner's quadrant, M1	1
Bore sight	1
Telescope, M70F	1
Azimuth Indicator, M19	1
Elevation quadrant, M9	1

Communications

Radio	SCR-508
Command tank	SCR-506
Interphone stations	5
Flag set, M238	24

Battery, Voltage Total | 24 |

Fire Protection and Decontamination

Fire Extinguisher—CO₂-10 lb. (fixed)	2
CO₂-4 lb. (hand)	2
Decontaminating Apparatus, M2, 1½ qts.	2

Track, Type | Rubber block
| Width | 16½ ins. |
| Pitch | 6 ins. |
No. of shoes per vehicle
158 (Medium Tank, M4A4, uses 166 shoes)

Suspension, Type | Volute spring
| Wheel or tire size | 20x9 |

Idler, Type | Fixed
| Wheel or tire size | 28⅛x9 |

Final Drive, Type | Herringbone
Gear ratio	2.84:1
Sprocket, no. of teeth	13
Pitch diameter	25.038

Differential, Controlled, Gear ratio | 3.53:1
Ring gear, no. of teeth	60
Pinion, no. of teeth	17
Steering ratio	1.515:1

Transmission, Type | Mechanical syncromesh
Gear ratios, First speed	7.56:1
Second speed	3.11:1
Third speed	1.78:1
Fourth speed	1.11:1
Fifth speed	.73:1
Reverse	5.65:1

MEDIUM TANKS M4 (105 MM HOW.), M4A3 (105 MM HOW.)—STANDARD

These modifications of Medium Tanks, M4 and M4A3, were designed to combine the firepower of a 105 mm howitzer with the performance characteristics of a medium tank. They are supplied in addition to the medium tanks with 75 mm guns authorized by Tables of Basic Allowances, and to replace the 75 mm Howitzer Motor Carriages, M8, in Battalion Headquarters Companies, Medium Tank Battalions.

The 105 mm Howitzer, M4, is mounted in a Combination Gun Mount, M52, with one cal. .30 Machine Gun, M1919A4, flexible, in a 360° hand-traversed turret. No gyrostabilizer is provided. The howitzer is a redesign of 105 mm Howitzer, M2A1.

Other armament is the same as for Medium Tanks, M4, and M4A3.

The cast turret has a partial turret basket. A fighting seat for the gunner, a convoy seat for the tank commander and a riding seat for the loader are provided. All seats traverse with the turret.

A commander's vision cupola is provided above the turret. Equipped with six prismatic vision blocks, of 3 inch, laminated, bullet-resisting glass, it affords a wide field of view.

There is a suitable floor over the stowage space on either side of the power tunnel. Pistol ports and lifting hooks are the same as for Medium Tanks, M4, and padding and safety belts are furnished wherever required. A pintle for towing an ammunition trailer is provided.

Construction of two pilot Medium Tanks, M4A4, mounting the 105 mm howitzer, was authorized by Ordnance Committee action in December, 1942. Designated Medium Tank, M4A4E1, the vehicle was tested at Aberdeen Proving Ground and at Fort Knox, Ky. Modifications deemed necessary were incorporated in new pilot models designated Medium Tank, M4E5. Standardization of the vehicles was approved in August, 1943.

MEDIUM TANK, M4 (105 mm HOW.), is based on Medium Tank, M4, using a Continental R975–C1 engine.

MEDIUM TANK, M4A3 (105 mm HOW.), is based on Medium Tank, M4A3, using a Ford GAA engine.

REFERENCES — OCM 17202, 17316, 19394, 21113, 21347.

MEDIUM TANK, M4 (105 MM HOWITZER), SHOWING DETAILS OF TOP OF HULL AND TURRET

TYPICAL CHARACTERISTICS

Crew   5

Physical Characteristics

Weight (gross, approx.)	M4—66,500 lb.
	M4A3—68,500 lb.
Length	M4—19 ft., 4 ins.
	M4A3—19 ft., 4½ ins.
Width	8 ft., 7 ins.
Height	9 ft., 2¹¹⁄₁₆ ins.
Ground clearance	17⅛ ins.
Tread (center to center of tracks)	83 ins.
Ground contact length	147 ins.
Ground pressure	M4—13.7 lb./sq. in.
	M4A3—14.1 lb./sq. in.

Armament

105 mm Howitzer, M4, and 1 cal. .30 Machine Gun, M1919A4 (flexible)	In Combination Gun Mount, M52
Elevation	– 10° to +35°
Traverse	360°
1 cal. .30 Machine Gun, M1919A4 (flexible)	In bow mount
1 cal. .50 Machine Gun, M2, HB (flexible)	On turret
1 Mortar, 2 inch, M3	
1 Tripod Mount, cal. .30, M2	
Provision for:	
1 cal. .45 Submachine Gun	

Ammunition, Stowage

105 mm Howitzer	66 rounds
Cal. .30	4,000 rounds
Cal. .50	300 rounds
Cal. .45	600 rounds
Grenades, Hand (Fragmentation, MK. II, 6; Smoke, W.P., M 15,6)	12
Smoke Bombs, 2 Inch, MK. I	18

Armor

	Actual	Basis
Hull, Front, Upper	2 ins.	2–4 ins.
Lower	1½–2 ins.	2–2½ ins.
Sides	1½–2 ins.	1½–2 ins.
Rear	1½ ins.	
Top	1 in.	
Bottom	½–1 in.	
Turret, Front	3 ins.	3¾ ins.
Sides	2 ins.	2 ins.
Top	1 in.	

Performance

Maximum speed on level—M4	24 m.p.h.
M4A3	26 m.p.h.
Maximum grade ability	60%
Trench crossing ability	7 ft., 5 ins.
Vertical obstacle ability	24 ins.
Fording depth (slowest forward speed)	36 ins.
Fuel capacity—M4	175 gals.
M4A3	174 gals.
Cruising range—M4	120 miles
M4A3	130 miles

Vision and Fire Control

Commander's vision cupola	1
Periscope, M6	6
Periscope, M4, with Telescope, T73	1
Gunner's Quadrant, M1	1

Communications

Radio	SCR-508, 528, or 538
Interphone stations	5
Flag Set	M238

Battery, Voltage, total   24

Fire Protection and Decontamination

Fire Extinguisher—CO_2-10 lb. (fixed)	2
CO_4-4 lb. (hand)	2
Decontaminating Apparatus, M2, 1½ qts.	2

(Other characteristics same as for Medium Tanks, M4 or M4A3.)

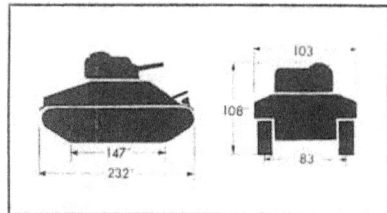

Office Chief of Ordnance -21-

MEDIUM TANK M4 (76 MM) SERIES

These modifications of the Medium Tank, M4, series, provide greatly increased firepower. The 76 mm gun uses 3 inch ammunition, with muzzle velocity, maximum range, and armor penetration considerably greater than that of 75 mm ammunition.

Principal armament is a 76 mm Gun, M1A1 or M1A2, with a cal. .30 Machine Gun, M1919A4 (flexible), with stabilizer, in a 360° power-operated turret. The guns may be elevated from −10° to +25°.

The 3 Inch A.P.C. Projectile, M62, fired from the 76 mm gun, has a muzzle velocity of 2,600 feet per second, and a maximum range of 16,100 yards. It will penetrate 4 inches of face-hardened armor plate at 1,000 yards.

Provision is made for fire control at 3,000 yards range, direct fire. By use of an azimuth indicator and elevation quadrant, indirect fire control can be had up to the maximum range.

A commander's vision cupola is mounted above the turret hatch. Equipped with six prismatic vision blocks of 3 inch laminated bullet-resistant glass, it affords a wide view.

Other armament and general characteristics are the same as on the respective variations of the Medium Tank, M4, series.

Water-protected ammunition racks are used. A traveling lock is provided on the front hull of the vehicle to support the gun when traveling in noncombat zones.

Medium Tank, M4 (76 mm), welded, and Medium Tank, M4A1 (76 mm), cast, are powered by Continental R975-C1 gasoline engines.

Medium Tank, M4A2, welded, is powered by a General Motors Diesel engine 6-71, 6046.

Medium Tank, M4A3, welded, is powered by a Ford GAA-III gasoline engine.

REFERENCES—OCM 18661, 18874, 20531, 20798, 22994.

MEDIUM TANK, M4 (76 MM), WITH GUN SUPPORTED BY TRAVELING LOCK

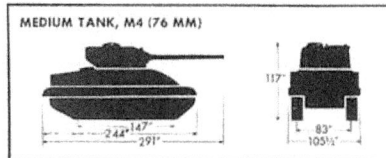
MEDIUM TANK, M4 (76 MM)

TYPICAL CHARACTERISTICS

MEDIUM TANKS, M4 (76 mm), M4A1 (76 mm)
Crew 5
Physical Characteristics
Weight (gross—approx.) ....70,000 lb.
Length—over end of gun ....24 ft., 3 ins.
excluding gun (with sand
shields) ....20 ft., 4 ins.
Width..................... 8 ft., 9½ ins.
Height.................... 9 ft., 9 ins.
Ground clearance .... 17⅛ ins.
Tread (center to center of tracks) ..... 83 ins.
Ground contact length .... 147 ins.
Ground pressure .... 14.4 lb./sq. in.
Armament
76 mm Gun, M1A1 or M1A2, ⎰ In Combination
and 1 cal. .30 Machine ⎱ Gun Mount,
Gun, M1919A4 (flex.) .... ⎰ M62, in turret
Elevation ....−10° to +25°
Traverse ....360°
1 cal. .30 Machine Gun,
M1919A4 (flex.) .... In ball mount on bow
1 cal. .50 Machine Gun,
M2, HB (flex.) ..... On turret, antiaircraft
1 Mortar, 2 in., M3
1 Tripod Mount, Cal. .30, M2
Provision for:
5 cal. .45 Submachine Guns
Ammunition, Stowage
76 mm (3 Inch, H.E., M42A1; 3 Inch,
A.P.C., M62; 3 Inch, Smoke, M8) 71 rounds
Cal. .30 ....6,250 rounds
Cal. .50 ....600 rounds
Cal. .45 ....900 rounds
Mortar, 2 Inch ....18 rounds
Grenades, Hand (Fragmentation, Mk. II, 4;
Offensive, Mk. III, w/fuze, detonation,

M6, 2; Smoke, H.C., M8, 4; Thermite,
Incendiary, 2) 12

Armor | **Actual** | **Basis**
Hull, Front .... | 2½ ins. | 4 ins.
Sides .... | 1½ ins. | 1½ ins.
Rear .... | 1½ ins. | 1½ ins.
Top .... | ¾ in. |
Bottom, Forward . | 1 in. |
Rear . | ½ in. |
Turret, Front..... | 2½ ins. |
Sides and rear .. | 2½ ins. |
Top ...... | 1 in. |

Performance
Maximum speed on level ....24 m.p.h.
Speed on 10% grade ....9 m.p.h.
Maximum grade ability 60%
Trench crossing ability ..... 7 ft., 6 ins.
Vertical obstacle ability ....24 ins.
Fording depth (slowest forward speed) .36 ins.
Turning radius ....31 ft.
Fuel capacity ....175 gals.
Cruising range ....85 miles
Vision and Fire Control
Periscopes, M6 6
Periscope, M4, w/M47 Telescope 1
Telescope, T92 (M71D) or M70H 1
Telescope Mount, T82 (M57) 1
Azimuth Indicator, M19 1
Elevation Quadrant, M9 1
Gunner's Quadrant, M1 1
Pistol port 1
Commander's vision cupola 1
Communications
Radio SCR-508
Command tank SCR-506
Interphone stations 5
Battery, Voltage, total 24

Fire Protection and Decontamination
Fire Extinguisher, CO₂-10 lb. (fixed).....2
CO₂-4 lb. (hand) 2
Decontaminating Apparatus, M2, 1½ qts....1
Engine, Make and Model Continental, R975-C1
(See additional engine characteristics on page 28.)
MEDIUM TANK, M4A2
Characteristics same as for Medium Tank, M4 (76 mm), except as noted:
Physical Characteristics
Weight (gross—approx.) ....72,800 lb.
Length—over end of gun ......24 ft., 7 ins.
excluding gun (with sand
shields) ....20 ft., 8 ins.
Width .... 8 ft., 9½ ins.
Ground pressure .... 14.9 lb./sq. in.
Performance
Maximum speed on level ....29 m.p.h.
Speed on 10% grade ....12 m.p.h.
Fording depth (slowest forward speed) .40 ins.
Fuel capacity ....148 gals.
Cruising range ....100 miles
Engine, Make and Model.........G.M. 6-71
MEDIUM TANK, M4A3
Characteristics same as for Medium Tank, M4 (76 mm), except as noted:
Physical Characteristics
Weight (gross—approx.) ....71,100 lb.
Length—over end of gun ...... 24 ft., 6½ ins.
excluding gun (with sand
shields) ....20 ft., 7½ ins.
Width .... 8 ft., 9½ ins.
Ground pressure .... 14.6 lb./sq. in.
Performance
Maximum speed on level ....26 m.p.h.
Speed on 10% grade ....10 m.p.h.
Fuel capacity ....174 gals.
Cruising range ....100 miles
Engine, Make and Model......Ford, GAA-III

HEAVY TANKS M6, M6A1, T1E1

HEAVY TANK M6 HAD CAST HULL AND DOUBLE TRACKS AND BOGIES. 3-INCH GUN WAS MOUNTED WITH 37-MM GUN IN POWER-TRAVERSED TURRET

Heavy Tanks M6 and M6A1 were standardized in May 1942, at which time they were the largest and most powerful tanks ever built in the U. S., weighing more than 60 tons each. Shortly afterward the Ordnance Committee authorized Limited Procurement of Heavy Tank T1E1, sometimes referred to as Heavy Tank M6A2. Because of changes in tactical thinking, comparatively few of these tanks were built and in December 1944 all three models were declared obsolete.

Heavy Tank M6 had a cast hull and a cast turret. Heavy Tank M6A1 had a welded hull and a cast turret. Each was powered by a Wright G-200 gasoline engine through a hydraulic torque converter and transmission. The torque converter, transmission, and final drive were mounted directly behind the engine, connected by a flexible coupling, without the use of a propeller shaft. A pedal, placed in the position usually occupied by a clutch pedal, served as a transmission brake pedal. Two forward speeds and one reverse speed were provided.

Heavy Tank T1E1 was similar to the M6 in general design, but used an electric drive. A large direct current generator was mounted directly behind the engine. This generator converted the mechanical output of the engine into electrical power for two traction motors, one for each track. The tank had varying speeds up to 22 m.p.h., and could turn in its own radius.

These vehicles had as their principal armament a 3-In. Gun M7 mounted with a 37-mm Gun M6. Additional firepower was provided by a cal. .30 machine gun on the turret for antiaircraft use, two cal. .50 machine guns in the bow, and a cal. .30 machine gun (flexible) in the bow. Provision was made for carrying two cal. .45 submachine guns.

The turret guns had elevations from $-10°$ to $+30°$ and could be traversed 360° by an electrically operated mechanism or by hand. A gyrostabilizer was provided.

The 3-In. Gun M7 was the same as used on the 3-In. Gun Motor Carriage M10, which proved so effective against Marshal Rommel's troops in North Africa. Fired from this gun, the 3-in. APC projectile had a muzzle velocity of 2,600 feet per second and at 45° elevation a maximum range of 16,100 yards. It could penetrate 3.9 inches of 20° obliquity homogeneous armor plate at 1,000 yards.

A horizontal volute spring suspension was used, with four bogie assemblies on each track. Each assembly had four bogie wheels, two wheels riding the outside half of the track and two the inside half. Two volute springs were mounted horizontally on each bogie assembly.

Each track block consisted, in effect, of two shoes held together by connecting pins. The pins were bare between the shoes, to provide space for a center track connector. Shoes were half rubber and half steel, the steel side making contact against the ground, and the rubber side riding against the bogie wheels and idlers.

The driving sprockets were at the rear of the vehicle. In addition to the main idler, provided to adjust each track, there was an auxiliary, non-adjustable idler between the main idler and the front bogie assembly. This gave additional track support when crossing rough terrain.

Maximum armor thickness was $3\frac{1}{4}$ in., as compared to $2\frac{1}{2}$ in. on Medium Tank M4. An armor plate skirting was used over each suspension.

Six periscopes were provided. There were four escape doors.

REFERENCES—TM 9–721; OCM 15842, 15946, 16040, 16200, 16297, 16477, 16655, 17812, 17906, 17952, 18059, 18283, 18544, 18984, 19199, 19625, 19981, 20034, 20680, 26039, 26357; SNL G–118, Vols. 1 and 2.

HEAVY TANK M6A1 WAS SIMILAR TO THE M6, BUT HAD A WELDED HULL. POWER WAS SUPPLIED BY WRIGHT G-200 ENGINE, THROUGH TORQUE CONVERTER

TYPICAL CHARACTERISTICS

Physical Characteristics
Weight (gross)	126,500 lb.
Length, Gun forward	27 ft., 8 in.
Hull only	24 ft., 9 in.
Width (overall)	10 ft., 2½ in.
Height, Top of turret	9 ft., 10 in.
Top of machine gun mount	10 ft., 7 in.
Turret ring diameter (inside)	69 in.
Ground clearance	20½ in.
Tread (center to center of tracks)	93 in.
Ground contact length	186 in.
Ground pressure	12.3 lb./sq. in.

Armament

3-In. Gun M7 and   In Combination
37-mm Gun M6   Gun Mount T49, in turret
1 Cal. .30 Machine Gun M1919A4
(flexible) .... In bow
1 Cal. .30 Machine Gun M1919A4
(flexible) .... On turret
2 Cal. .50 Machine Guns M2 HB
(fixed) .... In twin mount in bow
1 Cal. .30 Machine Gun Tripod Mount M2
Provision for:
2 Cal. .45 Submachine Guns M3

TORQUE CONVERTER AND FINAL DRIVE

Ammunition, Stowage
3-in.	75 rounds
37-mm	202 rounds
Cal. .50	5,700 rounds
Cal. .45	1,200 rounds
Cal. .30	7,500 rounds
Hand Grenades	12

Armor
	Actual	Basis
Hull, front, upper	3¼ in.	4 in.
Lower	2¾-4 in.	4 in.
Sides	1¾ in.	1¾ in.
Rear	1⅝ in.	2 in.
Top	1 in.	
Bottom	1 in.	
Turret, front	3¼ in.	3¼ in.
Sides and rear	3¼ in.	3¼ in.
Top	1 in.	

Performance
Maximum speed on level	22 m.p.h.
Maximum grade ability	60%
Trench crossing ability	11 ft.
Vertical obstacle ability	36 in.
Fording depth (slowest forward speed)	48 in.
Angle of approach	32°
Turning diameter	74 ft.
Fuel capacity	464 gal.
Cruising range (approx.)	100 miles

Vision and Fire Control
Periscope M6	5
Periscope M8, w/Telescope M39	1
Gunner's Quadrant M1, w/case	1
Bore Sight, 3-inch gun	1
Telescope M15	1

Communications
Radio	SCR-508, 528, or 538
Command tank	SCR-506
Interphone stations	6

Battery, Voltage, total | 24

Fire Protection and Decontamination
Fire Extinguisher
CO₂–10 lb. (fixed)	6
CO₂–4 lb. (hand)	2
Decontaminating Apparatus M2, 1½ qt.	4

Engine, Make and model | Wright G-200
Type	Radial, A.C.
No. of cylinders	9
Fuel (gasoline)	80 octane
Max. governed speed	2,300 r.p.m.
Gross hp	800 at 2,300 r.p.m.
Max. torque	1,850 lb.-ft. at 2,300 r.p.m.

Transmission, Type | Torque converter
Gear ratios
First speed	1.61:1
Second speed	0.22:1
Reverse	1.61:1

Gear Reduction Case, Type Twin Disc Clutch Co.

Torque Converter, Type Twin Disc Clutch Co.

Differential, Type | Controlled
Gear ratio	0.62:1
Steering ratio	1.62:1

Final Drive, Gear Ratio | 5:1
Sprocket, no. of teeth	14
Pitch diameter	26.806

Suspension, Type | Horizontal volute spring
Wheel or tire size	18x7x15

Idler, Type | Adjustable

Track, Steel bottom, rubber top, rubber bushed
Width	25¾ in.
Pitch	6 in.
No. of blocks per vehicle	198

HEAVY TANK **M26**—STANDARD

Standardization of Heavy Tank M26 in May 1945 culminated a consistent program of experimentation and development conducted over several years. Formally classified as Limited Procurement type in October 1944 and designated Heavy Tank T26E3, the vehicle embodies improvements which have been tested thoroughly on this and other tanks of the T20 series.

Compact in design, it is lower and wider than Heavy Tanks M6 and M6A1 and is not as heavy. It has greater fire power and heavier armor and has better mobility and maneuverability.

Weighing 46 tons, the vehicle has a ground pressure of 12.7 lb./sq. in. with 24-in. track and can be operated at speeds up to 25 m.p.h. Consideration is being given to reducing the unit ground pressure to 10.9 lb./sq. in. by using the T80E1 type of track with extended end connectors. It will climb a 60% grade and will cross a trench almost 8 feet wide.

Principal armament is a 90-mm Gun M3, mounted coaxially with a Cal. .30 Machine Gun M1919A4 in the turret. These guns can be depressed to −10° and elevated to +20° and can be traversed through 360°, either manually or by power. The gun is equipped with a muzzle brake.

The Shot, Fixed, HVAP-T, 90-mm, T30E16, fired from this gun, has a muzzle velocity of 3,350 feet per second. It will penetrate 7.2 inches of homogeneous armor plate at 30° obliquity at 1,000 yards.

A Cal. .30 Machine Gun M1919A4

HEAVY TANK M26, LEFT FRONT, SHOWING 90-MM GUN M3 WITH MUZZLE BRAKE

(flexible) is located in the bow. A Cal. .50 Machine Gun M2 HB (flexible) for antiaircraft use is mounted on the turret.

Provision is made for carrying five cal. .45 submachine guns and one cal. .30 carbine with grenade launcher.

The armor is placed at varying angles designed to provide the greatest possible protection against enemy projectiles. The front upper hull is 4 inches thick and has a basis of 6.9 inches. The turret front is 4 inches thick and has the additional protection of a gun mount shield with a 4½-inch basis.

The suspension is of the individually sprung torsion bar type, with bumper springs and double-acting shock absorbers to give additional protection. Center-guided track is used.

Power is supplied by a Ford GAF gasoline engine through a torqmatic transmission and a controlled differential, the tracks being driven by sprockets at the rear.

OVERHEAD VIEW, SHOWING COMMANDER'S VISION CUPOLA AND LOADER'S HATCH ON TURRET. TURRET IS TURNED TO REAR DURING TRAVEL

The commander, gunner, and loader are seated in the rotating turret, entrance to which is through the commander's hatch or a smaller hatch over the loader. The driver and assistant driver are seated in the lower front hull, access to which is through two hatches. Two emergency exit doors are located in the floor of the hull.

The commander's hatch is surmounted by a vision cupola, equipped with six laminated glass vision blocks, permitting vision in all directions. Periscopes for all crew members and a two-way radio are provided. When traveling in non-combat areas, the turret is turned to the rear and the 90-mm gun is secured in an exterior traveling lock.

Heavy Tank M26 is an outgrowth of the Medium Tank T20 series, which included Medium Tanks T20, T22, T23, and T25, and variations. Development of these tanks started in 1942, utilizing new components and new principles of design which were tested and proved satisfactory. The original Heavy Tank T26 was designed to use an electric drive, while the Heavy Tank T26E1 utilized a torqmatic transmission. Heavy Tank T26E3 was the production model of the T26E1, incorporating many improvements which were found advisable during tests. It is being used as the basis of additional tank developments, with the purpose of providing a well-rounded combat team.

REFERENCES—TM 9–735; OCM 24277, 24619, 26038, 26282, 27123, 27536.

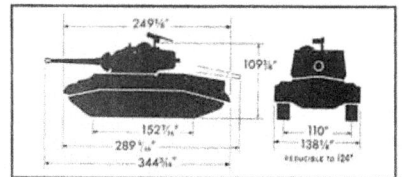

RIGHT REAR VIEW. NOTE DETAILS OF TORSION BAR SUSPENSION AND OF STOWAGE

TYPICAL CHARACTERISTICS

Crew. 5

Physical Characteristics

Weight (gross). . . . . .92,000 lb.	
Length, gun forward. . . . . . . .28 ft., 8 3/16 in.	
Gun to rear. . . . . .24 ft., 1 9/16 in.	
Hull only. . . . . .20 ft., 9⅛ in.	
Width (overall). . . . . .11 ft., 6¼ in.	
Reducible to. . . . . .10 ft., 4 in.	
Height. . . . . .9 ft., 1⅜ in.	
Turret ring diameter (inside). . . . . .69 in.	
Ground clearance. . . . . .17 3/16 in.	
Tread (center to center of tracks). . . . . .110 in.	
Ground contact length, right side. . .152 7/16 in.	
Left side. . . . . . . .148 7/16 in.	
Ground pressure. . . . . .12.7 lb./sq. in.	

Armament

1 90-mm Gun M3 and
1 Cal. .30 Machine Gun M1919A4 (flexible) } In Combination Gun Mount M67
- Elevation. . . . .—10° to +20°
- Traverse. . . . . .360°

1 Cal. .30 Machine Gun M1919A4 (flexible). . . . . .In bow

1 Cal. .50 Machine Gun M2 HB (flexible). . . . . .On turret

1 Cal. .30 Machine Gun Tripod Mount M2

Provision for:
5 Cal. .45 Submachine Guns M3
1 Cal. .30 Carbine M2 and Grenade Launcher M8

Ammunition, Stowage

90-mm. . . . . .70 rounds	
Cal. .50. . . . . .550 rounds	
Cal. .45. . . . . .900 rounds	
Cal. .30. . . . . .5,000 rounds	
Hand grenades. 12	
Signal flares. 12	

Armor

	Actual	Basis
Hull, front, upper.	4 in.	6.9 in.
Lower	3 in.	6.4 in.
Sides, forward.	3 in.	3 in.
Engine compartment	2 in.	2 in.
Rear.	2 in.	2 in.
Top.	⅞ in.	
Bottom. . . .	1 in. and ½ in.	
Turret, front.	4 in.	4.4 in.
Sides and rear.	3 in.	3 in.
Top.	1 in.	
Gun mount shield.		4½ in.

Performance

Maximum speed on level. . . . . .20 m.p.h.	
Maximum grade ability. 60%	
Trench crossing ability. . . . . .7 ft., 11 in.	
Vertical obstacle ability. . . . . .46 in.	
Fording depth (slowest forward speed). .48 in.	
Turning diameter. . . . . .60 ft.	
Fuel capacity. . . . . .186 gal.	
Cruising range (approx.). . . . . .75 miles.	

Vision and Fire Control

Commander's Vision Cupola. 1	
Periscope M6. 6	
Periscope M10F, w/Instrument Light M30. . .1	
(1 Periscope M4A1, w/Telescope M77F as spare)	
Telescope Mount T90. 1	
Elevation Quadrant M9, w/Instrument Light M30. 1	
Gunner's Quadrant M1. 1	
Azimuth Indicator M20. 1	
Aiming Post M1, w/Aiming Post Light M14. 2	
Fuze Setter M22. 1	
Pistol port. 1	

Communications

Radio. . . . . . .SCR-508, 528, 608B or British No. 19; AN/VRC-3	
Interphone stations. 5	

Battery, Voltage, total. 24	
Fire Protection and Decontamination	
Fire Extinguisher, CO₂-10 lb. (fixed). 2	
CO₂-4 lb. (hand). 2	
Decontaminating Apparatus M2, 1½ qt. . . .2	

Engine, Make and model. . . . . .Ford GAF

Type. . . . . .V-8, LC	
No. of cylinders. 8	
Fuel (gasoline). . . . . .80 octane	
Max. governed speed. . . . . .2,600 r.p.m.	
Gross hp. . . . . .500 at 2,600 r.p.m.	
Max. torque. . . . . .1,040 lb.-ft. at 2,200 r.p.m.	

Transmission, Type. . . . . .Torqmatic

Gear ratios
First speed. 1:1	
Second speed. . . . . . . .1:2.337 }	
Third speed. . . . . .1:4.105 } overdrive	
Reverse. . . . . .1:1.322 }	

Transfer Case
Gear ratio, engine to transmission. 1.38:1

Torque Converter,
Ratio. . . . . .Varies from 1:1 to 4.8:1

Differential, Type. . . . . .Controlled
Steering ratio. 1.78:1

Final Drive
Sprocket, No. of teeth. 13	
Pitch diameter. 25.068	
Gear ratio. 3.82:1	

Suspension, Type. . . . . .Torsion bar
Wheel or tire size. 26x6

Idler, Type. . . . . .Compensating
Wheel or tire size. 26x6

Track, Type. . . . . .T80E1 or T81
Width. . . . . .23 or 24 in.	
Pitch. . . . . .6 in.	
No. of shoes per vehicle. 164	

Radiator, Type. . . . . .Fin and tube

Brakes, Type. . . . . .External-contracting
Operation. . . . . .Manual lever

LIGHT TANK ENGINES

TYPICAL CHARACTERISTICS

	CONTINENTAL W-670-9A	GUIBERSON T-1020-4	CADILLAC Series 44†**	LYCOMING O-435-T
Type	Radial, A.C.	Radial, A.C.	V-8, L.C.	Opposed, A.C.
No. of cylinders	7	9	8	6
Cycle	4	4	4	4
Fuel, Octane or cetane	80 Octane	40 Cetane	80 Octane	80 Octane
Type	Gasoline	Diesel	Gasoline	Gasoline
Bore and stroke	5⅛ x 4⅝ in.	5⅛ x 5½ in.	3½ x 4½ in.	4⅞ x 3⅞ in.
Displacement	667 cu. in.	1,021 cu. in.	346 cu. in.	434 cu. in.
Compression	6.1:1	14.5:1	6.77:1	6.25:1
Max. governed speed	2,400 r.p.m.	2,200 r.p.m.	Not governed	2,800 r.p.m.
Gross hp	262 at 2,400 r.p.m.	245 at 2,200 r.p.m.	148 at 3,200 r.p.m.	192 at 2,800 r.p.m.
Max. gross torque	590 lb.-ft. at 1,700 r.p.m.	645 lb.-ft. at 1,300 r.p.m.	280 lb.-ft. at 1,200 r.p.m.	360 lb.-ft. at 2,100 r.p.m.
Crankshaft rotation (facing drive end)	C'Clockwise	C'Clockwise	C'Clockwise	C'Clockwise
Length	32 in.	37 in.	65³⁄₁₆ in.	48 in.
Width	53¼ in.*	45½ in.	25⅜ in.	35½ in.
Height	42⅜ in.	45½ in.	38³⁄₃₂ in.	31¼ in.
Ignition	Magneto	Compression	Battery	Battery
Weight, Dry	1,070 lb.	700 lb.	584 lb.	1,000 lb.
Weight, Installed	1,214 lb.			

*To outside of exhaust manifold.
†Data for Series 42, used on Light Tanks M5 and M5A1, essentially same except: Length, 63 in.; Width, 27¼ in.; Height 36 in.
**Two of these engines used in each Light Tank M24.

CONTINENTAL ENGINE W-670-9A, LIGHT TANK M3 SERIES

LYCOMING GASOLINE ENGINE O-43-T USED ON LIGHT TANK T9E1

CADILLAC ENGINE SERIES 44 USED ON LIGHT TANK M24

GUIBERSON ENGINE T1020-4 USED ON LIGHT TANK M3 (DIESEL)

MEDIUM AND HEAVY TANK ENGINES

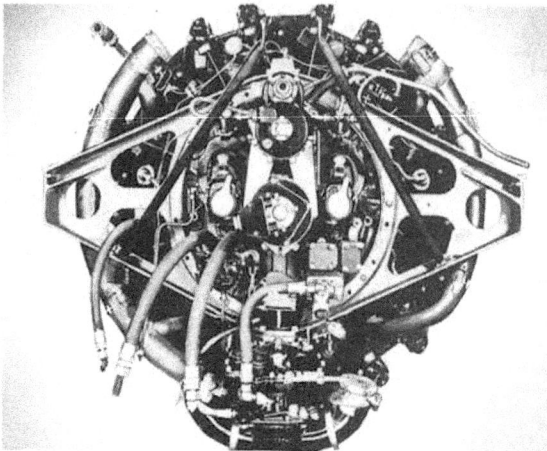

CONTINENTAL ENGINE FOR MEDIUM TANKS M4, M4A1

GENERAL MOTORS POWER UNIT FOR MEDIUM TANK M4A2

FORD GAA ENGINE IS USED IN THE MEDIUM TANK M4A3

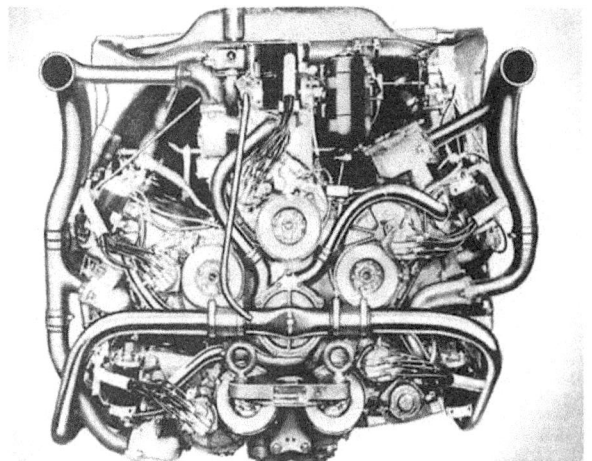

CHRYSLER POWER UNIT FOR MEDIUM TANK M4A4

TYPICAL CHARACTERISTICS

	CONTINENTAL R-975-C1*	G.M. DIESEL 6046	FORD GAA†	CHRYSLER A-57
Type	Radial, A.C.	2-line, L.C.	V-8, L.C.	5-line, L.C.
No. of cylinders	9	12	8	30
Cycle	4	2	4	4
Fuel, Octane or cetane	80 Octane	40 Cetane	80 Octane	80 Octane
Type	Gasoline	Diesel	Gasoline	Gasoline
Bore and stroke	5 x 5½ in.	4¼ x 5 in.	5.4 x 6 in.	3⁷⁄₁₆ x 4½ in.
Displacement	973 cu. in.	850 cu. in.	1,100 cu. in.	1,253 cu. in.
Compression	5.7:1	16:1	7.5:1	6.2:1
Max. governed speed	2,400 r.p.m.	2,100 r.p.m.**	2,600 r.p.m.	2,850 r.p.m.
Gross hp.	400 at 2,400 r.p.m.	410 at 2,900 r.p.m.	500 at 2,600 r.p.m.	425 at 2,850 r.p.m.
Max. gross torque	890 lb.-ft. at 1,800 r.p.m.	885 lb.-ft. at 1,900 r.p.m.	1,040 lb.-ft. at 2,200 r.p.m.	1,060 lb.-ft. at 1,400 r.p.m.
Crankshaft rotation (drive end)	C'Clockwise	C'Clockwise‡	C'Clockwise	C'Clockwise
Length	53 in.	65⅝ in.	60⅜ in.	54⅛ in.
Width	45 in.	59⁵⁄₃₂ in.	33¼ in.	58¾ in.
Height	45 in.	46¾ in.	47½ in.	56½ in.
Ignition	Magneto	Compression	Magneto	Battery
Weight, Dry	1,137 lb.	5,110 lb.	1,560 lb.	5,400 lb.

*R-975-C4 essentially same except: Gross hp., 460 at 2,400 r.p.m.; Max. torque, 1,025 lb.-ft. at 1,800 r.p.m.; Weight, dry, 1,212 lb.
**Crankshaft speed of each 6-cylinder half of power plant.
†Characteristics of Ford GAN engine are generally similar.

‡At power take-off flange out of transfer case, which couples both halves of the power plant, steps up the shaft speed, and reverses rotation with respect to the crankshafts of each half of the power unit.

The variety of medium tank engines shown here is a tribute to the resourcefulness of American industry, in cooperation with the Ordnance Department, in meeting an emergency.

When the program for the quantity production of medium tanks was inaugurated in 1940, it became necessary to find sources of sufficient engines. Medium Tank M3 used the Continental (Wright) R-975 engine, an aircraft type of engine adapted for use in tanks. Medium Tank M3 (Diesel) used the Guiberson T-1400 Diesel engine, but only a few of these were built.

To avoid conflicting with the Air Forces, whose need for engines was equally imperative, efforts were made to adapt commercial truck and passenger car engines, already in production, for use in tanks.

First such engine authorized for use as an alternate power plant was the G.M. 6046 Diesel engine, made up of two standard bus and truck type engines. In the medium tank installation, the engines, located one on either side of the engine compartment, are connected through a step-up gear and double clutch housing to a common propeller shaft. Originally authorized for use in Medium Tank M3A3 by Ordnance Committee action in December 1941, these engines are now used in Medium Tank M4A2 and in vehicles based on these tanks.

The Chrysler A-57 power unit consists of five conventional passenger car engines, geared together to operate as a single unit. Originally authorized for use in Medium Tank M3A4, it was used subsequently in Medium Tank M4A4.

The Ford GAA engine is an 8-cylinder, V-type engine designed specifically for tanks. It was introduced in Medium Tank M4A3 by Ordnance Committee action in January 1942. A modification known as the Ford GAN engine is being used in Medium Tank T23. Virtually the same engine, known as model GAF, is used in Heavy Tank T26E3.

Ordnance Committee action in May 1943 authorized the use of the RD-1820 Ordnance engine in Medium Tank M4A4 hulls, and designated this vehicle Medium Tank M4A6. This engine was formerly known as the Caterpillar D-200A engine.

Heavy Tanks M6 and M6A1 use Wright G-200 series engines, Model 781C9GC1. Heavy Tank T1E1, sometimes referred to as the M6A2, uses a modification of this engine, designated Model 795C9GC1, which is directly coupled to an electric generator.

REFERENCES—OCM 17503, 17578, 17678, 18283, 19200, 19439, 19630, 19631, 20607, 20796, 25785.

TYPICAL CHARACTERISTICS

	ORDNANCE ENGINE RD-1820	GUIBERSON T-1400	WRIGHT G-200 781C9GC1	WRIGHT G-200 795C9GC1**
Type	Radial, A.C.	Radial, A.C.	Radial, A.C.	Radial, A.C.
No. of cylinders	9	9	9	9
Cycle	4	4	4	4
Fuel, Octane and cetane	40 Cetane	40 Cetane	80 Octane	80 Octane
Type	Diesel	Diesel	Gasoline	Gasoline
Bore and Stroke	6⅛ x 6⅞ in.	5¾ x 6 in.	6⅛ x 6⅞ in.	6⅛ x 6⅞ in.
Displacement	1,823 cu. in.	1,400 cu. in.	1,823 cu. in.	1,823 cu. in.
Compression	15.5:1	14.3:1	4.92:1	4.92:1
Max. governed speed	2,000 r.p.m.*	2,400 r.p.m.	2,300 r.p.m.	1,950 r.p.m.
Gross hp	497 at 3,000 r.p.m.†	350 at 2,400 r.p.m.	800 at 2,300 r.p.m.	675 at 1,950 r.p.m.
Max. gross torque	945 lb.-ft. at 2,100 r.p.m.†	935 lb.-ft. at 1,400 r.p.m.	1,850 lb.-ft. at 2,300 r.p.m.	1,810 lb.-ft. at 1,950 r.p.m.
Crankshaft rotation (drive end)	C'Clockwise	C'Clockwise	C'Clockwise	C'Clockwise
Length	56 in.	41½ in.	52 in.	101⅛ in.
Width	55 in.	50 in.	55 in.	64¼ in.
Height	55 in.	50 in.	55 in.	58 in.
Ignition	Compression	Compression	Magneto	Magneto
Weight, Dry	3,536 lb.	1,100 lb.	1,350 lb.	7,900 lb.
Weight, Installed			1,711 lb.	8,261 lb.

*Engine crankshaft speed.
†These data refer to power take-off flange on output shaft out of step-up gear transfer case.
**Data for this power plant take into consideration the direct-coupled main propulsion generator.

RD-1820 ORDNANCE ENGINE USED IN MEDIUM TANK, M4A6

WRIGHT G-200 SERIES ENGINE USED IN HEAVY TANKS

TANK RECOVERY VEHICLES M31 SERIES—LIMITED STANDARD

TANK RECOVERY VEHICLE M31. RIGHT FRONT VIEW. NOTE DUMMY GUNS

LEFT REAR VIEW WITH BOOM IN TRAVELING POSITION, SHOWING TOOL BOXES

TYPICAL CHARACTERISTICS TANK RECOVERY VEHICLE M31

Crew 6

Physical Characteristics

Weight (gross)	60,000 lb.
Length	26 ft., 5 in.
Width	8 ft., 4 in.
Height	9 ft., 9 in.
Turret ring diameter (inside)	57 in.
Ground clearance	$17\frac{1}{8}$ in.
Tread (center to center of tracks)	83 in.
Ground contact length	147 in.
Ground pressure	12.5 lb./sq. in.

Armament

1 Cal. .30 Browning Machine Gun
  M1919A4 (flexible) . . . . .In bow
1 Cal. .30 Browning Machine Gun
  M1919A4 (fixed) . . . . .In turret
1 Cal. .30 Tripod Mount M2
Provision for:
  1 cal. .45 submachine gun

Ammunition, Stowage

Cal. .30	2,000 rounds
Cal. .45	600 rounds
Grenades, Hand (Smoke, M8, 10; Thermite, Incendiary, 4)	14
Smoke Pots, H.C., M1	3

Performance

Maximum speed on level	25 m.p.h.
Maximum grade ability	60%
Trench crossing ability	7 ft., 5 in.
Vertical obstacle ability	24 in.
Fording depth (slowest forward speed)	42 in.
Turning radius	35 ft.
Fuel capacity	185 gal.
Cruising range (approx.)	110 miles

Vision

Protectoscopes and direct vision slots

Communications

Radio	SCR-528 or 610 or British No. 19
Interphone stations	6
Flat Set M38	1

Battery, Voltage, total 24

Fire Protection and Decontamination

Fire Extinguishers, CO$_2$–10 lb. (fixed)	2
CO$_2$–4 lb. (hand)	3
Decontaminating Apparatus M2, $1\frac{1}{2}$ qt.	2

(Other characteristics same as for Medium Tanks M3, M3A3, and M3A5, respectively.)

These vehicles, designed for the recovery of disabled tanks on the battlefield, are modifications of medium tanks of the M3 series.

For camouflage purposes, the normal appearance of the tank is retained as far as possible. A simulated turret without cupola is used, and dummy 75-mm and 37-mm guns are mounted in place of the real guns. Actual armament is limited to a cal. .30 machine gun in the bow and one on the turret for antiaircraft purposes. Provision is made for carrying a cal. .45 submachine gun.

The right hull plate, on which the dummy 75-mm gun is mounted, opens as a door, giving access to the crew compartment. There is no turret basket.

A 60,000-pound-capacity winch is installed in the hull directly below and on the center line of the turret. A boom is mounted on a special mounting plate which replaces the 37-mm gun plate.

The vehicle may be used to tow light, medium, and heavy tanks across country and on highways and to winch tanks out of mudholes, sand, and soft ground, and up slopes. With the winch line threaded through the turret and over the boom, it may be used for various lifting operations, including removal of turrets from medium tanks and lifting a side, front, or rear of a medium tank for work on a track or suspension.

Tank Recovery Vehicle M31 is based on Medium Tank M3 (riveted), with a Continental R-975-C1 engine.

Tank Recovery Vehicle M31B1 is based on Medium Tank M3A3 (welded), with a G.M. 6046 Diesel engine.

Tank Recovery Vehicle M31B2 is based on Medium Tank M3A5 (riveted), with a G.M. 6046 Diesel engine.

The pilot vehicle was built by the Baldwin Locomotive Works.

References—OCM 18596, 18928, 20373, 21554, 21783.

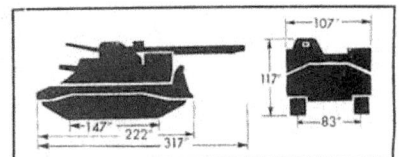

TANK RECOVERY VEHICLE **M32** SERIES—STANDARD

TANK RECOVERY VEHICLE, M32, WITH BOOM RAISED

LEFT FRONT VIEW, SHOWING 81 MM MORTAR, WITH BOOM IN CARRYING POSITION

These vehicles are modifications of medium tanks of the M4 series, designed primarily for recovery of tanks from battlefields.

The boom is of the "A" frame type, of 4½ inch tubular steel approximately 18 feet long. It is mounted on the forward sides of the sponsons and is pivoted. In the carrying position, laid back over the hull and supported by the sub "A" frame in the rear, it can be used for lifting and towing purposes where it is designed to carry a portion of the towed weight. When extended to its full raised position in front, the boom is held in position by cables.

An 81 mm mortar is mounted on the front plate. Other armament includes a cal. .50 machine gun on the turret, and a cal. .30 machine gun in the bow.

A rounded front fixed turret is provided in place of the customary tank turret.

A 60,000 pound capacity winch is installed on the floor directly in back of the driver. Operation of the winch and of the "A" frame boom is controlled by the driver. The vehicle may be driven and the winch operated at the same time.

Chock blocks are supplied to keep the vehicle from moving during winching operations. Telescopic hold-off poles are furnished to keep towed vehicles from getting too close to the recovery vehicle.

Tank Recovery Vehicle, M32, is a modification of Medium Tank, M4, welded hull, with a Continental R975–C1 engine.

Tank Recovery Vehicle, M32B1, is based on Medium Tank, M4A1, cast hull, with a Continental R975–C1 engine.

Tank Recovery Vehicle, M32B2, is a modification of Medium Tank, M4A2, welded hull, powered by a GMC 6–71 6046 Diesel engine.

Tank Recovery Vehicle, M32B3, is a modification of Medium Tank, M4A3,

welded hull, with a Ford GAA engine.

Tank Recovery Vehicle, M32B4, is based on Medium Tank, M4A4, welded hull, with Chrysler Multibank engine.

The pilot vehicle was built by the Lima Locomotive Works.

REFERENCES — OCM 19995, 20011, 20245, 20374, 20980, 21554, 21713.

CHARACTERISTICS OF TANK RECOVERY VEHICLE, M32

Crew 4

Physical Characteristics

Weight (gross) . . . . .62,000 lb.
Length of hull . . . . .19 ft., 1¼ ins.
Width. . . . . .8 ft., 7 ins.
Height. . . . . .8 ft., 8³⁄₁₆ ins.
Length of boom . . . . .18 ft.
Turret ring diameter (inside) . . . . .68 ins.
Ground clearance . . . . .17⅛ ins.
Tread (center to center of tracks) . . . . . .83 ins.
Ground contact length. . . . . .147 ins.
Ground pressure . . . . .13.3 lb./sq. in.

Armament

1 cal. .50 Machine Gun, M2, HB,
(flexible). . .On Ring Mount, M49, on turret
1 81 mm Mortar, M1 . . . .On front plate of hull
  Elevation . . . .+40° to +80°
  Traverse . . . . .130 mils
1 cal. .30 Machine Gun, M1919A4
(flexible). . . . . .In ball mount in bow
1 81 mm Mortar Mount, M1, w/o base plate
1 Carriage and cradle assembly
1 Tripod Mount, cal. .30, M2
Provision for:
1 cal. .45 submachine gun

Ammunition, Stowage

Cal. .30 . . . . .2,000 rounds
Cal. .50 . . . . .300 rounds
Cal. .45 . . . . .600 rounds
81 mm Mortar, W.P., M57. . . . . . . .30 rounds
Grenades, Hand (Fragmentation Mk. II, 5;
  Smoke, WP, M15, 15). 20
Smoke Pots, H.C., M1 6

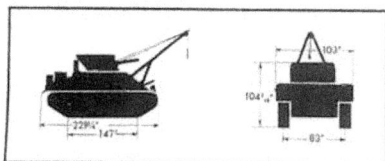

Armor	Actual	Basis
Hull, Front, Upper	2 ins.	2–4 ins.
Lower.	1½–2 ins.	2–2½ ins
Sides	1½ ins.	1½ ins.
Rear	1–1½ ins.	1–1½ ins.
Top	¾ in.	
Bottom	½ in.	
Turret, Front	1¼ ins.	1¼ ins.
Sides and Rear	1¼ ins.	1¼ ins.

Performance

Maximum speed on level. . . . . .24 m.p.h.
Maximum grade ability. 60%
Trench crossing ability . . . . .6 ft., 2 ins.
Vertical obstacle ability. . . . . .24 ins.
Fording depth (slowest forward speed) . .48 ins.
Turning radius. . . . . .31 ft.
Fuel capacity. . . . . .175 gals.
Cruising range. . . . . .120 miles

Vision and Fire Control

Periscopes, M6 4
Sight, M4. 1

Communications

Radio . . . . .SCR 528, 538 (less Radio Receiver
             BC-603), 610 or British 19
Interphone stations 4
Flag Set, M238. 1

Battery, Voltage, total. 24

Fire Protection and Decontamination

Fire Extinguisher, CO₂–10 lb. (fixed) 2
  CO₂–4 lb. (hand) 3
Decontaminating Apparatus, M2, 1½ qts.. . .3

(Other characteristics same as for respective variation of Medium Tank, M4, Series.)

45-TON TANK TRANSPORTER TRUCK, TRAILER M19—LIMITED STANDARD

45-TON TANK TRANSPORTER TRUCK, TRAILER, M19, IS CAPABLE OF HAULING MEDIUM TANKS AND SIMILAR EQUIPMENT ALONG THE HIGHWAY

Manufactured originally by the Quartermaster Corps for the British, these vehicles were authorized for limited procurement and designated Substitute Standard, in September, 1942. The vehicles were reclassified as Limited Standard in June, 1943, upon standardization of the M25 vehicle.

Consisting of 12-Ton, 6x4 (4DT) Truck, M20, and 45-Ton, 12 Wheel (12DT) Trailer, M9, the complete tank transporter is approximately 52 feet, 9 inches long, and has a train weight, with 90,000 pound payload, of 160,000 pounds.

Its main use is the evacuation of heavy equipment from points along the axis of evacuation and supply. Its use in battlefield recovery is limited because it is not designed for travel over rough or muddy terrain.

REFERENCES — OCM 18552, 18626, 20129, 20375, 20717.

12-TON, 6x4 (4DT) TRUCK, M20, serves as the prime mover for the tank transporter trailer, and may also be used for many independent operations.

It is powered by a Hercules DXFE Diesel engine. The main transmission has four speeds forward and one in reverse. An auxiliary transmission, for low-range driving, has three forward speed selections, and also powers the 40,000 pound capacity winch, mounted at the rear.

The winch cable may be threaded through a roller alongside the radiator for operations requiring a front winch. A torque control stops the winch if the line pull becomes excessive.

Skid pans are used to help anchor the transporter during winch operations.

TYPICAL CHARACTERISTICS

12-TON, 6x4 (4DT) TRUCK, M20
Crew 3
Physical Characteristics
Weight—empty . . . . 26,650 lb.
   loaded . . . . 45,000 lb.
Length . . . . 23 ft., 3¾ ins.
Width . . . . 8 ft., 4 ins.
Height . . . . 3 ft., 4 ins.
Ground clearance . . . . 11⅛ ins.
Wheelbase . . . . 179¼ ins. (52 in. bogie)
Tread (center to center, rear) . . . . 74 ins.
Tire equipment . . . . 12.00 x 20, 14 ply

Performance
Maximum speed on level . . . . 23 m.p.h.
Speed on 3% grade . . . . 6 m.p.h.
Speed on 10% grade . . . . 2 m.p.h.
Maximum grade ability, with towed load . . 25%
  without towed load 65%
Fording depth (slowest forward speed) . . 32 ins.
Angle of approach . . . . 40½°
Angle of departure . . . . 51°
Turning radius . . . . 33 ft.
Fuel capacity . . . . 150 gals.
Cruising range . . . . 300 miles
Payload . . . . 18,350 lb.
Max. towed load . . . . 115,000 lb.
Winch capacity . . . . 40,000 lb.

Battery, Voltage, total 24

Engine, Make and Model . . . . Hercules, DFXE
No. of cylinders 6

Fuel (Diesel) . . . . 45 Cetane
Max. governed speed . . . . 1,600 r.p.m.
Net hp. . . . . 178 at 1,600 r.p.m.
Max. torque . . . . . 685 lb.-ft. at 1,200 r.p.m.

Transmission, Gear ratios
First speed 5.55:1
Second speed 3.27:1
Third speed 1.76:1
Fourth speed 1:1
Reverse 6.58:1

Transfer Case, Gear ratios .77:1; 1:1; 1.99:1

Rear Axle, Gear ratio 11.66:1

Brakes, Service, Type . . . . Air
Parking, Type . . . . Disk

45-TON, 12 WHEEL (12DT) TRAILER, M9
Physical Characteristics
Weight—empty (approx.) . . . . 25,000 lb.
  payload . . . . 90,000 lb.
Length—overall (approx.) . . . . . . 29 ft., 8 ins.
Width . . . . 9 ft., 6 ins.
Height (trailer only) . . . . 4 ft., 9½ ins.
Height of deck . . . . 39 ins.
Ground clearance . . . . 18 ins.
Wheelbase . . . . 187 ins. (40 in. bogie)
Tire equipment . . . . 8.25 x 15, 14 ply

Brakes, Service, Type . . . . Air
Parking, Type . . . . Wheel-operated

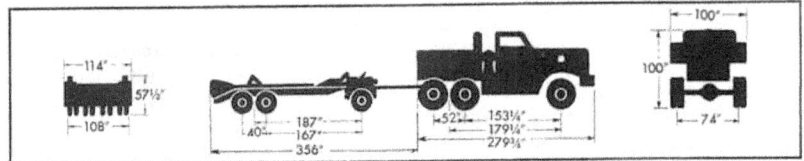

The truck has accommodations for a crew of three. Pintles are provided at the front and rear. The vehicle has air-brake controls for the trailed load.

45-TON, 12 WHEEL (12DT) TRAILER, M9, is designed to transport medium and light tanks. It may be used with the above truck, or with a tractor or similar prime mover. It is fastened behind the towing vehicle by a draw bar and safety chains.

Two ramps, hinged at the rear of the trailer, facilitate loading. Four chock blocks are provided to keep the load in position while traveling.

Air brakes, controlled from the towing vehicle, stop the trailer automatically if it breaks away.

TRACTOR TRUCKS **M26**—LIMITED STANDARD; **M26A1**—STANDARD
SEMITRAILER **M15**—LIMITED STANDARD
45-TON, 8-WHEEL, TRANSPORTER SEMITRAILER **M15A1**—SUBSTITUTE STANDARD

TRACTOR TRUCK M26 HAS ARMORED CAB WITH RING MOUNT

TRACTOR TRUCK M26A1 HAS UNARMORED, "SOFT TOP" CAB

Tractor Truck M26 and Semitrailer M15 were standardized in June 1943 as components of the 40-Ton Tank Transporter Truck-Trailer M25. In October 1944 Tractor Truck M26A1 was standardized and Tractor Truck M26 was reclassified as Limited Standard, and at the same time the practice of assigning nomenclature to the combination of tractor truck and semitrailer was discontinued. Previously the 45-Ton, 8-Wheel, Transporter Semitrailer M15A1 was classified as Substitute Standard to replace Semitrailer M15 in production, and arrangements were made to reclassify the M15 as Limited Standard when production of the M15A1 got under way.

The tractor truck and semitrailer were designed for use in combination in recovering and evacuating disabled materiel over all types of terrain, but can be used separately. When separated from the semitrailer, the tractor truck can perform most of the functions of a heavy wrecker.

REFERENCES—OCM 18047, 18079, 18319, 18552, 18732, 20129, 20676, 20680, 20717, 20802, 21002, 21008, 21871, 24053, 24938, 25029, 25258, 25332; SNL G–160.

TRACTOR TRUCK M26 is a 6x6 vehicle designed to supply the power and equipment needed for a variety of recovering and wrecking operations. It has an armored cab, all openings of which are protected against lead splash, to permit operation in combat areas. A Ring Mount M49 for a cal. .50 machine gun is mounted on the roof for protection against aircraft.

Accommodations are provided for a crew of seven, including the driver.

The vehicle uses divided rim type wheels with beadlocks. Single wheels are used at the front and dual wheels on

SEMITRAILER M15 WILL CARRY TWO LIGHT TANKS OR ONE MEDIUM TANK

SEMITRAILER M15A1 HAS RAMPS FOR LOADING HEAVY TANK OVER TIRES

the rear. Power is applied to all wheels.

A heavy duty universal type semi-automatic fifth wheel is provided for towing the semitrailer. Air brakes are provided on the four rear wheels and there is an air-brake valve connection for the semitrailer.

Power is supplied by a Hall Scott, 440, in-line, 6-cylinder, water-cooled engine. The transmission has four speeds forward and one reverse speed. In connection with an auxiliary transmission, twelve forward

speeds and three reverse speeds are available.

A front-mounted winch, controlled from the cab, has a capacity of 35,000 pounds on the first layer. Its primary purpose is the recovery of the truck and semitrailer when stuck in terrain which they cannot negotiate. It may also be used for recovery of other loads if the terrain makes the use of the rear winches unfeasible.

Two winches mounted behind the cab are controlled from the operations platform and have a capacity of 60,000 pounds on the first layer. These are generally used for loading and unloading the semitrailer and for doing the bulk of the recovery work. They may be used in tandem or independently of each other.

The pilot vehicle was built by the Knuckey Truck Co. Production vehicles were built by the Pacific Car and Foundry Co.

TRACTOR TRUCK M26A1 is a modification of the M26 with an unarmored "soft top" cab. A Ring Mount M49 for a cal. .50 machine gun is provided.

SEMITRAILER M15 is an eight-wheeled semitrailer designed especially for use with the Tractor Truck M26.

It will carry loads up to 80,000 pounds.

Hinged ramps at the rear are lowered to the ground for use in loading, the winch cables from the tractor truck being threaded through rollers at the front of the trailer and to the disabled vehicle. The semitrailer wheels may be moved closer together or farther apart to accommodate vehicles of different widths.

The semitrailer may be loaded and made ready for travel in the absence of the tractor truck, inasmuch as its front end may be made to rest on skis supported by collapsible legs.

Wheel covers, skid rails, and bed rails are used to provide a smooth surface, and to protect the tires when vehicles without

wheels or tracks are winched onto the semitrailer.

The vehicle uses divided rim type wheels and has air brakes operated from the tractor.

The pilot vehicle was built by the Fruehauf Trailer Co.

45-TON, 8-WHEEL, TRANSPORTER SEMITRAILER M15A1 is a modification of Semitrailer M15 designed to accommodate Heavy Tank T26E3. The trailer bed is strengthened to support the weight of the Heavy Tank T26E3. Hinged ramps are provided over the outer wheels so the tank may be loaded over the wheels. All of the functions of the Semitrailer M15 are preserved.

TYPICAL CHARACTERISTICS

	M26	M26A1
Crew	7	7
Physical Characteristics		
Weight (gross)	48,300 lb.	45,000 lb.
Length (overall)	25 ft., 4 in.	25 ft., 7 in.
Width	10 ft., 10¾ in.	10 ft., 10½ in.
Height, To top of ring mount	10 ft., 4 in.	10 ft., 8 in.
To top of cab	9 ft., 6 in.	9 ft., 6 in.
Ground clearance	14 in.	14 in.
Tread (center to center, rear)	98½ in.	98½ in.
Wheelbase	172 in.	172 in.
Tire equipment	14.00x24, 20-ply	14.00x24, 20-ply
Armament		
Ring Mount M49	1	1
Provision for:		
Cal. .50 Machine Gun HB M2 (flexible)	1	1
Cal. .50 Tripod Mount M3	1	1
Cal. .45 submachine gun	1	1
Cal. .30 carbine		1
Ammunition, Stowage		
Cal. .50	1,500 rounds	700 rounds
Cal. .45	600 rounds	600 rounds
Grenades	24	
Armor, Actual Thickness		
Front	¾ in.	¾ in.
Sides, rear, and top	¼ in.	¼ in.
Performance		
Maximum speed on level	26 m.p.h.	26 m.p.h.
Speed on 3% grade	12 m.p.h.	12 m.p.h.
Maximum grade ability	30%	30%
Vertical obstacle ability	22 in.	22 in.
Fording depth	56 in.	56 in.
Angle of approach	35°	32°
Fuel capacity	120 gal.	120 gal.
Cruising range (approx.)	250 miles	270 miles
Maximum drawbar pull (with trailer coupled)	60,000 lb.	60,000 lb.
Payload	55,000 lb.	58,000 lb.
Normal towed load	115,000 lb.	132,675 lb.
Communications		
Flag Set M238	1	1
Battery, Voltage, total	12	12
Fire Protection and Decontamination		
Fire Extinguisher, CO_2–4 lb. (hand)	4	3
Decontaminating Apparatus M2, 1½ qt.	2	2

	M26	M26A1
Engine, Make and model	Hall Scott, 440	Hall Scott, 440
Type	In-line, L.C.	In-line, L.C.
No. of cylinders	6	6
Fuel (gasoline)	70–72 octane	70–72 octane
Max. governed speed	2,100 r.p.m.	2,100 r.p.m.
Net hp.	230 at 2,100 r.p.m.	230 at 2,100 r.p.m.
Max. torque	810 lb.–ft. at 1,100 r.p.m.	810 lb.–ft. at 1,100 r.p.m.
Transmission, Type	Selective sliding	Selective sliding
Gear ratios		
First speed	5.55:1	5.55:1
Second speed	3.27:1	3.27:1
Third speed	1.76:1	1.76:1
Fourth speed	1:1	1:1
Reverse	6.58:1	6.58:1
Transfer Case		
Gear ratios	0.75:1, 1:1, 2.62:1	0.75:1, 1:1, 2.29:1
Rear Axle, Gear ratio	7.69:1	
Including chain reduction		14.65:1
Brakes, Service, Type	Air	Air
Parking, Type	Drum	Drum

SEMITRAILERS

	M15	M15A1
Physical Characteristics		
Weight (gross, without tank load)	35,000 lb.	42,675 lb.
With load	115,000 lb.	132,675 lb.
Length	38 ft., 9 in.	39 ft., 6½ in.
Length of bed	27 ft., 5 in.	27 ft., 5 in.
Width, Normal operating	12 ft., 6½ in.	12 ft., 6½ in.
Emergency operating	10 ft., 4 in.	10 ft., 4 in.
Width of bed	10 ft., 4 in.	10 ft., 4 in.
Height (overall)	9 ft., 6 in.	9 ft., 6 in.
Height of bed	3 ft., 6 in.	3 ft., 6 in.
Ground clearance	14 in.	14 in.
Tread (center to center, rear)	131 in.	131 in.
Wheelbase (center of bogie to king pin)	372 in.	372 in.
Tire equipment	14.00x24, 20-ply	14.00x24, 20-ply
Performance		
Payload	80,000 lb.	90,000 lb.
Brakes, Type	Two-shoe, fixed anchor	Two-shoe, fixed anchor
Operation	Internal-expanding, air	Internal-expanding, air

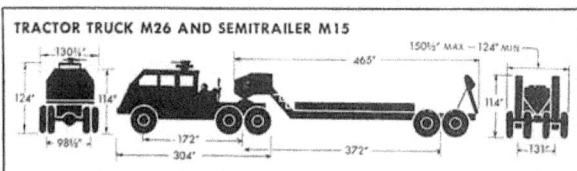
TRACTOR TRUCK M26 AND SEMITRAILER M15

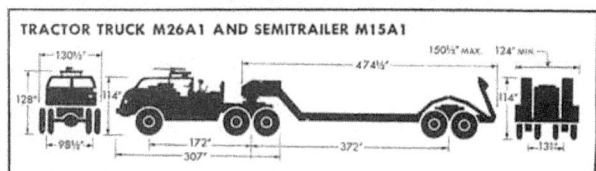
TRACTOR TRUCK M26A1 AND SEMITRAILER M15A1

75-MM GUN MOTOR CARRIAGES M3, M3A1

75-MM GUN MOTOR CARRIAGE M3, WITH MODIFIED GUNSHIELD FOR INDIRECT SIGHTING DEVICE; THE M3A1 DIFFERED ONLY IN GUN MOUNT

TYPICAL CHARACTERISTICS

Crew 5

Physical Characteristics
Weight (gross) . . . . .20,000 lb.
Length . . . . .20 ft., 5½ in.
Width . . . . .7 ft., 1 in.
Height . . . . .8 ft., 2⅝ in.
Height of center line of bore . . . . .82 in.
Ground clearance . . . . .11³⁄₁₆ in.
Tread, Front . . . . .64½ in.
   Rear .63¹³⁄₁₆ in.
Wheelbase . . . . .135½ in.
Ground contact length . . . . .46¾ in.
Tire equipment . . . . . .8.25x20, 12-ply, combat

Armament
1 75-mm Gun M1897A4, on Mount M3 or M5
Provision for:
   1 Cal. .30 Rifle M1903
   4 Cal. .30 Carbines M1

1 Grenade Launcher . . . . .For rifle

Ammunition, Stowage
75-mm (H.E., Mk. 1; H.E., M48; Chem.,
   Mk. II; A.P.C., M61; A.P., M72) .59 rounds
Grenades (Hand: Fragmentation, Mk. II, 5;
   Smoke, M8, 5; Thermite, Incendiary, 2;
   Rifle: M9A1, 10) 22

Armor, Front, sides, and rear . . . . ¼ in.
Windshield shield . . . . ½ in.
Wingshields . . . . ¼ in.
Top, engine compartment . . . . ¼ in.
Gun shield, Front . . . . ⅝ in.
   Sides and top . . . . ¼ in.

Performance
Maximum speed on level . . . . .45 m.p.h.
Speed on 4% grade . . . . .25 m.p.h.
Maximum grade ability 60%
Vertical obstacle ability . . . . .12 in.

Fording depth (slowest forward speed) . . .32 in.
Turning radius . . . . .30 ft.
Fuel capacity . . . . .60 gal.
Cruising range . . . . .200 miles

Vision and Fire Control
Direct—Slits in windshield and wingshields
Telescope M33 1
Telescope Mount M36 1
Instrument Light M17 1

Communications
Radio SCR-510
Flag Set M238 .1

Fire Protection and Decontamination
Fire Extinguisher, CO₂-2 lb. 1
Decontaminating Apparatus M2, 1½ qt. 1

(Other characteristics same as for Half-Track Personnel Carrier M3.)

The 75-mm Gun Motor Carriage M3, the first standardized American self-propelled antitank weapon used in World War II, provided high mobility for the 75-mm gun. Standardized in November 1941, it was put into production in time to aid in the rout of Rommel's troops in North Africa.

It was reclassified as Limited Standard in March 1944 upon the standardization of 76-mm Gun Motor Carriage M18, and was declared obsolete in September 1944.

The gun was carried on Mount M3, a mount adapted from the 75-mm Gun Carriage M2A3. It could be elevated from −10° to +29° and could be traversed 19° to the left and 21° to the right.

The 75-mm Gun Motor Carriage M3A1, which was also declared obsolete in September 1944, used Gun Mount M5, adapted from Gun Carriage M2A2. Its gun could be elevated from 6½° to +29° and traversed 21° right and 21° left. Both vehicles had a gunshield that gave protection against cal. .30 armor-piercing bullets at 250 yards and overhead protection from frontal attack by aircraft. The shield traversed with the gun.

An A. P. C. projectile fired from the gun had a muzzle velocity of 2,000 feet per second, and would penetrate 3 inches of face-hardened plate at 1,000 yards.

The gun was loaded and operated from the crew compartment. Stowage space was provided for 59 rounds of ammunition and for a cal. .30 rifle and four cal. .30 carbines, which were the personal equipment of the crew.

Body armor was the same as on Half Track Personnel Carrier M3, including hinged protective shields for the windshield and doors. A detachable canvas top was provided. The vehicle was equipped with a two-way radio.

The pilot vehicle was built by the Autocar Co.

REFERENCES—TM 9–306, 9–710; M3: OCM 16970, 17054, 17377, 17450, 17878, 18072, 18160, 20680, 21002. M3A1: OCM 18682, 20253, 22918, 23202, 24942, 25260; SNL G–102, Vols. 8 and 9.

37-MM GUN MOTOR CARRIAGE M6

37-MM GUN MOTOR CARRIAGE M6 WAS BASED ON ¾-TON, 4x4, TRUCK

OVERHEAD VIEW, SHOWING GUN MOUNT AND STOWAGE OF AMMUNITION

This vehicle was standardized in February 1942, to provide greater mobility for the 37-mm antitank gun, previously used on a gun carriage towed behind a separate vehicle.

It depended on its speed to travel quickly to a point of vantage, deliver firepower sufficient to knock out a light tank, and retire before heavier firepower could be concentrated against it. It was reclassified as Limited Standard in September 1943 and was declared obsolete in January 1945.

The 37-mm Antitank Gun M3 had a muzzle velocity of 2,900 feet per second. The A. P. C. projectile fired from this gun would penetrate 1.8 inches of face-hardened armor plate at 1,000 yards.

The gun was mounted on the chassis of a standard ¾-Ton, 4x4, Truck by means of a Pedestal Mount M25 or M26 bolted to the floor. The cradle or top assembly was identical with the top carriage of 37-mm Carriage M4. The mount afforded elevations from −10° to +15° and a traverse of 360°. Normal firing was to the rear because full depression could not be obtained to the front.

A ¼-inch armor plate shield gave upper and lower frontal and partial flank protection, including overhead protection against frontal attack by low-flying aircraft.

Power was supplied by a 6-cylinder, L-head gasoline engine. A take-off from the engine supplied the power to operate the 5,000-pound-capacity winch.

Normal crew consisted of a commander, gunner, loader, and driver. The vehicle was equipped with a two-way radio. Provision was made for carrying a rifle and three carbines and also for blankets, a water bucket, and pioneer tools.

The pilot vehicle was manufactured by the Fargo Division, Chrysler Motor Co.

REFERENCES — TM 9-750A; OCM 16802, 16835, 16933, 17273, 17303, 17359, 17495, 17579, 17847, 19048, 19134, 20680, 21002, 21266, 21457, 25889, 26359.

TYPICAL CHARACTERISTICS

Crew..................................4

Physical Characteristics
Weight (gross).....................7,350 lb.
Length..........................14 ft., 10 in.
Width...............................7 ft., 4 in.
Height...........................6 ft., 10¾ in.
Height of center line of bore......5 ft., 4½ in.
Ground clearance....................10⅝ in.
Tread (center to center, rear).......64¾ in.
Wheelbase.............................98 in.
Tire equipment........9.00x16, 8-ply, combat

Armament
1 37-mm Gun M3........On Pedestal Mount
M25 or M26
Elevation..................−10° to +15°
Traverse.........................360°
Provision for:
1 Cal. .30 Rifle M1903A1
1 Grenade Launcher
3 Cal. .30 Carbines M1

Ammunition, Stowage
37-mm (A.P.C. M51B1, with tracer; H.E.
M63, with BD Fuze M58; Canister M2;
A.P. M74, with tracer)..........80 rounds
Grenades (Hand: Fragmentation, 5; Smoke,
W.P., M8, 5; Thermite Incendiary, 2;
Rifle: M9A1, 10)....................22

Armor
Gun shield, Front and top.............¼ in.

Performance
Maximum speed on level...........55 m.p.h.
Speed on 10% grade...............20 m.p.h.
Maximum grade ability................60%
Vertical obstacle ability............12 in.
Fording depth (slowest forward speed)..35 in.
Angle of approach...................36½°
Angle of departure....................31°
Turning radius.......................22 ft.
Fuel capacity.......................30 gal.
Cruising range....................180 miles
Payload..........................1,200 lb.

Vision and Fire Control
Telescope M6...........................1
Telescope Mount M19....................1
Bore Sight.............................1

Communications
Radio............................SCR-510
Flag Set M238..........................1

Battery, Voltage, total...............6

Fire Protection and Decontamination
Carbon tetrachloride, 1 qt............1
Decontaminating Apparatus M2, 1½ qt....1

Engine, Make and model........Dodge T-214
Type.........................In-line, L
No. of cylinders......................6
Fuel (gasoline)................72 octane
Net hp..............99 at 3,300 r.p.m.
Max. torque......184 lb.-ft. at 1,400 r.p.m.

(Other characteristics same as for ¾-Ton, 4x4, Truck.)

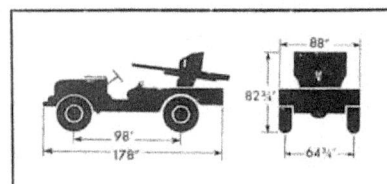

105-MM HOWITZER MOTOR CARRIAGES **M7, M7B1**— SUBSTITUTE STANDARD

105-MM HOWITZER MOTOR CARRIAGE **M37**—STANDARD

Standardization in January 1945 of 105-mm Howitzer Motor Carriage M37 added another vehicle to the combat team built upon the Light Tank M24 chassis and continued the line of powerful weapons started with 105-mm Howitzer Motor Carriage M7, which helped rout Rommel in Libya.

All are lightly-armored, open-top vehicles in which a 105-mm howitzer is the principal armament. The pulpit-like appearance of the machine gun compartment caused the M7 to be nicknamed "The Priest" by British troops.

105-MM HOWITZER MOTOR CARRIAGE M7 was standardized in April 1942 and was reclassified as Substitute Standard in January 1945. The vehicle is based on a Medium Tank M3 chassis which has a Continental R–975–C1 gasoline engine, syncromesh transmission, and a vertical volute spring suspension.

Principal armament is a 105-mm Howitzer M2A1 mounted at the front of the crew compartment. The howitzer can be elevated from −5° to +35° and can be traversed 30° to the right and 15° to the left. An HE shell, fired from this howitzer, has a muzzle velocity of 1,550 feet per second at an elevation of 44° and a maximum range of 12,205 yards.

A Cal. .50 Machine Gun M2 HB (flexible) on a ring mount is provided for use against low-flying aircraft. Provision is made for 3 cal. .45 submachine guns.

The crew of seven consists of the driver, chief of section, gunner, and four cannoneers. The crew compartment is protected by ½-in. armor at the front, sides, and rear, and is open at the top. The upper portion of the side and rear armor is hinged and held in position by lock pins. Grip handles, which serve as ladders leading to the crew compartment, are at both sides of the vehicle.

Direct vision for the driver is through a removable windshield and indirect vision through a protectoscope. The vehicle has five speeds forward and one reverse, the maximum speed being 24 m.p.h.

The pilot vehicle was manufactured by the American Locomotive Co.

References—TM 9-731E; OCM 17760, 18007, 18120, 18151, 18226, 19327, 19525, 20680, 21002, 21211, 23540, 23712, 24984, 25812, 26429; SNL G–128.

105-MM HOWITZER MOTOR CARRIAGE M7B1 is based on the Medium Tank M4A3 chassis and is powered by a Ford GAA, V–8, gasoline engine. Stand-

105-MM HOWITZER MOTOR CARRIAGE M7 USES MEDIUM TANK M3 CHASSIS

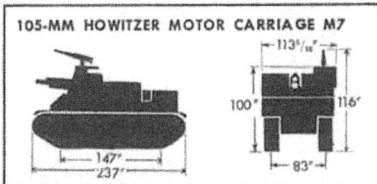

105-MM HOWITZER MOTOR CARRIAGE M7

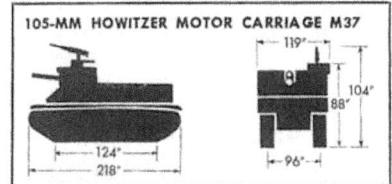

105-MM HOWITZER MOTOR CARRIAGE M37

105-MM HOWITZER MOTOR CARRIAGE M37 HAS LIGHT TANK M24 CHASSIS

ardized in September 1943, it was reclassified as Substitute Standard in January 1945.

Physical characteristics and performance of this vehicle are generally similar to those of 105-mm Howitzer Motor Carriage M7, the only difference being in the variations of the respective tanks.

References—TM 9-749; OCM21720, 25812, 26429; SNL G–199.

105-MM HOWITZER MOTOR CARRIAGE M37 was standardized in January 1945. It is a lighter, more mobile, and less expensive 105-mm howitzer motor carriage than the earlier vehicles, which were based on medium tank chassis, and has better armor protection.

It is a full track-laying vehicle, with individual torsion bar suspension, driven from the front sprocket. Like the Twin 40-mm Gun Motor Carriage M19, it has a chassis similar to the Light Tank M24, forming another member of a combat team of vehicles designed for maximum interchangeability.

OVERHEAD VIEW OF THE M37, SHOWING OPEN FIGHTING COMPARTMENT

a muzzle velocity of 1,550 feet per second and at an elevation of 44°, has a range of 12,205 yards. The howitzer, which is carried on Mount M5, can be elevated from −10° to +45° and can be traversed 22½° left and 22½° right. A Cal. .50 Machine Gun M2 HB (flexible) on a concentric ring mount is provided. Provision is made for carrying one cal. .45 submachine gun and six cal. .30 carbines.

Power is supplied by twin Cadillac engines through Hydra-Matic transmissions and a transfer unit with synchronizer that provide eight forward speeds up to 35 m.p.h. and four reverse speeds up to 18 m.p.h.

Indirect vision for the driver is provided by a periscope.

Provision is made for installing a telephone and reel unit, with interphone communication for the chief of section and the driver. A British No. 19 wireless set may be installed if 24 rounds of ammunition are removed.

Shorter but wider than the 105-mm Howitzer Motor Carriages M7 and M7B1, the M37 provides greater working space for the crew members and increased space for ammunition stowage. Armor plate ½ in. thick affords protection at the front, sides, and rear of the vehicle, and also over the driver's compartment.

Principal armament is a 105-mm Howitzer M4, which when firing the HE shell at

REFERENCES—OCM 20679, 21009, 22304, 22435, 24883, 25812, 26429.

CHARACTERISTICS OF 105-MM HOWITZER MOTOR CARRIAGES M7, M7B1, M37

	M7*, M7B1**		M37†		
Crew	7		7		
Physical Characteristics					
Weight	50,634 lb.		40,000 lb.		
Length	19 ft., 9 in.		18 ft., 2 in.		
Width	9 ft., 5 5/16 in.		9 ft., 11 in.		
Height	8 ft., 4 in.		7 ft., 4 in.		
Over A. A. gun	9 ft., 8 in.		8 ft., 8 in.		
Ground clearance	17⅛ in.		17 in.		
Tread (center to center of tracks)	83 in.		96 in.		
Ground contact length	147 in.		124 in.		
Ground pressure	10.4 lb./sq. in.		10.1 lb./sq. in.		
Armament					
105-mm Howitzer	M2A1 in Mount M4		M4 in Mount M5		
Elevation	−5° to +35°		−10° to +45°		
Traverse	30° right, 15° left		22½° right, 22½° left		
1 Cal. .50 Machine Gun M2 HB (flexible)	On ring mount		On ring mount		
Provision for:					
Cal. .45 submachine guns	3		1		
Cal. .30 carbines	0		6		
Ammunition, Stowage					
105-mm	69 rounds		90 rounds		
Cal. .50	300 rounds		900 rounds		
Cal. .45	1,620 rounds		600 rounds		
Hand Grenades	8		8		
Armor	**Actual**	**Basis**	**Actual**	**Basis**	
Hull, front, upper	½ in.	½ in.	½ in.	1¼ in.	
Lower	2–4¼ in.	2–4½ in.	½ in.	⅞ in.	
Sides, upper	½ in.	½ in.	½ in.	½ in.	
Lower	1½ in.***	1½ in.	½ in.	½ in.	
Rear, upper	½ in.	½ in.	½ in.	½ in.	
Lower	1½ in.***	1½ in.	½ in.	⅞ in.	
Bottom, front	1 in.	1 in.	½ in.	½ in.	
Rear	½ in.	½ in.	⅜ in.	⅜ in.	
Top, forward			½ in.		
Gun mount shield			½ in.	½ in.	
Performance					
Maximum speed on level	25 m.p.h.		35 m.p.h.		
Maximum grade ability	60%		60%		
Trench crossing ability	7 ft., 6 in.		7 ft.		
Vertical obstacle ability	24 in.		42 in.		
Fording depth (slowest forward speed)	48 in.		42 in.		
Turning diameter	62 ft.		40 ft.		
Fuel capacity	179 gal.		115 gal.		
Cruising range (approx.)	85–125 miles		100–150 miles		

		M7	M37
Vision and Fire Control			
Periscope M6	0		2
Protectoscope	1		0
Panoramic Telescope M12-A2, w/Instrument Light M19	1		1
On Mount M21A1, w/8-in. filler piece	1		0
On Mount T96	0		1
Telescope M76G (3-power), on Mount T95, w/Instrument Light M33	0		1
Elbow Telescope M16 or M16A1C	1		0
Telescope Mount M42	1		0
Instrument Light M36 (for M16A1C)	1		0
Aiming Post M1, w/Aiming Post Light M14	2		2
Range Quadrant M4	1		0
Range Quadrant T14, w/Instrument Light M18	0		1
Gunner's Quadrant M1	1		1
Fuze Setter M22	1		1
Communications			
Flag Set M238	1		1
Panel Set AP50A	0		1
Provision for:			
Telephone EE-8-( ) and Reel Unit RL-39	0		1
Interphone RC-99	0		1
British Wireless Set No. 19	0		1 ††
Battery, Voltage, total	24		24
Fire Protection and Decontamination			
Fire Extinguisher			
CO₂–10 lb. (fixed)	2		2
CO₂–4 lb. (hand)	2		2
Decontaminating Apparatus, 1½ qt.	3		2

*Other characteristics same as for Medium Tank M3.
**Characteristics of M7B1 same as for M7 except: weight, 50,000 lb.; length, 20 ft., 3 ¾ in.; ground pressure, 10.3 lb./sq. in.; maximum speed, 26 m.p.h.; fording depth, 36 in.; fuel capacity, 168 gal.
***Soft plate, minimum ballistics of ½-inch armor.
†Other characteristics same as for Light Tank M24.
††Displaces 18 rounds of 105-mm ammunition.

105-MM HOWITZER MOTOR CARRIAGE T19

105-MM HOWITZER MOTOR CARRIAGE T19, SHOWING HOWITZER AT 0° ELEVATION. THIS VEHICLE WAS NEVER STANDARDIZED.

This weapon was designed as an expedient to provide a 105-mm howitzer on a self-propelled mount. It was superceded by the 105-mm Howitzer Motor Carriage M17 and is no longer in use.

The weapon consisted of a 105-mm Howitzer M2A1 mounted on a Half-Track Personnel Carriage M3.

Authority to construct the weapon was requested in September 1941. This request was originally disapproved, but was later approved by the Adjutant General and the project was initiated by the Ordnance Committee in October, 1941.

Test firing at Aberdeen Proving Ground gave results better than expected. A test run showed that the frame sagged considerably, and to remedy this it was directed that subsequent vehicles should have reinforced frames and spread out gun mounts.

The Ordnance Committee, in March 1942, recorded authority for purchase of 324 of these howitzer motor carriages as an expedient.

Principal armament was a 105-mm Howitzer M2A1 or 105mm Howitzer Mount T2. The Howitzer had elevations from — 5° to + 35° and a traverse of 20° right and 20° left.

An HE Shell M1, fired from this howitzer, had a muzzle velocity of 1,550 feet per second and, at an elevation of 14°, a maximum range of 12,315 yards, but this was limited to 11,700 yards at the max-

TYPICAL CHARACTERISTICS

Crew..6

Physical Characteristics
Weight (gross).................... 20,000 lb.
Length...........................19 ft., 9½ in.
Width.............................7 ft., 1 in.
Height............................7 ft., 8 in.
Height to center line of bore.......6 ft., 7 in.
Ground clearance.................11¾ in.
Wheelbase........................135½ in.
Ground contact length............46¾ in.
Tread (center to center, rear)...63⅛ in.
Tire equipment..........8.25x10, combat

Armament
105-mm Howitzer M2A1.........................
......On 105-mm Howitzer Mount T2
    Elevation.................—5° to +35°
    Traverse..............20° right, 20° left
1 Cal. .50 Machine Gun M2 HB (Res.)
    On Pedestal Mount M25, modified
1 Cal. .45 submachine gun
Provision for
4 Cal. .30 Carbines M1 or
    4 Cal. .30 Rifles M1

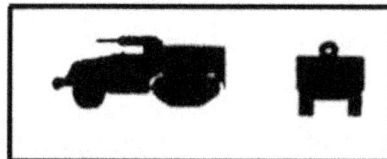

elevation of the mount.

Other armament included a Cal. .50 Machine Gun M2 HB, on a pedestal mount, for anti-aircraft protection and a cal. .45 submachine gun. Provisions were made for carrying four cal. .30 carbines or four cal. .30 rifles, which were the personal equipment of crew members.

The vehicle had a crew of six men. It

Ammunition, Stowage
105-mm..........................8 rounds
Cal. .50.........................300 rounds
Cal. .45.........................300 rounds

Armor
Windshield......................½ in.
Sides and rear..................¼ in.

Performance
Maximum speed on level.........45 m.p.h.
Speed on 4% grade.............25 m.p.h.
Maximum grade ability..........60%
Vertical obstacle ability.........12 in.
Fording depth (slowest forward speed)....32 in.
Turning diameter................60 ft.
Fuel capacity....................60 gal.
Cruising range..................200 miles

Vision and Fire Control
Vision.................Slits in windshield shield
Telescope Mount M2............................1
Panoramic Telescope M12A2.................1
Range Quadrant M4...........................1
Gunner's Quadrant M1.......................1
Telescope Mount M23........................1
Elbow Telescope M16.........................1

Fire Protection
Fire Extinguisher, Carbon Tetrachloride.......1 qt.

(Other characteristics same as for Half-Track Personnel Carrier M3.)

was never standardized.

Due to a sub-standard original, this page has been recreated.

REFERENCES TM 9-710; OCM 17391. 18017; SNL G-102, Vol II.

75-MM HOWITZER MOTOR CARRIAGE T30

Due to a sub-standard original, this page has been recreated.

75-MM HOWITZER MOTOR CARRIAGE T30, SHOWING HOWITZER AND SHIELD

Designed as an expedient to provide a 75-mm howitzer on a self-propelled mount, this vehicle was superseded by the 75mm Howitzer Motor Carriage M8 and is no longer in use.

It consisted of a 75mm Howitzer M1A1 mounted on a Half-Track Personnel Carrier M3. It had a crew of five men.

The project was initiated in October 1941 at the rquest of the Armored Force Board, substantiated by verbal instructions from the Office of the Assistant Chief of Staff, G-1.

Contract for the manufacture of two pilot vehicles was let to the Autocar Co. in December 1941.

The Ordnance Committee, in January 1942, outlined military characteristics and authorized construction of pilot vehicles. Various designs of gunshields were constructed and tested at the Aberdeen Proving Ground. Subsequently, 500 of the vehicles were manufactured.

The howitzer had elevations from −9° to +50° and a traverse of 221/2° right and 221/2° left. Firing a 14.6-pound projectile, with a muzzle velocity of 1,250 feet per second and at an elevation of 43 1/2", the howitzer had a maximum range of 9,610 yards.

Other armament included one Cal. .50 Machine Gun M2 HB (flexible) on a pedestal mount for antiaircraft protection and one cal. .45 submachine gun. Provisions were made for carrying four cal. .30 rifles or four cal. .30 carbines, which were the personal equipment of crew members.

Armor was the same as on the Half-

TYPICAL CHARACTERISTICS

Crew 5

Physical Characteristics
Weight (approx.) .... 19,500 lb.
Length .... 19 ft., 9 1/2 in.
Width .... 7 ft., 1 in.
Height .... 8 ft., 3/4 in.
Ground clearance .... 11 3/16 in.
Wheelbase .... 135 1/2 in.
Tread (center to center, rear) .... 63 13/16 in.
Ground contact length (track) .... 46 3/4 in.

Armament
75-mm Howitzer M1A1
  Elevation .... −9° to +50°
  Traverse .... 221/2° right and 221/2° left
1 Cal. .50 Machine Gun M2 HB (flex.)
          on Pedestal Mount M25, modified
Provision for:
1 Cal. .45 submachine gun
4 Cal. .30 Carbines M1 or
  4 Cal. .30 Rifles M1

Ammunition
75-mm .... 60 rounds
Cal. .50 .... 300 rounds
Cal. .45 .... 200 rounds

Armor
Windshield .... 1/2 in.
Gunshield .... 3/8 in.
Sides and rear .... 1/4 in.

Performance
Maximum speed on level .... 45 m.p.h.
Speed on 41/2% grade .... 25 m.p.h.
Maximum grade ability 60%
Vertical obstacle ability .... 12 in.
Fording depth (slowest forward speed) .. 32 in.
Fuel capacity .... 60 gal.
Cruising range .... 200 miles
Turning diameter .... 60 ft.

Vision and Fire Control
Vision .... Slits in windshield shield
Panoramic Telescope M1 1
Gunner's Quadrant 1
Range Quadrant M3 1
Elbow Telescope M5 1
Telescope Mount M16 1

Communications
Radio SCR-510

Fire Protection
Fire Extinguisher - Carbon Tetrachloride .. 1 qt.

(Other characteristics same as for Half-Track Personnel Carrier M3.)

Track Personnel Carrier M3 with the addition of a gunshield designed to give protection against cal. .30 AP ammunition at 250 yards and overhead protection against low-flying aircraft.

REFERENCES — OCM 17665, 17809, 18073, 18188

75 MM HOWITZER MOTOR CARRIAGE **M8**—STANDARD

75 MM HOWITZER MOTOR CARRIAGE, M8, IS BASED ON LIGHT TANK, M5, CHASSIS

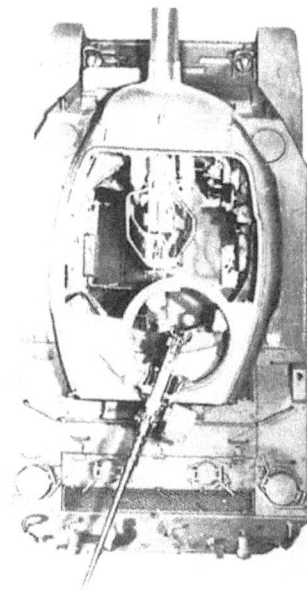

TOP VIEW, SHOWING SEMI-OPEN TURRET

This is a highly mobile 75 mm howitzer motor carriage capable of being used as assault or support artillery with full protection against small arms fire.

It is similar to Light Tank, M5, but has a redesigned turret to mount a 75 mm howitzer.

Principal armament is a 75 mm Howitzer, M2 or M3, with a rate of fire of 25 rounds per minute. Firing an H.E. shell, M48, with a muzzle velocity of 1,250 feet per second, it has a maximum range of 9,610 yards. The howitzer has an elevation of from −20° to +40°.

The turret is of welded armor, open at the top except for a partial roof to support the cal. .50 HB antiaircraft machine gun ring mount. It has a traverse of 360°.

The hull is of armor plate and is a completely welded structure except for portions of the front, top and rear which are removable for service operations.

The vehicle is powered by two Cadillac engines, each of which is connected to a Hydra-Matic transmission, providing six forward speeds and one reverse speed. It is wired for radio and for an interphone system. Four periscopes are provided.

The pilot model was manufactured by the Cadillac Motor Car Division, General Motors Corp.

REFERENCES — TM 9-732B; OCM 17236, 17315, 17966, 18049, 18098, 18188, 19368, 19398, 19979, 21838.

TYPICAL CHARACTERISTICS

Crew 4

Physical Characteristics
Weight (gross)	34,600 lb.*
Length	14 ft., 6¾ ins.
Width	7 ft., 4¼ ins.
Height	7 ft., 6½ ins.
Turret ring diameter (inside)	54½ ins.
Ground clearance	16½ ins.
Tread (center to center of tracks)	73 ins.
Ground contact length	121 ins.
Ground pressure	11.6 lb./sq. in.

Armament
75 mm Howitzer, M2 or M3, in
  75 mm Howitzer Mount, M7
    Elevation . . . . −20° to +40°
    Traverse . . . . 360°
1 cal. .50 Machine Gun, M2,
  HB (flexible) . . . . On Turret (antiaircraft)
Provision for:
1 cal. .45 Submachine Gun
3 cal. .30 Carbines, M1

Ammunition, Stowage
75 mm (H.E., M48; A.P.C., M61;
  A.P., M72) . . . . 46 rounds
Cal. .50 (in 50 round boxes) . . . . 400 rounds
Cal. .45 (in 20 or 30 round clips) . . 600 rounds
Cal. .30 (in cartridge belts) . . . . . . 735 rounds
Grenades, Hand (Fragmentation, Mk. II, 2;
  Smoke, H.C., M8, 4; Thermite,
  Incendiary, 2) 8

Armor
	Actual	Basis
Hull, Front, upper	1⅛ ins.	2½ ins.
lower	1¾ ins.	2½ ins.
Sides	1 in.	1⅛ ins.
Rear	1 in.	
Top	½ in.	
Bottom	⅜–½ in.	
Turret, Front	1½ ins.	
Sides and rear	1 in.	
Top	⅜ in.	

Performance
Maximum speed on level	40 m.p.h.
Maximum grade ability	60%
Trench crossing ability	5 ft., 4 ins.
Vertical obstacle ability	18 ins.
Fording depth (slowest forward speed)	36 ins.
Fuel capacity	89 gals.
Cruising range	100 miles

Vision and Fire Control
Periscopes, M9	4
Bore Sight	1
Panoramic Telescope, M12A5	1
Telescope, M70C	1
Gunner's Quadrant, M1	1

Communications
Radio	SCR–510 or 210
Interphone stations	3

Battery, Voltage, total 12

Fire Protection and Decontamination
Fire Extinguisher—CO₂–10 lb. (fixed)	1
CO₂–4 lb. (hand)	1
Decontaminating Apparatus, 1½ qts., M2	3

*With T16 Tracks.

(Other characteristics same as for Light Tank, M5.)

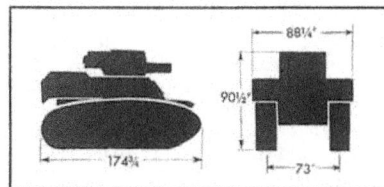

3 INCH GUN MOTOR CARRIAGES M10, M10A1—STANDARD

3 INCH GUN MOTOR CARRIAGE, M10A1, SHOWING CIRCULAR BOSSES ON SIDES FOR ATTACHING AUXILIARY ARMOR

This weapon, designed for use against tanks and armored vehicles, embodies heavy firepower, excellent mobility and sloping armor with good ballistic qualities.

It consists of a 3 Inch Gun, M7, mounted in a semi-open turret on a medium tank chassis.

3 Inch Gun Motor Carriage, M10, is based on a Medium Tank, M4A2, chassis, with twin General Motors Diesel engines. The pilot vehicle was manufactured by the Fisher Body Co.

3 Inch Gun Motor Carriage, M10A1, is based on a Medium Tank, M4A3, chassis, with a Ford GAA gasoline engine. The pilot vehicle was manufactured by the Ford Motor Co.

Physical characteristics and performance of the models vary only slightly, in accordance with the variations in the respective tanks.

The 3 Inch Gun, M7, is mounted in a semi-open turret, with elevations from −10° to +19°. Fired from it, the A.P.C. projectile has a muzzle velocity of 2,600 feet per second and a maximum range of 16,100 yards. It will penetrate 4 inches of face-hardened armor plate at 1,000 yards.

A cal. .50 machine gun is mounted at the rear of the turret for protection against low-flying planes.

The armor protection may be increased by attaching auxiliary armor of varying thickness to bosses on the basic armor.

REFERENCES—M10:TM9-752A;OCM 17462, 17642, 18006, 18061, 18313, 18332, 18435, 18597, 18944, 19045, 19055, 19167, 19242, 19245, 20067, 20281, 20310, 20680, 21002, 21461. M10A1: TM 9-731G; OCM 20515.

TYPICAL CHARACTERISTICS

3 INCH GUN MOTOR CARRIAGE, M10

Crew 5

Physical Characteristics

Weight . . . . .66,000 lb.
Length . . . . 19 ft., 7 ins.
Width . . . . 10 ft.
Height . . . . 8 ft., 1½ ins.
Height of center line, 3 inch gun . . . 82½ ins.
Turret ring diameter (inside) . . . . .69 ins.
Ground clearance . . . . 17⅛ ins.
Tread (center to center of tracks) . . . . . . 83 ins.
Ground contact length . . . . 147 ins.
Ground pressure . . . . 12.3 lb./sq. in.

Armament

3 Inch Gun, M7, in Mount, M5 . . . . . .In turret
  Elevation . . . . −10° to +19°
  Traverse . . . . .360°
Cal. .50 Machine Gun, M2, HB
  (flexible) . . . . On turret (Antiaircraft)
1 Tripod Mount, cal. .50, M3
Provision for:
5 cal. .30 Carbines, M1

Ammunition, Stowage

3 inch (A.P.C., M62, and H.E.,
  M42A1) . . . . .54 rounds
Cal. .50 (in 50 round boxes) . . . . . 300 rounds
Cal. .30 (Carbine, M1) . . . . 450 rounds
Grenades, Hand (Smoke, W.P., M15, 6;
  Fragmentation, Mk., II, 6) 12
Smoke Pots, H.C., M1 4

Armor	Actual	Basis
Hull, Front . . .	½–2 ins.	3¼ ins.
Sides . . .	¾–1 in.	1–1⅜ ins.
Rear . . .	1–1½ ins.	
Top . . .	⅜–¾ ins.	
Bottom . . .	¼ in.	
Turret, Front . . .	2½ ins.	4½ ins.
Sides and rear . . .	1 in.	1⅛–1¾ ins.
Top . . .	¾ in.	

Performance

Maximum speed on level . . . . .30 m.p.h.
Speed on 3% grade . . . . .20 m.p.h.
Maximum grade ability 60%
Trench crossing ability . . . . 7 ft., 6 ins.
Vertical obstacle ability . . . . .24 ins.
Fording depth (slowest forward speed) .36 ins.
Turning radius . . . . 31 ft.
Fuel capacity . . . . .164 gals.
Cruising range (approx.) . . . . .200 miles

Vision and Fire Control

Periscopes, M6 3
Telescope, M51 1
Bore Sight 1
Gunner's Quadrant, M1 1

Communications

Radio . . . . .SCR-510 or 610 or British 19
Interphone stations 5
Flag Set, M238 1

Battery, Voltage, total 24

Fire Protection and Decontamination

Fire Extinguisher—CO₂-10 lb. (fixed) 2
  CO₂-4 lb. (hand) 2
Decontaminating Apparatus, 1½ qts., M2 . . .2

Engine, Make and Model . . . .G.M. 6-71-6046

3 INCH GUN MOTOR CARRIAGE, M10A1

Characteristics same as for 3 Inch Gun Motor Carriage, M10, except as noted:

Weight (gross) . . . . .64,000 lb.
Fuel capacity . . . . .192 gals.
Cruising range . . . . .160 miles
Engine, Make and Model . . . . . . .Ford GAA

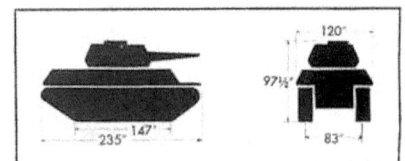

155 MM GUN MOTOR CARRIAGE M12—CARGO CARRIER M30—STANDARD

155 MM GUN MOTOR CARRIAGE, M12, WITH GUN IN TRAVELING LOCK. GUN IS ELEVATED, AND SPADE AT REAR LOWERED, WHEN FIRING

TYPICAL CHARACTERISTICS

155 mm GUN MOTOR CARRIAGE, M12
Crew..6

Physical Characteristics
Weight (gross).........................58,000 lb.
Length............................22 ft., 1 in.
Width..............................8 ft., 9 ins.
Height............................8 ft., 10 ins.
Height of center line of bore........7 ft., 1½ ins.
Ground clearance.....................17⅛ ins.
Ground contact length.................147 ins.
Tread (center to center of tracks)....83 ins.
Ground pressure.................116 lb./sq. in.

Armament
155 mm Gun, M1918M1, M1917A1
  or M1917................On Mount, M4
 Elevation...................−5° to +30°
 Traverse...........................28°
Provision for:
 5 cal. .30 carbines........Equipment of crew
 1 Grenade Launcher, M8......For carbine

Ammunition, Stowage
155 mm (H.E., Mk. IIIA1 or M101) 10 rounds
 Grenades (Hand: Fragmentation, Mk. II, 4;
  Offensive, Mk. III, w/fuze, M6, 2;
  Smoke, WP, M8, 4; Thermite, Incendi-
  ary, 2; Rifle: M9A1, 10).................22

Armor

	Actual	Basis
Hull, Front	1½–2 ins.	3½ ins.
Sides	1 in.	1 in.
Rear	¾ in.	¾ in.
Top	½ in.	½ in.
Bottom	½–1 in.	½–1 in.
Shield	¾ in.	

Performance
Maximum speed on level..............24 m.p.h.
Maximum grade ability.................60%
Trench crossing ability...........7 ft., 6 ins.
Fording depth (slowest forward speed)..36 ins.
Fuel capacity......................200 gals.
Turning radius........................35 ft.
Cruising range (approx.)............140 miles

Vision and Fire Control
Panoramic Telescope, M6 (with Instrument
 Light, M9, and one 14-in. extension
 bar).............................1
Telescope, M53........................1
Telescope Mount, M40..................1
Aiming Post, M1 (with Aiming Post
 Light, M14).........................1
Gunner's Quadrant, M1, w/case.........1
Quadrant Sight, M1918A1, w/cover,
 M1918..............................1
Fuze Setter, M21 or M14...............1
Bore Sight............................1
Vision Slots..........................2

Communications
Flag Set, M113........................1

Battery, Voltage, total...............24

Fire Protection and Decontamination
CO₂—10 lb. (Fixed)....................2
Fire Extinguisher, CO₂—4 lb. (Hand)....2
Decontaminating Apparatus, M2, 1½ qts...2

Engine, Make and Model..Continental R975-C1
Type...........................Radial A.C.
No. of cylinders......................9
Cycle.................................4
Fuel (gasoline)...................80 octane
Max. governed speed.........2,400 r.p.m.
Net hp............353 at 2,400 r.p.m.
Max. torque.....850 lb.-ft. at 1,800 r.p.m.
(See additional engine characteristics on page
 28.)

Transmission, Type...........Syncromesh
Gear ratios
 First speed.....................7.56:1
 Second speed....................3.11:1
 Third speed.....................1.78:1
 Fourth speed....................1.11:1
 Fifth speed......................73:1
 Reverse.........................5.65:1

Differential, Type...............Controlled

Final Drive, Type............Herringbone

Suspension, Type.........Volute spring

Idler, Type....................Fixed

Track, Type.............Rubber block

Brakes, Type.............Mechanical

CARGO CARRIER, M30
Physical Characteristics
Weight (gross).........................47,000 lb.
Length...........................19 ft., 10 ins.
Width.............................8 ft., 9 ins.
Height—ring mount up, with gun.......10 ft.
 ring mount, lowered, without gun 8 ft., 6 ins.
Ground pressure.................10 lb./sq. in.

Armament
Provision for:
 5 cal. .30 carbines........Equipment of crew
 1 Grenade Launcher, M8......For carbine
 1 cal. .50 Machine Gun, M2,
  HB (flexible).............On ring mount

Ammunition, Stowage
155 mm (H.E., Mk. IIIA1 or M101) .40 rounds
Cal. .50.......................1,000 rounds
Grenades (Hand: Fragmentation, Mk. II, 4;
 Offensive, Mk. III w/fuze, M6, 2; Smoke,
 4; Thermite Incendiary, 2; Rifle: M9A1,
 10)................................22

Vision
Protectoscopes.........................2

Communications
Radio...........................SCR-610

(Other characteristics same as for 155 mm Gun
Motor Carriage, M12.)

CARGO CARRIER, M30, SHOWING MACHINE GUN ON MOUNT

155 mm GUN MOTOR CARRIAGE, M12, IN FIRING POSITION

155 mm GUN MOTOR CARRIAGE, M12, provides increased mobility and maneuverability for the powerful 155 mm gun.

It is intended for use principally (a) where the tactical situation calls for quick-moving, long-range fire and (b) as a special purpose weapon for beach defense.

The weapon consists of a 155 mm Gun, M1918M1, M1917A1 or M1917, mounted on 155 mm Gun Mount, M4, on a modified Medium Tank, M3, chassis.

The 155 mm gun has an elevation from −5° to +30° and a traverse of 28°. Using a 95 pound projectile, with a muzzle velocity of 2,410 feet per second, it has a maximum range of 20,100 yards. Provisions are made for carrying five cal. .30 carbines and one cal. .30 rifle.

A spade at the rear is used to stabilize the weapon against recoil. This may be elevated out of the way when the vehicle is in motion. A hinged platform is provided for the gun crew when the spade is lowered.

Direct and indirect vision are provided for the driver and assistant driver. Seats for four other crew members are provided. Additional ammunition, and additional personnel needed to serve the gun, are carried in a companion vehicle, Cargo Carrier, M30.

The pilot model was manufactured by Rock Island Arsenal.

REFERENCES—TM9–751;OCM16859,16912, 18074, 18584, 18727, 19399, 21546, 21835.

CARGO CARRIER, M30, is the companion vehicle for 155 mm Gun Motor Carriage, M12, and like it is built on a modified Medium Tank, M3, chassis.

It is used to transport additional personnel needed to operate the 155 mm gun, and adequate ammunition and equipment for it. The tail gate may be lowered to facilitate access to the cargo.

A ring mount for a cal. .50 machine gun is provided for antiaircraft and ground protection. Provision is made for carrying a cal. .30 rifle, and four cal. .30 carbines.

The pilot vehicle was designed at Rock Island Arsenal, and built by the Pressed Steel Car Company.

REFERENCES—TM9–751;OCM18628,18731, 21444, 21628.

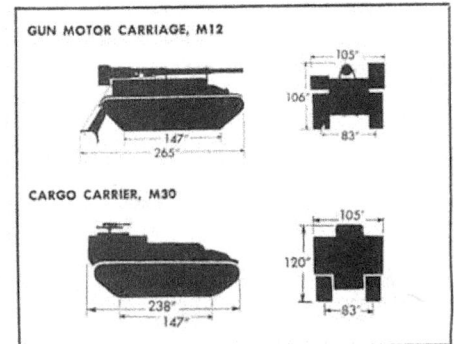

GUN MOTOR CARRIAGE, M12

CARGO CARRIER, M30

57 MM GUN MOTOR CARRIAGE T48—LIMITED PROCUREMENT

57 mm GUN MOTOR CARRIAGE, T48, FROM ABOVE, SHOWING GUN IN TRAVELING POSITION, GUN SHIELD, AND STOWAGE

This vehicle consists of a 57 mm Gun, M1, on 57 mm Gun Mount, T5, on a Half Track Personnel Carrier, M3.

Its development was initiated by Ordnance Committee action in April, 1942, as an expedient mounting for the 57 mm gun pending the development of a more suitable motor carriage for the weapon.

The pilot vehicle was constructed at the Aberdeen Proving Ground.

It was originally expected that the vehicle would be manufactured to fill both United States and British requirements, but later developments resulted in requirements for the British only. In accordance with requests from the British Army Staff, and in accordance with requirements of the Army Supply Program, production of the vehicles for the British was initiated. O.C.M. 19063, dated 18 October 1942, gave military characteristics as required for British use.

The 57 mm Gun, M1, has an elevation from −5° to +15° and may be traversed 27½° right and 27½° left. Using A.P. projectile, M70, with a muzzle velocity of 2,800 feet per second, it will penetrate 2.2 inches of face-hardened armor plate at 1,000 yards. Provision is made for carrying five British cal. .30 rifles.

The 57 mm gun is mounted on the center of the vehicle, immediately behind the front bulkhead, and fires to the front. A pivoted gunner's seat is provided, and swings independently of the gun.

The gun shield is of sloping, face-

TYPICAL CHARACTERISTICS

Crew 5

Physical Characteristics
Weight (gross) . . . . 19,000 lb.
Length . . . . 21 ft., ⅝ in.
Width . . . . 7 ft., 1 in.
Height . . . . 7 ft.
Height—to center of gun bore . . . . . . 72 ins.
Ground clearance . . . . 11¾₁₆ ins.
Wheelbase . . . . 135½ ins.
Tread (center to center rear) . . . . 63¹³⁄₁₆ ins.
Ground contact length—tracks . . . . 46¾ ins.
Tire equipment . . . 8.25 x 20, 12 ply, (combat)

Armament
57 mm Gun, M1 . . . . On mount, T5
  Elevation . . . . −5° to +15°
  Traverse . . . . . 27½° right, 27½° left
Provision for:
5 cal. .30 Rifles, British . . . . . Equipment of crew
1 Grenade Launcher . . . . For rifle

Ammunition, Stowage
57 mm (A.P., M70) . . . . 99 rounds
Grenades (Hand: Fragmentation, Mk. II, 5;
  Smoke, M8, 5; Thermite, Incendiary, 2;
  Rifle: M9A1, 10) 22

Armor
Vehicle—same as Half Track Personnel Carrier, M3
Gun shield, Front . . . . ⅝ in.
Sides and top . . . . ¼ in.

Performance
Maximum speed on level . . . . 45 m.p.h.
Speed on 4% grade . . . . 25 m.p.h.
Maximum grade ability 60%
Vertical obstacle ability . . . . 12 ins.
Fording depth (slowest forward speed) . . 32 ins.
Angle of approach . . . . 37°
Angle of departure . . . . 32°
Turning radius . . . . 30 ft.
Fuel capacity . . . . 60 gals.
Cruising range (approx.) . . . . 200 miles

Vision and Fire Control
Telescope, M18 1
Telescope Mount, M24 1
Bore Sight 1

Communications
Radio . . . . British Wireless Set, No. 19
Flag Set, M238 1

Battery, Voltage, total 12

Fire Protection and Decontamination
Fire Extinguisher, CO₂-2 lb. (hand) 1
Decontaminating Apparatus, M2, 1½ qts. . . 1

(Other characteristics same as for Half Track Personnel Carrier, M3.)

hardened armor plate, ⅝ inch thick at the front, and ¼ inch at the sides and overhead.

Other armor is essentially the same as on Half Track Personnel Carrier, M3. Space for the gun tube is allowed between the two windshields.

A traveling lock, with a quick release mechanism, holds the gun in place above

the hood when not in use. It may be pulled away when the gun is being fired.

Removable headlights are provided, as well as removable blackout lights which may be fitted into the headlight brackets.

The vehicle is equipped with a British Wireless Set, No. 19.

REFERENCES — OCM 18099, 18149, 19063, 20680, 21002.

MULTIPLE GUN MOTOR CARRIAGE M15—LIMITED STANDARD
COMBINATION GUN MOTOR CARRIAGE M15A1—SUBSTITUTE STANDARD

COMBINATION GUN MOTOR CARRIAGE, M15A1, MOUNTS 37 mm GUN AND TWO CAL. .50 MACHINE GUNS, IN LOW SILHOUETTE, ROTATING TURRET MOUNT

MULTIPLE GUN MOTOR CARRIAGE, M15—LIMITED STANDARD—This highly mobile weapon, capable of a concentration of rapid fire, was designed primarily for vehicular antiaircraft column defense.

It is comprised mainly of a Half Track Personnel Carrier, M3, chassis, and the top carriage of the 37 mm Gun Carriage, M3E1 (designated Combination Gun Mount, M42), mounting a 37 mm Gun, M1A2, and two cal. .50 Machine Guns, M2, HB, and Sighting System, M6.

The mount is manually operated and has an elevation from 0° to +85° and a traverse of 360°. Depression at the front is limited to +20°.

The H.E. shell, fired from the 37 mm gun, has a maximum range, vertical, of about 6,200 yards, and, horizontal, of about 8,875 yards. The cal. .50 guns have a maximum range each of 7,200 yards.

REFERENCES—TM 9-708; OCM 17313, 18152, 18477, 18698, 18957, 19087, 19115, 19198, 21281, 21563.

COMBINATION GUN MOTOR CARRIAGE, M15A1—SUBSTITUTE STANDARD—This is similar to Multiple Gun Motor Carriage, M15, but embodies several improvements. Combination Gun Mount, M54, is used. This mount consists of the top carriage of a 37 mm Gun Carriage, M3A1, mounting a 37 mm Gun, M1A2, two cal. .50 Machine Guns, M2, HB, and Sighting System, M5.

The vehicle is lighter and more stable than the M15, and is regarded as better in appearance because of its lower silhouette. It does not require gear box controls. Interference between the guns and other equipment has been eliminated at several points.

A platform is provided for a loader for the 37 mm gun and for the lead setter, and ammunition chests have been separated so as to provide sufficient room for him to stand. A rail is provided in the rear of the mount for convenience of the gun crew in getting on the mount. The lead setter's seat is raised to facilitate operation of the sight.

REFERENCES — OCM 16367, 16428, 21226, 21281, 21563, 21850, 22628, 23746, 24133.

TYPICAL CHARACTERISTICS

COMBINATION GUN MOTOR CARRIAGE, M15A1

Crew...........................7

Physical Characteristics
Weight (gross)...............20,800 lb.
Length..............20 ft., 3½ ins.
Width...............7 ft., 4½ ins.
Height (overall)..........7 ft., 10 ins.
Ground clearance..........11³⁄₁₆ ins.
Wheelbase................135½ ins.
Tread, front.............64½ ins.
   rear.............63¹³⁄₁₆ ins.
Ground contact length.........46¾ ins.
Tire equipment....8.25 x 20, 12 ply (combat)

Armament
37 mm Gun, A.A., M1A2, and
2 cal. .50 Machine Guns, M2, HB*
   On Combination Gun Mount, M54
   Elevation...............−5° to +85°
   Traverse....................360°
Provision for:
4 cal. .30 carbines........Equipment of crew

*With side plate triggers.

GUN MOTOR CARRIAGE, M15A1

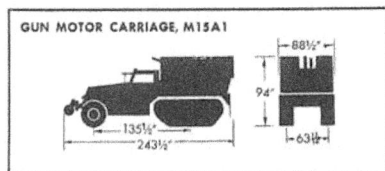

Ammunition, Stowage
37 mm (H.E., M54; A.P., M74;
   A.P.C., M59)............200 rounds
Cal. .50.................1,200 rounds
Armor
Chassis—Same as Half Track Personnel Carrier, M3, omitting side and rear body armor.
Gun Shield—rotating...............¼ in.
Vision and Fire Control
Computing Sight, M14............1
Bore Sight.......................1
Communications
Radio...................SCR-510
Battery, Voltage, total................12
Fire Protection and Decontamination
Fire Extinguisher, CO₂-2 lb............1
Decontaminating Apparatus, M2, 1½ qts...1

(Other characteristics essentially same as for Half Track Personnel Carrier, M3.)

MULTIPLE GUN MOTOR CARRIAGE, M13, consists of a Twin cal. .50 Machine Gun Mount, M33, developed by the W. L. Maxson Co., on a modified Half Track Personnel Carrier, M3. Standardized in September, 1942, it was redesignated Substitute Standard upon standardization of Multiple Gun Motor Carriage, M16.

Principal armament is two cal. .50 Machine Guns, M2, HB (TT), in a power-operated turret. The turret has a traverse of 360° and may be elevated from −10° to +90°, except in front where depression is limited to +5° because of the projection of the cab. The guns may be elevated and traversed at infinitely variable speeds ranging from 0° to 60° per second.

Each gun will fire 400 to 500 rounds per minute, and has a maximum range of 7,200 yards. Standard ammunition feed boxes of 200 rounds capacity each are provided. Fire control is by a Navy Mark IX reflex sight. Provision is made for carrying a cal. .45 submachine gun, a cal. .30 rifle and three cal. .30 carbines.

The crew consists of a gunner, two loaders, a driver and the commander.

Armor is the same as on Half Track Personnel Carrier, M3, except that the upper sides and rear are hinged and can be folded downward to permit firing at −10°. A ¼-inch frontal armor shield is provided for the protection of the gunner.

The vehicles are manufactured by the Autocar Co., the Diamond T Motor Co. and the White Motor Co.

REFERENCES — OCM 17848, 17928, 18627, 18681, 18839, 19264, 19430.

MULTIPLE GUN MOTOR CARRIAGE, M14, consists of a twin cal. .50 Machine Gun Mount, M33, mounted on a Half

Track Personnel Carrier, M5. It is similar to the M13, except for the variations in the basic vehicles.

It was designated Substitute Standard in October, 1942. The vehicles are manufactured by the International Harvester Co.

REFERENCES—TM 9–707; OCM 18694.

MULTIPLE GUN MOTOR CARRIAGE, M17, consists of four cal. .50 Machine Guns, M2, HB (TT), in a Multiple Mount, M45, mounted on a Half Track Personnel Carrier, M5.

It is similar to Multiple Gun Motor Carriage, M16, except for the variations in the basic vehicles.

It was designated as Substitute Standard by Ordnance Committee action in December, 1942. The vehicles are manufactured by the International Harvester Co.

REFERENCES—TM 9–707; OCM 19264, 19430.

TWIN CAL. .50 MACHINE GUN MOUNT ON MULTIPLE GUN MOTOR CARRIAGE, M13 OR M14

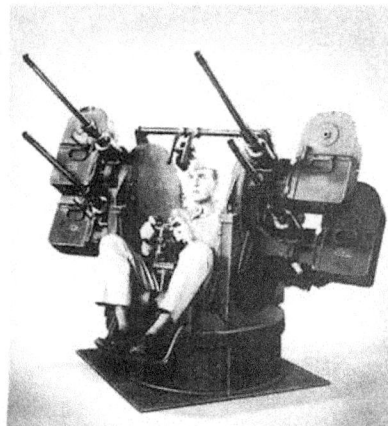

MULTIPLE CAL. .50 MACHINE GUN MOUNT, M45

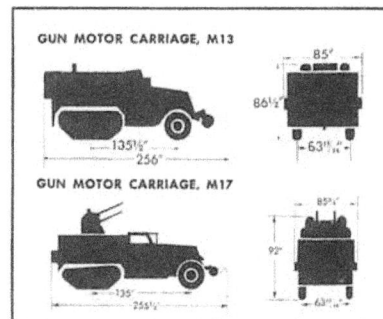

GUN MOTOR CARRIAGE, M13

GUN MOTOR CARRIAGE, M17

TYPICAL CHARACTERISTICS
GUN MOTOR CARRIAGES, M13, M14
Crew. 5

Armament
  2 cal. .50 Machine Guns, M2, HB (TT),
    w/Edgewater adapter
      On Twin cal. .50 Machine Gun Mount, M33
  Provision for:
  1 cal. .45 Submachine Gun } Equipment of crew
  1 cal. .30 Rifle, M1903 } Equipment of crew
  3 cal. .30 Carbines
  1 Grenade Launcher, M1. . . . . .For rifle

Ammunition, Stowage
  Cal. .50. . . . . .5,000 rounds
  Cal. .45. . . . . .480 rounds
  Grenades (Hand: Fragmentation, Mk. II,
    12; Smoke, M8, 12; Thermite, Incendi-
    ary, 2; Rifle: M9A1, 10). 36

Vision and Fire Control
  Reflex Sight, Mark IX (Navy)

Communications
  Radio. . . . . .SCR-528 or British 19
  Flag Set, M238. .1

GUN MOTOR CARRIAGE, M17
Crew. 5

Armament
  4 cal. .50 Machine Guns, M2, HB (TT),
    w/o Edgewater Adapter. On Multiple cal.
      .50 Machine Gun Mount, M45
  Provision for:
  1 cal. .45 Submachine Gun } Equipment of crew
  1 cal. .30 Rifle, M1903 } Equipment of crew
  3 cal. .30 Carbines, M1
  1 Grenade Launcher, M1. . . . . .For rifle

Ammunition, Stowage
  Cal. .50. . . . . .5,000 rounds
  Cal. .45. . . . . .420 rounds
  Grenades (Hand: Fragmentation, Mk. II,
    12; Smoke, M8, 12; Thermite, Incendi-
    ary, 2; Rifle: M9A1, 10). 36

Vision
  Direct. . . . . .Slits in shields

Communications
  Radio. . . . . .SCR-528 or British 19
  Flag Set, M238. .1

MULTIPLE GUN MOTOR CARRIAGE M16—STANDARD

MULTIPLE GUN MOTOR CARRIAGE, M16, MOUNTS 4 CAL. .50 MACHINE GUNS IN MAXSON TURRET; HAS FOLDING ARMOR AT SIDES AND REAR

This weapon consists of four cal. .50 Machine Guns, M2, HB (TT), in a Multiple Mount, M45, mounted on a Half Track Personnel Carrier, M3.

The mount, known as the Maxson turret, is essentially the same as that used on Multiple Gun Motor Carriage, M13, which it replaced in production, but is modified to permit the use of four cal. .50 guns, instead of two.

Each gun will fire 400 to 500 rounds per minute, and has a maximum range of 7,200 yards. The turret may be elevated from −10° to +90°, and has a traverse of 360° at a maximum speed of 60° per second. Interrupter switches prevent firing when the guns enter the driver's compartment-area. Provision is made to align the guns with each other and with the sight by means of adjustment for vertical and horizontal alignment.

The gunner sits in a 45° reclining position on a fabric seat adjustable to his height. The seat is arranged to provide a comfortable position and to permit the gunner to rest his elbows against the seat or his body while aiming. This results in stability of control and minimum fatigue.

The sight and guns pivot about an axis running approximately through the gunner's ears. He can conveniently follow the sight in any position without moving.

Control grips are mounted on a handlebar located on a post between the gunner's knees. Each grip contains a "dead man's" switch and a trigger switch, either of which will fire all guns. Rotation of the handlebars in the vertical plane controls elevation and in the horizontal plane controls traverse. The guns may be trained precisely when following a target and yet may be slewed rapidly to pick up a new target.

The crew consists of five men, the driver and commander, two loaders, and the gunner. Provision is made for carrying one cal. .45 submachine gun, one cal. .30 rifle with grenade launcher, and three cal. .30 carbines.

The gunner is protected from the front against small arms fire by a shield of armor plate. The vehicular armor is substantially the same as on Half Track Personnel Carrier, M3. Armor at the sides and rear of the vehicle may be folded down when the guns are in use. Two cargo boxes are provided at the rear of the vehicle.

REFERENCES — OCM 17848, 17928, 17969, 18020, 18627, 18681, 18839, 18845, 18964, 19140, 19264, 19430, 20680, 20726, 21002.

TYPICAL CHARACTERISTICS

Crew 5

Physical Characteristics
Weight (gross) . . . . 19,800 lb.
Length . . . . 21 ft., 4 ins.
Width . . . . 7 ft., 1 in.
Height . . . . 7 ft., 8 ins.
Height of center line of bore . . . . . . 6 ft., 3 ins.
Ground clearance . . . . 11$\frac{3}{16}$ ins.
Tread, rear . . . . 63$\frac{13}{16}$ ins.
Wheelbase . . . . 135$\frac{1}{2}$ ins.
Tire equipment . . . . 8.25 x 20, 12 ply (combat)

Armament
4 cal. .50 Machine Guns, M2, HB (TT),
  w/o Edgewater Adapter . . On Multiple cal.
               .50 Machine Gun Mount, M45
Provision for:
1 cal. .45 Submachine Gun ⎫
1 cal. .30 Rifle, M1903 ⎬Equipment of crew
3 cal. .30 Carbines, M1   ⎭
1 Grenade Launcher, M1 . . . . For rifle

Ammunition, Stowage
Cal. .50 . . . . 5,000 rounds
Cal. .45 . . . . 420 rounds
Grenades (Hand: Fragmentation, Mk. II,
  12; Smoke, M8, 12; Thermite, Incendi-
  ary, 2; Rifle: M9A1, 10) 36

Vision—Direct . . . . Slits in shields

Communications—Radio SCR-528 or British 19
  Flag Set, M238 1

Fire Protection and Decontamination
Fire Extinguisher, CO₂-2 lb. (hand) 1
Decontaminating Apparatus, M2, 1½ qts. . . . 1

———

(Other characteristics same as for Half Track Personnel Carrier, M3.)

76 MM GUN MOTOR CARRIAGE M18—STANDARD

76 MM GUN MOTOR CARRIAGE, M18, HAS SLOPING ARMOR AND USES TORSION BAR SUSPENSION; MOUNTS MACHINE GUN ABOVE OPEN TURRET

This is a highly mobile, low-silhouette, lightly armored 76 mm gun motor carriage designed for tank destroyer use.

It is of the full track-laying type, using a torsion bar independent suspension, front-sprocket driven. Sloping armor is used, affording good ballistic qualities.

Principal armament is a 76 mm Gun, M1A1 or M1A2, in an open-top turret with a partial turret basket. The gun can be elevated from $-10°$ to $+19\frac{1}{2}°$. The turret can be traversed through 360°. A ring mount for a cal. .50 machine gun is provided on the top of the open turret for antiaircraft protection. Provision is made for carrying five cal. .30 carbines.

The A.P.C. projectile, M62, fired in the 76 mm gun, with a muzzle velocity of 2,600 feet per second, will penetrate 4-inch face-hardened armor plate at 1,000 yards.

Driver and assistant driver occupy seats in the hull, and the gunner, loader, and commander in the turret. Two escape hatches are in the hull roof and one in the floor. Periscopes, M6, are provided for the driver and assistant, and a Periscope, M4 or M4A1, with Telescope, M47 or M47A2, for the gunner.

Power is supplied by a Continental R975–C1 or –C4 gasoline engine. Transmission is torqmatic, with three speeds forward and one reverse.

An SCR–610 or British No. 19 Radio is provided, as well as interphone stations.

The pilot vehicle was built by the Buick Motor Division, General Motors Corp.

REFERENCES — OCM 19185, 19319, 19438, 19628, 20584, 21523, 22918, 23202.

TYPICAL CHARACTERISTICS

Crew 5

Physical Characteristics
Weight (gross, approx.) . . . . 40,000 lb.
Length—to end of gun . . . . 21 ft., 10 ins.
   excluding gun . . . . 17 ft., 4 ins.
Width . . . . 9 ft., 2 ins.
Height . . . . 8 ft., 5 in. over A.A. Gun
Ground clearance . . . . 14 ins.
Tread (center to center of tracks) . . . . . . 95 ins.
Ground contact length . . . . 116 ins.
Ground pressure . . . . 12.5 lb./sq. in.

Armament
76 mm Gun, M1A1 or M1A2, in open top
  turret (with partial basket) . . . . In Mount, M1
  Elevation . . . . $-10°$ to $+19\frac{1}{2}°$
  Traverse . . . . 360°
1 cal. .50 Machine Gun,
  M2, HB . . . . On Ring Mount
1 Tripod Mount, cal. .50, M3
Provision for:
5 cal. .30 Carbines, M1

Ammunition, Stowage
76 mm (A.P.C., M62; A.P., M79; H.E.,
  M42A1; Smoke, M88) . . . . 45 rounds

Cal. .30 Carbine . . . . 450 rounds
Cal. .50 Machine Gun . . . . 800 rounds
Grenades, Hand (Smoke, WP, M8, 6;
  Fragmentation, Mk. II, 6) 12
Smoke Pots 4

Armor   **Actual**
Hull,
  Front, sides, and rear . . . . $\frac{1}{2}$ in.
  Top . . . . $\frac{5}{16}$ in.
  Bottom . . . . $\frac{1}{4}$ in.
Turret
  Front w/gunshield . . . . $\frac{3}{4}$–1 in.
  Sides and rear . . . . $\frac{1}{2}$ in.

Performance
Sustained speed on level . . . . 50 m.p.h.
Speed on 10% grade . . . . 15 m.p.h.
Maximum grade ability 60%
Vertical obstacle ability . . . . 36 ins.
Fording depth (slowest forward speed) . 48 ins.
Fuel capacity . . . . 165 gals.
Cruising range . . . . 150 miles

Vision and Fire Control
Periscope, M6 2
Periscope, M4 or M4A1, w/Telescope,
  M47 or M47A2, and Instrument
  Light, M30 for M4A1 1

Telescope, M76C, w/Instrument Light,
  M33, or Telescope, M70H, w/Instrument
  Light, M32 1
Telescope Mount, M55 1
Elevation Quadrant, M9, w/Instrument
  Light, M30 1
Azimuth Indicator, M20 or M18 1

Communications
Radio . . . . SCR–610 or British No. 19
Interphone stations 5

Battery, Voltage, total 24

Fire Protection and Decontamination
Fire Extinguisher, CO₂–10 lb. (fixed) 1
  CO₂–4 lb. (hand) 1
Decontaminating Apparatus, M2, 1½ qts. . . 1

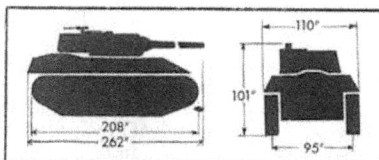

TWIN 40 MM GUN MOTOR CARRIAGE M19—STANDARD

TWIN 40 MM GUN MOTOR CARRIAGE, M19, SHOWING GUNS IN TRAVELING POSITION. VEHICLE USES LIGHT TANK, M24, CHASSIS

This lightly armored, low silhouette, high-speed, twin 40 mm gun motor carriage, designed for protection of armored force and motor columns against aircraft, was standardized in June, 1944, to replace Combination Gun Motor Carriage, M15A1.

It consists of one 40 mm Dual Automatic Gun, M2, on Twin 40 mm Gun Mount, M4, on a modified Light Tank, M24, chassis. The gun can be elevated from −5° to +85°, and has a traverse of 360° in a power-operated turret.

The 40 mm A.P. Shot, M81A1, fired from the gun, has a muzzle velocity of 2,870 feet per second. It has a maximum range of 9,475 yards horizontal, and will penetrate 1.6 inches of 20° obliquity face-hardened armor plate at 1,000 yards. The 40 mm H.E. Shell, Mk. II, also has a muzzle velocity of 2,870 feet per second. It has a horizontal range of 10,820 yards and a vertical range of 7,625 yards. The dual gun can be fired at the rate of 240 rounds per minute. It can be traversed at speeds up to 40° per second.

Provision is made for carrying four carbines. Sheet-metal, dust-proof and water-proof ammunition containers are furnished.

The crew consists of six men. The driver and assistant driver occupy seats in the front of the hull. The commander and gun crew members occupy seats in the semi-open turret, which is at the rear of the vehicle. A 5/16-in. belt of vertically disposed plate incloses the gun mount on all sides. Additional ½-in. frontal shields protect the gunners.

An individually sprung, compensated torsion bar suspension is used, together with a single-pin, rubber-bushed, center guide track.

The driver and assistant driver have direct vision, and are provided with a periscope each for use in combat areas. A Computing Sight, M13, and Local Control System, M16, are furnished for use by the gun crew.

REFERENCES — OCM 19046, 19133, 19846, 20035, 20297, 20394, 20583, 20705, 22629, 20446, 21699, 23746, 24133, 24244.

TYPICAL CHARACTERISTICS

Crew 6

Physical Characteristics

Weight (gross, approx.)	38,500 lb.
Length	17 ft., 11 ins.
Width	9 ft., 4 ins.
Height (overall)	9 ft., 9½ ins.
Turret ring diameter (inside)	31 ins.
Ground clearance	17 ins.
Tread (center to center of tracks)	96 ins.
Ground contact length	124 ins.
Ground pressure	9.7 lb./sq. in.

Armament

1 40 mm Dual Automatic Gun, M2, on Twin 40 mm Gun Mount, M4
    Elevation . . . . −5° to +85°
    Traverse . . . . 360°
Provision for:
4 cal. .30 Carbines, M1
1 Grenade Launcher for Carbine
1 cal. .45 Submachine Gun, M3

Ammunition, Stowage

40 mm	336 rounds
Cal. .30 carbine	480 rounds
Grenades, Hand (Smoke, WP, M15, 6; Fragmentation, Mk. II, 6; Rifle, M9A1, 10)	22
Cal. .45 (in 30-rd. clips)	570 rounds

Armor

Hull, Front	½ in.
Sides	½ in.
Rear	¼ in.
Top (over driver)	½ in.
Roof (over engine compartment)	¼ in.
Bottom, forward of 2nd suspension	½ in.
remainder	⅜ in.
Turret, Sides	5/16 in.
Gun shields	½ in.

Performance

Maximum speed on level	35 m.p.h.
on 3% grade	18 m.p.h.
on 10% grade	11 m.p.h.
Maximum grade ability	60%
Trench crossing ability	8 ft.
Vertical obstacle ability	40 ins.
Fording depth (slowest forward speed)	42 ins.
Turning radius	20 ft.
Fuel capacity	115 gals.
Cruising range (approx.)	100-160 miles
Maximum tractive effort	26,950 lb.

Vision and Fire Control

Periscopes, M6	2
Computing Sight, M13	1
Local Control System, M16	1

Communications

Radio	SCR–510 or 528 or British No. 19
Interphone stations	4

Battery, Voltage, total 24

Fire Protection and Decontamination

Fire Extinguisher, CO₂–10 lb. (fixed)	1
CO₂–4 lb. (hand)	2
Decontaminating Apparatus, M2, 1½ qts.	3

(Other characteristics same as for Light Tank, M24.)

90 MM GUN MOTOR CARRIAGE M36—STANDARD

90 MM GUN MOTOR CARRIAGE, M36. RIGHT FRONT VIEW, WITH COVER OVER MACHINE GUN. WHILE TRAVELING, TURRET IS TURNED TOWARD REAR

This is a modification of the 3-Inch Gun Motor Carriage, M10A1, designed to provide a more powerful self-propelled antitank gun. It was standardized in June, 1944.

Principal weapon is the 90 mm Gun, M3, in 90 mm Gun Mount, M4, in a semi-open top turret with 360° power traverse.

The gun can be elevated from $-10°$ to $+20°$. Using A. P. C. projectile, M82, with a muzzle velocity of 2,670 feet per second, it has a maximum range of 15,600 yards. This projectile is capable of penetrating 3 inches of homogeneous armor at ranges up to 4,700 yards. A cal. .50 Machine Gun, M2, HB (flexible), on a pedestal mount on the turret, is provided.

A new turret with a partial turret basket is used. Seats, traversing with the turret, are provided for the gunner, loader, and commander.

The chassis is essentially the same as that of the 3-Inch Gun Motor Carriage, M10A1. To provide for the stowage of 90 mm ammunition, the sponson stiffener brackets were moved forward. An auxiliary generator was installed in the engine compartment, and a bracket installed to hold the trunnions of the slip ring. The hull electrical installation was modified to accommodate the auxiliary generator and the slip ring. The hinging of the sub-floor doors was changed, and the fixed fire extinguisher cover was modified.

Power is supplied by a Ford GAA gasoline engine.

Pilot vehicles were manufactured by the Chevrolet Division of the General Motors Corporation.

TYPICAL CHARACTERISTICS

Crew 5

Physical Characteristics

Weight (gross)	62,000 lb.
(net)	57,000 lb.
Length	20 ft., 2 ins.
Width	10 ft.
Height—pedestal A. A. gun folded	8 ft., 11 ins.
Ground clearance	17⅛ ins.
Tread (center to center of tracks) . .	83 ins.
Ground contact length	147 ins.
Ground pressure	12.7 lb./sq. in.

Armament

90 mm Gun, M3, in Mount, M4	In turret
Elevation	$-10°$ to $+20°$
Traverse	360°
Cal. .50 Machine Gun, M2, HB (flexible)	On pedestal mount
1 Tripod Mount, Cal. .50, M3	
Provision for:	
5 cal. .30 Carbines, M1A2	

Ammunition, Stowage

90 mm (H.E., M71; A.P.C., M82) .	47 rounds
Cal. .50	1,000 rounds
Cal. .30 Carbine, M1	450 rounds
Grenades, Hand (Fragmentation, Mk. II, 6; Smoke, M15, 6)	12
Smoke Pots, H.C., M1	4

Armor

	Actual	Basis
Hull, Front, Upper . . .	1½ ins.	3¼ ins.
Lower	2 ins.	3¾ ins.
Sides, Upper	¾ ins.	1⅜ ins.
Lower	1½ ins.	
Rear, Upper	¾ in.	1 in.
Lower	1½ ins.	
Top, Forward . . .	¾ in.	
Rear	⅜ in.	

Bottom	½ in.	
Turret, Front	3 ins.	
Sides	1¼ ins.	1½ ins.
Top	1⅛ ins.	
Rear	4 ins.	

Performance

Maximum speed on level	30 m.p.h.
Speed on 3% grade	20 m.p.h.
10% grade	12 m.p.h.
Maximum grade ability	60%
Trench crossing ability	7 ft., 5 ins.
Vertical obstacle ability	24 ins.
Fording depth (slowest forward speed)	36 ins.
Fuel capacity	192 gals.
Cruising range	150 miles

Vision and Fire Control

Periscopes, M6	3
Telescope, M71C or M76D or M76F, w/Instrument Light, M33	1
Telescope Mount, M64 (T92)	1
Elevation Quadrant, M9, w/Instrument Light, M30	1
Azimuth Indicator, M20 or M18	1
Gunner's Quadrant, M1	1

Communications

Radio . . SCR-510 or 610 (with Reel Assembly, RL-106/V1) or British No. 19	
Interphone stations	5
Flag Set, M238	1

Fire Protection and Decontamination

Fire Extinguisher—10 lb.-CO_2 (fixed)	2
4 lb.-CO_2 (hand)	2
Decontaminating Apparatus, M2, 1½ qts. . . .	1

(Other characteristics same as for Medium Tank, M4A3.)

REFERENCES—OCM 18944, 19055, 19845, 20144, 21210, 21512, 22129, 22336, 22588, 22632, 23978, 24206, 24985.

HALF TRACK 81 MM MORTAR CARRIERS M4, M4A1—LIMITED STANDARD
HALF TRACK 81 MM MORTAR CARRIER M21—STANDARD

HALF TRACK 81 MM MORTAR CARRIER, M21, HAS MORTAR MOUNTED TO FRONT

OVERHEAD VIEW, SHOWING STOWAGE

These vehicles are designed to give greater mobility to the 81 mm Mortar, M1, which can be used on the vehicle or separate from it.

HALF TRACK 81 mm MORTAR CARRIER, M4, consists of the 81 mm Mortar, M1, mounted on a Half Track Car, M2, to fire to the rear. It was designed in 1940 with provisions made to fire the weapon from the vehicle in extreme emergencies only. The traverse is limited to that contained in the bipod (130 mils). Standardized in October, 1940, it was reclassified as Limited Standard in December, 1942.

HALF TRACK 81 mm MORTAR CARRIER, M4A1, is generally the same as the Half Track 81 mm Mortar Carrier, M4, with modifications to permit the weapon to be placed in action with greater rapidity.

The 81 mm Mortar, M1, has a traverse of 600 mils, and can be elevated from +40° to +80°. It can be fired from the chassis in all ordinary firing problems. Using H.E. projectile, M43A1, with a muzzle velocity of 700 feet per second, it has a range of 3,288 yards at 45° elevation.

A cal. .30 Browning machine gun is provided, which can be used from the gun rail which surrounds the top of the body, or separate from the vehicle. Provisions are made for carrying a Rocket Launcher, A.T., 2.36", M1, and a cal. .45 submachine gun, which are the personal equipment of the crew members.

Armor is the same as on Half Track Car, M2, and performance is essentially the same.

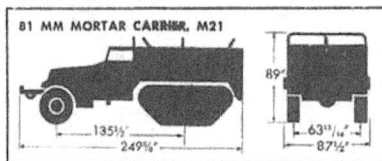

Standardized in December, 1942, it was reclassified as Limited Standard in July, 1943.

HALF TRACK 81 mm MORTAR CARRIER, M21, standardized in July, 1943, is based on the Half Track Personnel Carrier, M3, with winch, instead of the Half Track Car, M2, and is modified to allow the mortar to fire to the front.

Principal armament consists of the 81 mm Mortar, M1, with 81 mm Mortar Mount, M1, designed so that the base plate of the mount can be used in firing from the ground. It has an elevation of +40° to +85°, and a traverse of 60° to the front. Fire control is provided by Sight, M6.

A cal. .50 Machine Gun, M2, HB (flexible), is provided and can be used from a pedestal mount on the vehicle, or from a Tripod Mount, M3, on the ground. Provisions are made for carrying a cal. .45 submachine gun and a Rocket Launcher, M1.

Armor is the same as on Half Track Personnel Carrier, M3, and the vehicle performance characteristics are the same. A two-way radio is provided.

The pilot vehicles were manufactured by the White Motor Co.

REFERENCES—TM 9–710; OCM 16112, 16187, 18312, 18963, 19607, 19821, 19980, 20064, 20846, 21142; SNL G–102, vol. 15.

CHARACTERISTICS OF HALF TRACK 81 MM MORTAR CARRIER, M21

Crew. 6
Physical Characteristics
  Weight (gross). . . . . .18,500 lb.
  Length, with winch. . . . . . .20 ft., 9⅝ ins.
  Width. . . . . .7 ft., 3½ ins.
  Height—over bows. . . . . .7 ft., 5 ins.
  Ground clearance. . . . . .11⁵⁄₁₆ ins.
  Tread—front. . . . . .64½ ins.
    rear. . . . . .63¹³⁄₁₆ ins.
  Wheelbase. . . . . .135½ ins.
  Ground contact length. . . . . . . .46¾ ins.
  Tire equipment. . . . .8.25x20, 12 ply (combat)
Armament
  81 mm Mortar, M1, with 81 mm Mortar
    Mount, M1 (Base plate of mount to be
    used in firing from ground)
    Elevation. . . . .+40° to +85°
    Traverse. . . . . .60° to front
  1 cal. .50 Machine Gun, M2, HB (flexible),
    on Pedestal Mount
  1 cal. .50 Tripod Mount, M3
  Provision for:
    1 cal. .45 Submachine Gun
    1 Rocket Launcher, M1
Ammunition, Stowage
  81 mm (H.E., M43A1; W.P., M57,
    or H.E., M58). . . . . .97 rounds
  Cal. .50. . . . . .400 rounds
  Cal. .45. . . . . .600 rounds
  Grenades, Hand (Offensive, Mk. III, 2; Frag-
    mentation, Mk. II, 4; Smoke, HC, M8, 4;
    Thermite Incendiary, 2). 12
  Rockets, A.T., 2.36-in.. 6
  Mines, A.T., M1A1. 12
Fire Control
  Sight, M6. .1
Communications
  Radio, SCR-509 or SCR-510, less Battery
    Case, CS-79. 1
  Flag Set, M238. 1
Fire Protection and Decontamination
  Fire Extinguisher
    CO₂-2 lb. (hand). 1
  Decontaminating Apparatus, M2, 1½ qts.. .3

(Other characteristics same as for Half Track Personnel Carrier, M3.)

VEHICULAR MACHINE GUN MOUNTS

Development of the machine gun mounts shown in these pages converts each vehicle so equipped into a potent weapon against aircraft and against personnel.

The principal types, as illustrated, are the pedestal truck mounts, the dash mount, and the ring mounts for trucks and other vehicles.

PEDESTAL TRUCK MOUNTS

Each mount consists essentially of a pintle or cradle-pintle assembly and a pedestal body. The pintle is rotatable in a socket of the pedestal body, and can be locked at any point of traverse by means of a clamping screw.

PEDESTAL TRUCK MOUNT M24 was designed for the ½-Ton, 4x4, Weapons Carrier Truck.

Inasmuch as the vehicle was classified as Limited Standard, Pedestal Truck Mount M24 was reclassified as Limited Standard in July 1942.

The mount is suitable for mounting the Cal. .50 Machine Gun M2 HB, the Cal. .30 Machine Gun M1919A4, the Cal. .30 Machine Gun M1917A1, and the Browning automatic rifle. The mount is attached to the front panel of the truck body, to the rear of and between the driver's and assistant driver's seats.

REFERENCES—TM 9–224; OCM 16294, 16373, 18357, 18563; SNL A–55, Sec. 16, Add.

PEDESTAL TRUCK MOUNT M24C is the designation applied to Pedestal Truck Mount M24 when Pintle D38579 is replaced by the improved cradle, pintle, and ammunition box holder assembly E10014. The latter assembly provides for use of standard Ammunition Boxes M1 and M2, although normally only the Cal. .50 Machine Gun M2 HB will be used with this mount.

REFERENCES—OCM 24118, 24328.

PEDESTAL TRUCK MOUNT M24A1 is a modification of Pedestal Mount M24 to adapt it for use on the ¾-Ton, 4x4, Truck. Standardized in July 1942, it was reclassified as Limited Standard in December 1943.

It is suitable for mounting the Cal. .30 Machine Guns M1917A1 and M1919A4 and the Browning automatic rifle. Because of excessive dispersion, it is not suitable for the cal. .50 machine gun.

REFERENCES—TM 9–224; OCM 18357, 18563, 21990, 22263; SNL A–55, Sec. 16, Add.

PEDESTAL TRUCK MOUNT M24A2 is a redesign of Pedestal Truck Mount M24A1 strengthened for use with the cal. .50 machine gun as well as the cal. .30 machine gun. A new cradle and pintle assembly with an ammunition box holder suitable for use with standard cal. .30 and cal. .50 ammunition boxes is included. The mount is adaptable to the ¾-Ton, 4x4, and 1½-Ton, 6x6, Trucks. It was standardized in December 1943.

REFERENCES — OCM 20147, 21990, 22263.

PEDESTAL TRUCK MOUNT M25 is designed for Half-Track Personnel Carriers M3 and M5. It mounts the Cal. .30 Machine Gun M1919A4.

REFERENCES—TM 9–224; OCM 16575; SNL A–55, Sec. 17, Add.

PEDESTAL TRUCK MOUNT M31 is designed for mounting a machine gun on the ¼-Ton, 4x4, Truck. It is used by all services other than the Infantry.

It consists of a vertical pedestal, with attachments for mounting and bracing the gun, fastened to the floor by a base plate and given additional support by three steel braces. The mount is fastened at the front of the cargo compartment, with one supporting brace positioned between the two seats in the driver's compartment.

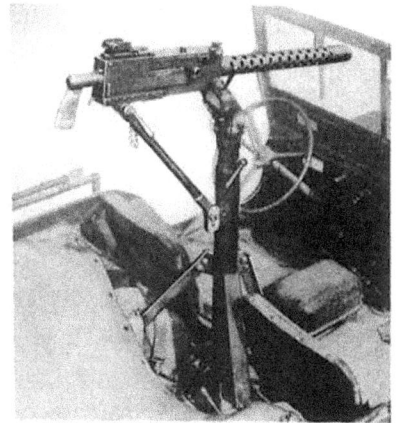

PEDESTAL MOUNT M31 ON ¼-TON TRUCK

This mount is suitable for mounting Cal. .30 Machine Guns M1917A1 and M1919A4, the Cal. .50 Machine Gun M2 HB, and the Browning automatic rifle.

One ammunition tray each for the Cal. .30 Machine Gun M1919A4 and the Cal. .50 Machine Gun M2 is supplied with each mount.

REFERENCES—TM 9–224; OCM 16805, 16914, 18338, 18479; SNL A–55, Sec. 18, Add.

PEDESTAL TRUCK MOUNT M31C is the designation applied to Pedestal Truck Mount M31 when Pintle D38579 is replaced by the improved cradle, pintle, and ammunition box holder assembly E10014. The latter assembly provides for use of standard Ammunition Boxes M1 and M2, although normally only the Cal. .50 Machine Gun M2 HB will be used with this mount.

REFERENCE—OCM 24118, 24328.

MACHINE GUN MOUNT M35 consists of a carriage and cradle assembly designed for use on skate rails, as on Scout Car

CAL. .30 MACHINE GUN MOUNT M48 ON DASH OF ¼-TON TRUCK

PEDESTAL MOUNT M24A2 WITH CAL. .50 MACHINE GUN

MACHINE GUN MOUNT M35 ON SKATE RAIL OF HALF-TRACK CAR M2

RING MOUNT M66 ON HIGH SPEED TRACTOR M4. NOTE BACK REST

M3A1, Half-Track 81-mm Mortar Carrier M4A1, Half-Track Car M2, and Landing Vehicles, Tracked. It will mount either the Cal. .50 Machine Gun M2 HB or the Cal. .30 Machine Gun M1919A4.

REFERENCES—OCM 18312; SNL A-55, Sec. 28.

MACHINE GUN MOUNT M35C is the designation applied to the M35 when Cradle Assembly D54075 is replaced by cradle, pintle, and ammunition box holder assembly E10014. The latter assembly provides for use of standard Ammunition Boxes M1 and M2, although normally only the Cal. .50 Machine Gun M2 HB will be used with this mount.

REFERENCES—OCM 24118, 24328.

DASH MOUNT

CAL. .30 MACHINE GUN MOUNT M48 is a dash mount for the Cal. .30 Machine Guns M1917A1 and M1919A4 and the Browning automatic rifle, for use on the ¼-Ton, 4x4, Truck. It was designed by the Infantry Board and revised slightly after

TRUCK MOUNT M36 ON OPEN CAB TRUCK

testing at the Aberdeen Proving Ground. The mount was standardized in March 1943 for use by the Infantry.

The mount is attachable to the extreme right side of the instrument panel of the truck, and is intended for fire against ground targets and limited use against aerial targets. It consists of a bracket employing the pintle supplied with Pedestal Truck Mounts M24, M24A1, and M31, and is attached by bolts to the dash.

By means of an adapter developed by Aberdeen Proving Ground, the Cal. .30 Ammunition Box M1 can be used with the Cal. .30 Machine Gun M1919A4 on this mount. The cradle assembly of the Tripod Mount M1917A1 will ordinarily be used in lieu of the Pintle D38579 to mount the Machine Gun M1917A1. This cradle assembly permits mounting of the Cal. .30 Ammunition Box M1 thereon, and eliminates the necessity for an adapter with this weapon.

REFERENCES—TM 9-224; OCM 18388, 18479, 19746, 19991, 20727, 21412; SNL A-55, Sec. 32.

RING MOUNTS

Each mount consists essentially of a circular track on which is mounted a carriage assembly, a cradle assembly, and an ammunition box for a machine gun.

The cradle, which allows elevations from −20° to + 85°, is rotatable in the pintle sleeve of the carriage, which is guided on the track by means of rollers, providing a traverse of 360°.

The mount is supported above a vehicle in such a manner as to permit the machine gunner to stand within the ring while operating the gun, firing against a fast-moving aerial target, without moving from his position.

The designation, Ring Mount, is applied to those components which are common to all vehicle installations without reference to the supporting structure.

REFERENCES—TM 9-224; OCM 17761, 18562, 20099, 20721, 20722, 21420, 21954, 23016, 23802, 24570, 24776; SNL A-55, Sec. 19.

RING MOUNT M49 is the basic ring mount used on truck mounts as well as on half tracks and various other vehicles.

RING MOUNT M49C designed for use on high-speed tractors, makes use of a track with a slightly different cross-section from the original ring. It is provided with a continuous flange throughout its entire circumference, to provide a seal against water and foreign matter when installed in the roof of a vehicle.

RING MOUNT M66 is a roller-bearing mount for the Cal. .50 Machine Gun M2 HB. It is similar in appearance and size to the Ring Mount M49C, but because of its roller-bearing construction the entire inner ring is turned to traverse the gun. The gun is mounted at the front of the inner ring in an equilibrated cradle assembly similar to that used on light and medium tanks. A padded back rest, which is fastened to the rear of the inner ring, enables the gunner to control the traverse of the weapon through 360° by the use of his body. This mount was standardized in August 1944 for use on the Armored Utility Car M20, 18-Ton High-Speed Tractor M4, and 38-Ton High-Speed Tractor M6.

TRUCK MOUNTS

The designation, Truck Mount, is applied to a ring mount together with the supporting structure designed for use on a particular truck. The mount is supported above the assistant driver's seat, and is manned by the assistant driver, standing on the seat cushion or on a firing platform provided by folding the seat back and down over the cushion. It is suitable for either the cal. .30 or cal. .50 machine gun.

VEHICULAR MACHINE GUN MOUNTS (Continued)

TRUCK MOUNT M32 IS USED ON 2½-TON, CLOSED CAB TRUCKS

TRUCK MOUNT M37 ON SHORT WHEELBASE, CLOSED CAB TRUCK

REFERENCES—TM 9–224; OCM 17600, 17720, 17761, 18562, 20100, 20582, 22212, 24052, 24263; SNL A–55, Sec. 19.

TRUCK MOUNT M32 is designed for 2½-ton, 6x6, long wheelbase, closed cab trucks, with conventional steel bodies.

TRUCK MOUNT M36 is designed for 2½-ton, or larger, trucks with open cabs, as follows:

2½-ton, 6x6, G.M.C., long wheelbase, short wheelbase, cab-over-engine, water tank, gasoline tank, dump, and amphibian types with open cabs.

4-ton, 6x6, Diamond T, short wheelbase, long wheelbase and wrecker, with open cabs.

4–5 ton, 4x4, open cab tractor (Federal and Autocar).

5-ton, 4x2, open cab tractors, short wheelbase, heavy duty and light duty (International).

5–6 ton, 4x4, open cab tractor (Autocar).

6-ton, 6x6, open cab prime mover (White and Corbitt).

7½-ton, 6x6, open cab prime mover (Mack).

Heavy Wrecking Truck M1A1.

10-ton, 6x4, G.S.L.C., open cab (Mack).

12-ton, 6x4, Truck M20, open cab.

TRUCK MOUNT M37 is designed for 2½-ton, 6x6, short wheelbase, closed cab trucks, with conventional steel bodies.

TRUCK MOUNT M37A1 is designed for 2½-ton, 6x6, short wheelbase, closed cab trucks, with wood bodies.

TRUCK MOUNT M37A2 is designed for 2½-ton, 6x6, long wheelbase, closed cab trucks, with wood bodies.

TRUCK MOUNT M37A3 is designed for the camouflaged 2½-ton, 6x6, 750-gallon gasoline tank truck and 700-gallon water tank truck.

TRUCK MOUNT M50 is designed for the 1½-ton, 6x6, truck.

TRUCK MOUNT M56 is designed for closed cab, 4-ton, 6x6, trucks; cargo, short wheelbase; cargo, long wheelbase; and wrecker (Diamond T).

TRUCK MOUNT M57 is designed for 6-ton, 6x6, closed cab prime mover and 2,000-gal. gasoline tank trucks (White).

TRUCK MOUNT M58 is designed for 6-ton, 6x6, closed cab, prime mover truck (Corbitt).

TRUCK MOUNT M59 is designed for 6-ton, 6x6, closed cab, bridge erecting truck (Brockway).

TRUCK MOUNT M60 is designed for 4-5 ton, 4x4, closed cab tractor truck (Federal).

TRUCK MOUNT M61 is designed for 4-5 ton, 4x4, closed cab tractor truck and 5-6 ton, 4x4, closed cab tractor truck (Autocar).

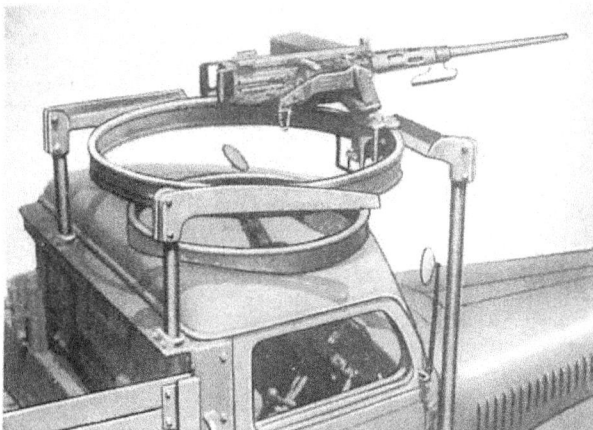

TRUCK MOUNT M56 ON 4-TON, 6 X 6, CLOSED CAB CARGO TRUCK

TRUCK MOUNT M57 ON 6-TON, 6 X 6, CLOSED CAB PRIME MOVER

ARMORED TRAILER M8—LIMITED STANDARD

ARMORED TRAILER M8, WITH PINTLE HITCH FOLDED BACK ON FRAME

TYPICAL CHARACTERISTICS

Physical Characteristics

Weight (gross) . . . . 5,058 lb.
(Trailer, 2,640 lb.; tank hitch, 218 lb.;
payload 2,200 lb.)
Length (over front lunette and
rear pintle) . . . . 9 ft., 10¼ in.
Width . . . . 7 ft., 4⅝ in.
Height . . . . 4 ft., 4¼ in.
Inside Body Dimensions
Length . . . . 4 ft., 8 in.
Width . . . . 5 ft., ¾ in.
Depth . . . . 2 ft., 4½ in.
Ground clearance . . . . 16½ in.

Tread (center to center of tires) . . . . 75 in.
Tire equipment—combat tires . . . . . . 9.00 x 20

Armor

Cargo body—sides and rear . . . . ⅜ in.
front and top . . . . ¼ in.

Coupling Devices

Lunette on frame in front
Pintle on rear (for tandem use)
Pintle hitch assembly with quick release pintle
provided with trailer (carried on lunette frame
when not in use)

Brakes, Parking . . . . Hand

SIDE VIEW, WITH PINTLE HITCH EXTENDED FOR ATTACHING TO TANK

Armored Trailer M8 is a two-wheeled, rubber-tired vehicle, designed to be towed behind tanks and other combat vehicles or trucks. Standardized in September 1942, it was reclassified as Limited Standard by Ordnance Committee action in November 1943.

It is suitable for transporting fifty-four 5-gallon Quartermaster gasoline cans or the following rounds of ammunition:

105-mm howitzer, 42 rounds;
75-mm gun, 93 rounds;
37-mm gun, 360 rounds;
Cal. .50 machine gun, 25,200 rounds;
81-mm mortar, 222 rounds.

The body is constructed of ⅜-inch armor at the sides and rear, and ¼-inch armor at the front and top. The floor is not armored, but consists of a ⅛-inch steel floor plate with an additional ⅛-inch skid plate under the frame to prevent snagging. The body is mounted on a channel iron framework to which the axle also is welded. Two hinged covers permit access to the body. Web straps, inside the body and on the covers, hold the cargo in place.

The trailer is provided with a lunette frame, for use when towed by a vehicle equipped with a pintle. To permit use of the trailer with tanks not equipped with pintles, a hitch incorporating a pintle is supplied as a part of each trailer, and may be attached to the towing lugs on the rear of any type of tank. The hitch is equipped with a cable release, operated from the towing vehicle. The hitch may be folded back on the lunette frame when not in use.

A pintle on the rear of the trailer permits towing in tandem. There is a retractable pole prop for supporting the front of the trailer when detached from the vehicle.

The vehicle is equipped with parking brakes, operated by a hand lever located on the front of the body. Standard combat zone safety lights on the rear are operated from batteries carried on the trailer.

The vehicle was manufactured by John Deere & Co.

References—TM 9-791; OCM 17970, 18063, 18350, 18520, 18840, 19781, 19986, 22361.

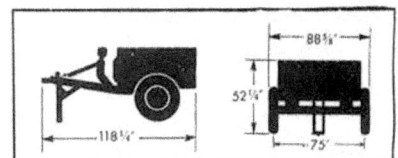

LIGHT ARMORED CAR **M8**—STANDARD

Light Armored Car M8 is designed as a light, highly mobile, armored reconnaissance vehicle which may also be used as a 37-mm gun motor carriage.

It consists of a welded hull and cast turret on a 6-wheel (6x6) chassis. The vehicle uses a conventional type of steering wheel and a Hercules model JXD engine.

Principal armament consists of a 37-mm Gun M6, mounted with a cal. .30 machine gun in a combination mount in the turret. The guns have an elevation from −10° to +20°. The machine gun can be removed from the combination mount and used on a Tripod Mount M2 if required.

The 37-mm gun, using A.P.C. shot M51B1 or M51B2, with a muzzle velocity of 2,900 feet per second, will penetrate 1.8 inches of face-hardened armor plate at 1,000 yards. A folding cal. .50 antiaircraft machine gun mount is provided.

The commander and gunner occupy positions in the open-top turret, which has a traverse of 360°. Driver and assistant are seated forward in the hull. In combat zones, the direct-vision slot shutters and hatch covers can be closed, and vision afforded by protectoscopes.

The vehicle is equipped with a radio and an intracar speaking tube. It is provided with a removable folding canopy of heavy canvas for covering the turret.

LIGHT ARMORED CAR M8, WITH PEDESTAL MOUNT FOR MACHINE GUN AT REAR OF TURRET

A pintle hook is affixed to the rear of the vehicle for towing a trailer.

The pilot vehicle was manufactured by the Ford Motor Co.

REFERENCES—TM 9–743; OCM 17303, 17359, 17718, 17929, 18133, 18314, 18340, 18511, 19432, 20680, 21002, 22248, 22381, 23333, 23570; SNL G-136.

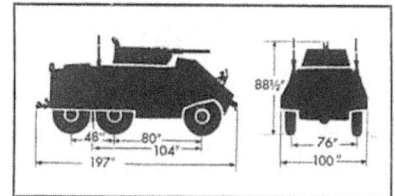

TYPICAL CHARACTERISTICS

Crew 4

Physical Characteristics
Weight (gross) . . . . 17,400 lb.
Length . . . . 16 ft., 5 in.
Width . . . . 8 ft., 4 in.
Height . . . . 7 ft., 4½ in.
Ground clearance . . . . 11½ in.
Tread (center to center of tracks) . . . . . 76 in.
Wheelbase, front to rear axle . . . . . . 128 in.
   Front to intermediate axle . . . . . 80 in.
Ground pressure at 3-inch
   penetration . . . . 13.6 lb./sq. in.
Tire equipment . . . . . 9.00x20, 12-ply (combat)

Armament
1 37-mm Gun M6 and
1 Cal. .30 Browning Machine Gun
  M1919A4 (flexible)
  In Combination Mount M23A1 in turret
  Elevation . . . . −10° to +20°
  Traverse . . . . 360°
1 Cal. .50 Machine Gun M2 HB (flexible)
  on turret, antiaircraft
1 Tripod Mount, Cal. .30, M2
1 Tripod Mount, Cal. .50, M3
Provision for:
  4 Cal. .30 Carbines . . . . . . Equipment of crew

Ammunition, Stowage
37-mm (A.P.C., M51B1 or M51B2;
  H.E., M63; and Can., M2) . . . . . 80 rounds*
Cal. .30 carbine . . . . 400 rounds

Cal. .30 machine gun . . . . 1,500 rounds
Cal. .50 . . . . 400 rounds
Grenades, Hand (Fragmentation, Mk. II, 6;
  Smoke, WP, 6) 12
Mines, Antitank, H.E., M1A1 6
Smoke Pots M1 or M2 4

Armor   **Actual**
Hull, Front, Upper . . . . ⅝ in.
    Lower . . . . ¾ in.
Sides . . . . ⅜ in.
Rear . . . . ⅜ in.
Top . . . . ¼ in.
Bottom . . . . ⅛–¼ in.
Turret, Front . . . . ¾ in.
   Sides and rear . . . . ¾ in.

Performance
Maximum speed on level . . . . 55 m.p.h.
Speed on 3% grade . . . . 30 m.p.h.
Maximum grade ability 60%
Vertical obstacle ability . . . . 12 in.
Fording depth (slowest forward speed) . . 24 in.
Turning radius . . . . 28 ft.
Fuel capacity . . . . 56 gal.
Cruising range . . . . 350 miles

Vision and Fire Control
Protectoscopes 2
Telescope M70D, w/Instrument Light M39C . . 1

Communications
Radio . . . . SCR-506 and/or 508, 510, 608, 610
Interphone stations 4
Flag Set M238 1

*Vehicles with two radios carry only 16 rounds of 37-mm ammunition.

Battery, Voltage, total 12

Fire Protection and Decontamination
Fire Extinguisher, CO₂-4 lb. (hand) 1
Decontaminating Apparatus M2, 1½ qts. . . . 2

Engine, Make and model . . . . . . Hercules JXD
Type . . . . In-Line,"L"
No. of cylinders 6
Fuel (gasoline) . . . . 70 octane
Net hp. . . . . 110 at 3,000 r.p.m.
Max. torque . . . . 238 lb.-ft. at 1,100 r.p.m.

Transmission, Type . . . . . . Selective sliding gear
Gear ratios
   First speed 6.499:1
   Second speed 3.543:1
   Third speed 1.752:1
   Fourth speed 1.000:1
   Reverse 6.987:1

Transfer Case, Gear ratios
   High gear 1.000:1
   Low gear 1.956:1

Suspension, Type . . . . Leaf springs
Wheel construction . . . . Divided rim

Master Clutch, Type . . . . Dry, single plate

Radiator, Type . . . . Tube and fin
Capacity of system . . . . 23 qt.

Brakes, Type . . . . Hydraulic

ARMORED UTILITY CAR M20—STANDARD

ARMORED UTILITY CAR M20, WITH RING MOUNT M49. LATER VEHICLES USE RING MOUNT M66

TYPICAL CHARACTERISTICS

Crew . . . . .2 to 6

Physical Characteristics
Weight (unloaded). . . . . .12,800 lb.
Weight (loaded—depending on use)
. . . . .14,500 to 17,500 lb.
Length. 16 ft., 5 in.
Width. . . . . 8 ft., 4 in.
Height. . . . . 7 ft., 7 in.
Ground clearance. . . . . .11½ in.
Tread (center to center, rear). . . . . 76 in.
Wheelbase, front to rear axle. . . . . . . .128 in.
Wheelbase, front to intermediate axle. . .80 in.
Ground pressure at 3-in. penetration
(depending on load) 12.7 to 14.35 lb./sq. in.
Tire equipment. . . . . .9.00x20, 12-ply, combat

Armament
1 Ring Mount M49 or M66 for Cal. .50
Machine Gun M2 HB (flexible)
Provision for:
1 Cal. .50 Machine Gun M2 HB (flexible)
1 Cal. .50 Tripod Mount M3
5 Cal. .30 Carbines
1 2.36-In. Rocket Launcher M9A1

Ammunition, Stowage
Cal. .50. . . . . .1,000 rounds
Cal. .30 carbine. . . . . .500 rounds
Grenades (Hand: Fragmentation, Mk. II, 6;
Smoke, WP, 6; Rifle: M9A1, 3). 15
Rockets, A.T., 2.36-In., M6A3. 10
Mines, A.T., M1A1. 3
Smoke Pots M1 or M2. 4

Armor   **Actual**
Hull, Front, Upper. . . . . .⅝ in.
Lower. . . . . .¾ in.
Sides. . . . . .⅜ in.
Rear. . . . . .⅜ in.
Top. . . . . .¼ in.
Bottom. . . . . ⅛-¼ in.

Performance
Maximum speed on level. . . . . 55 m.p.h.
On 3% grade. . . . . 30 m.p.h.
Maximum grade ability. 60%

Vertical obstacle ability. . . . . .12 in.
Fording depth (slowest forward speed). . .24 in.
Turning radius. 28 ft.
Fuel capacity. . . . . 56 gal.
Cruising range (approx.). . . . . .350 miles

Vision and Fire Control
Protectoscopes. .2

Communications
Radio. . . .SCR-506 and/or 508, 510, 608, 610
Flag Set M238. 1

Battery, Voltage, total. 12

Fire Protection and Decontamination
Fire Extinguisher, CO₂-4 lb. (hand). 1
Decontaminating Apparatus M2, 1½ qt. 2

Engine, Make and model. . . . . . .Hercules JXD
Type. . . . . .In-line, "L"
No. of cylinders. 6
Fuel (gasoline). . . . . 70 octane
Net hp. . . . . .110 at 3,000 r.p.m.
Max. torque. . . . . . .238 lb.-ft. at 1,100 r.p.m.

Transmission, Type. . . . . .Selective sliding gear
Gear ratios
First speed. 6.499:1
Second speed. 3.543:1
Third speed. 1.752:1
Fourth speed. 1.000:1
Reverse 6.987:1

Transfer Case, Gear ratios
High gear. 1.000:1
Low gear. 1.956:1

Suspension, Type. . . . . .Leaf springs
Wheel construction. . . . . .Divided rim

Master Clutch, Type. . . . . . . .Dry, single plate

Radiator, Type. . . . . .Tube and fin
Capacity of system. . . . . .23 qt.

Brakes, Type. . . . . .Hydraulic

This vehicle, which is based on the chassis of Light Armored Car M8, is designed to combine the functions of a command car and of a personnel and cargo carrier.

Following the standardization of Light Armored Car M8, the Tank Destroyer Command requested the development of three vehicles—a command car, a personnel and cargo carrier, and an anti-aircraft multiple machine gun mount—based on the same chassis.

Of these, it was proposed that the command car should be essentially the same as Armored Car M8, the principal change being the substitution for the 37-mm gun of a cal. .50 machine gun on a ring mount on top of the turret. The proposed personnel and cargo carrier was to be without a turret. Subsequently the Tank Destroyer Board indicated a preference for a turretless command car. This permitted the combination of the two functions in a single vehicle, with provision for stowage as required for the two different uses.

The vehicle was originally standardized in April 1943 as Armored Utility Car M10. To avoid confusion with the 3-Inch Gun Motor Carriage M10 in tank destroyer organizations, the designation was changed to Armored Utility Car M20.

A Ring Mount M49 or M66, for the Cal. .50 Machine Gun M2 HB (flexible), is provided over the rear of the open cargo compartment, for protection against low-flying aircraft. Provision is made for carrying a 2.36-in. rocket launcher and five cal. .30 carbines.

The car will accommodate two to six men, depending on the use for which it is intended. Protectoscopes and direct vision are provided for the driver and assistant driver.

Like the Armored Car M8, the vehicle is of the six-wheeled type, with power from a Hercules JXD gasoline engine being supplied to all six wheels.

The pilot vehicle was manufactured by the Ford Motor Co.

REFERENCES—TM 9-743; OCM 18314, 18390, 19347, 19431, 19993, 20077, 20203, 20363, 20446, 20680, 20982, 21002, 21178, 21339, 24570, 24776, 25471, 25641; SNL G-176.

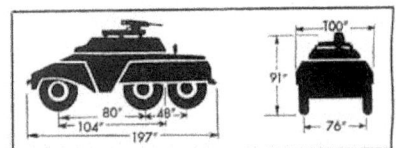

ARMORED CARS T17, T17E1, T17E2—LIMITED PROCUREMENT

As the result of reports from war areas, particularly North Africa, indicating the need for armored, wheeled vehicles for reconnaissance and combat, the Ordnance Committee, in July 1941, set forth military characteristics for medium and heavy armored cars.

In September 1941, authority was given to procure pilot models. A six-wheeled vehicle, built by the Ford Motor Co., was designated Armored Car T17, and a four-wheeled vehicle, built by the Chevrolet Motor Co., was designated Armored Car T17E1.

On 15 October 1942, a board, composed of Armored Force, Cavalry, Tank Destroyer, and Ordnance representatives was appointed to consider armored cars in production or in development. As the medium and heavy armored cars were considered too large, the contract for Armored Car T17, then in production, was reduced to 250 cars, which the British agreed to accept. None were sent overseas, however. The guns were removed, and the vehicles were assigned for military police use in this country.

Limited procurement of Armored Car T17E1 was authorized for International Aid. Ordnance Committee action in June 1943 recorded authority for procurement of a quantity of these vehicles with a Fraser-Nash turret instead of a tank type turret, and designated the modified vehicle Armored Car T17E2.

REFERENCES — OCM 16987, 17091, 17217, 17473, 18229, 19780, 20645, 20680, 21002, 22818.

ARMORED CAR T17 is a 6x6 vehicle which originally mounted a 37-mm Gun M6 and a cal. .30 machine gun (fixed) in a Combination Mount M24, with gyro-stabilizer, in a tank type turret. A cal. .30 machine gun (flexible) was mounted in the bow and another was provided for antiaircraft use. Provision was made for carrying a cal. .45 submachine gun.

Power is supplied by two Hercules JXD engines, each having its own clutch and four-speed transmission. Gears are shifted by a single lever, and either transmission can be put into neutral. A transfer case provides eight forward and two reverse speeds. Steering is by means of a hydraulic-boosted, worm and roller type gear and a conventional steering wheel.

REFERENCES—TM 9-740; OCM 16987, 17091, 18229, 19780, 20680, 21002, 22818; SNL G-134.

ARMORED CAR T17E1 is a 4x4 vehicle designed for distant reconnaissance, convoy escort, and police purposes. The hull is so constructed that a frame is not required, the springs, steering gear, transfer case, and other units being attached directly to the hull.

Principal armament is a 37-mm Gun M6 and a Cal. .30 Machine Gun M1919A4 (fixed), in a combination mount in a power-operated turret. A Cal. .30 Machine Gun M1919A4 (flexible) is mounted in the bow and one on the turret.

Direct-vision doors, with protected vision slots, and six periscopes are provided. The vehicle is intended for British use, and was modified to satisfy British requirements.

REFERENCES—TM 9-741; OCM 17217, 17473, 18229, 19780, 22818; SNL G-128.

ARMORED CAR T17, WITH VISION SLOTS OPEN, SHOWING TURRET AND BOW GUNS

ARMORED CAR T17, 146", 218", 102", 91", 86"

ARMORED CAR T17E1, 120", 216", 106", 93", 89"

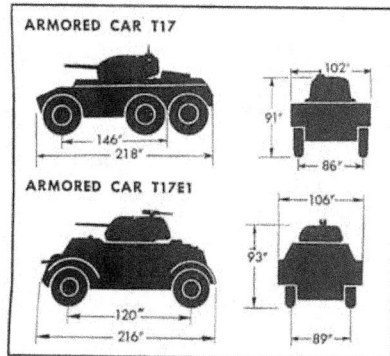

ARMORED CAR T17E1, HAS 37-MM AND CAL. .30 GUNS IN TURRET

ARMORED CAR T17E2 HAS TWO CAL. .50 A. A. GUNS IN TURRET

ARMORED CAR T17E2 is similar to Armored Car T17E1, but has a Fraser-Nash type of power turret mounting two cal. .50 antiaircraft guns.

One thousand of these vehicles were manufactured at the request of the British.

The cal. .50 machine guns can be elevated from $-10°$ to $+75°$ at a speed of 30° per second, and can be traversed 360° at a rate of 43° per second.

REFERENCES—TM 9–741; OCM 20645, 21848, 22203, 22818; SNL G-122.

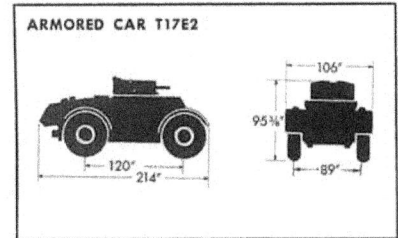

ARMORED CAR T17E2

TYPICAL CHARACTERISTICS

	T17	T17E1	T17E2
Crew	5	5	3
Physical Characteristics			
Weight (gross)	32,000 lb.	30,705 lb.	26,558 lb.
Length	18 ft., 2 in.	18 ft.	17 ft., 10 in.
Width	8 ft., 6 in.	8 ft., 10 in.	8 ft., 10 in.
Height	7 ft., 7 in.	7 ft., 9 in.	7 ft., 11⅜ in.
Ground clearance	13½ in.	15 in.	15 in.
Tread	86 in.	89 in.	89 in.
Wheelbase	146 in.	120 in.	120 in.
Tire equipment (combat)	12.00 x 20	14.00 x 20	14.00 x 20
Ground pressure at 4 in. penetration	17.7 lb./sq. in.	17.95 lb./sq. in.	15.4 lb./sq. in.
Armament			
37-mm Gun M6 and Cal. .30 Machine Gun M1919A4 (fixed)	1 each, in Combination Mount M24, in turret	1 each, in Combination Mount M24A1, in turret	
Cal. .50 Machine Guns M2 HB, TT (special)			2, in Fraser-Nash turret
Elevation	$-10°$ to $+45°$	$-7°$ to $+40°$	$-10°$ to $+75°$
Traverse	360°	360°	360°
Cal. .30 Machine Gun M1919A4 (flexible)	1, in bow / 1, on turret (antiaircraft)	1, in bow / 1, on turret (antiaircraft)	
Tripod Mount, cal. .30, M2	1		
2-In. Mortar M3		1	
Provision for: Cal. .45 submachine guns	1	1	1
Ammunition			
37 mm	111 rounds	103 rounds	
Cal. .30	4,750 rounds	5,250 rounds	
Cal. .45	450 rounds	450 rounds	450 rounds
Cal. .50			2,610 rounds
Grenades, Hand	12	12	12
2-In. Mortar		14 rounds	
Armor	**Actual**	**Actual**	**Actual**
Hull, Front	¾ in.	⅞–⅝ in.	⅞–⅝ in.
Sides	¾ in.	¾ in.	¾ in.
Rear	½ in.	⅜ in.	⅜ in.
Top	⅝ in.	½ in.	½ in.
Bottom	¼ in.	½–¼ in.	½–¼ in.

	T17 Actual	T17E1 Actual	T17E2 Actual
Armor			
Turret, Front	1¼ in.	1¾ in.	1¼ in.
Sides and rear	1¼ in.	1¼ in.	1¼ in.
Top	¾ in.	½ in.	
Shield		1 in.	
Performance			
Maximum speed	60 m.p.h.	55 m.p.h.	55 m.p.h.
Speed on 3% grade	35 m.p.h.	35 m.p.h.	35 m.p.h.
Maximum grade	60%	57%	57%
Vertical obstacle	18 in.	21 in.	21 in.
Fording depth	32 in.	32 in.	32 in.
Turning radius	30 ft.	27.5 ft.	27.5 ft.
Fuel capacity	75 gal.	137 gal.	137 gal.
Cruising range	250 miles	450 miles	450 miles
Vision and Fire Control			
Direct vision slots	2	2	2
Periscope M6	6	6	3
Periscope M4, with Telescope M40	1	1	
Sight, Illuminated, Mk. IX (24-volt)			1
Communications			
Radio	British No. 19	British No. 19	British No. 19
Interphone stations	5	5	3
Flag Set M238	1	1	1
Battery, Voltage	24	24	24
Fire Protection and Decontamination			
Fire Extinguisher, CO₂ –10 lb. (fixed)	2	2	2
CO₂–4 lb. (hand)	1	1	1
Decontaminating Apparatus M2	1	1	1
Engine, Make	Hercules JXD (2)	G.M.C. 270 (2)	G.M.C. 270 (2)
Type	In-line, L, L.C.	In-line, L.C.	In-line, L.C.
No. of cylinders (each engine)	6	6	6
Fuel (gasoline)	70–80 octane	70–80 octane	70–80 octane
Displacement (each engine)	320 cu. in.	270.5 cu. in.	270.5 cu. in.
Net hp. at r.p.m. (each engine)	110 at 3,000	97 at 3,000	97 at 3,000
Max. torque at r.p.m. (each engine)	238 lb.-ft. at 1,100	216.3 lb.-ft. at 1,000	216.3 lb.-ft. at 1,000

LIGHT ARMORED CAR M38—STANDARD

Light Armored Car M38, which was standardized in March 1945, is the result of efforts to develop a 6-wheel-drive reconnaissance vehicle with superior qualities for cross-country operation.

Its excellent mobility and riding qualities are largely the result of the spacing of the axles on the chassis. Unlike Light Armored Car M8, which it is expected to replace, the M38 has axles evenly spaced from front to back to provide better distribution of weight, whereas the rear axles of the M8 are close together, as on a conventional 6-wheel-drive transport vehicle.

This improvement gives not only better flotation in soft terrain but also greater ability to cross craters and trenches and to surmount obstacles. Light Armored Car M38 can surmount a 24-in. vertical obstacle and cross a 50-in. trench; Light Armored Car M8 can surmount only a 12-in. vertical obstacle and has negligible trench-crossing ability. To prevent undue wear on the tires that would otherwise result from the even spacing of the axles, the wheels on the two forward axles pivot for steering.

Other improvements that contribute to the good riding qualities are the independent suspension of the wheels, the oversize tires (12.00x20 as against 9.00x20 on the M8), and light weight. Combat loaded, the M38 weighs approximately 2,000 lb. less than the M8.

Some of the decrease in weight has been obtained by cutting down the thickness of armor. The M38 has ⅜-in. armor on many portions of the hull and turret where the M8 has ⅝- and ¾-in. plate. Increased angles, however, retain comparable ballistic characteristics to a large extent.

Except that the M38 has a Cadillac V-8 engine and a Hydra-Matic transmission instead of a Hercules JXD engine and selective sliding gear transmission, characteristics of the two armored cars are much the same. Principal armament of the M38 is the 37-mm Gun M6 in a combination mount with a Cal. .30 Machine Gun M1919A4 (flexible). A cal. .50 machine gun for protection against low-flying aircraft is mounted on the turret. Tripod mounts for a cal. .30 and a cal. .50 machine gun are also provided, along with adequate stowage for ammunition.

The vehicle has a top speed of 60 m.p.h. and a cruising range of 300 miles. It carries a crew of four.

The pilot vehicle was built by the Chevrolet Division, General Motors Corporation.

REFERENCES — OCM 19581, 19955, 20794, 25967, 26849.

NEW TYPE OF SUSPENSION GIVES LIGHT ARMORED CAR M38 GREAT MOBILITY

TYPICAL CHARACTERISTICS

Crew. 4
Physical Characteristics
Weight (combat loaded). . . . . .15,300 lb.
Length. . . . . .16 ft., 9¼ in.
Width. . . . . .8 ft.
Height. .6 ft., 6 in.
Turret ring diameter. . . . . .56 in.
Ground clearance. . . . . .14½ in.
Tread (center to center of tires). . . . . .80 in.
Wheelbase (59 in. between axles). . .118 in.
Ground pressure at
3-in. penetration. . . . . .8.1 lb./sq. in.
Tire equipment 12.00x20, new standard combat
Armament
37-mm Gun M6 and
1 Cal. .30 Machine Gun M1919A4 (flexible)
In Combination Mount M23A2, in turret
Elevation. . . . .−10° to +20°
Traverse. .360°
1 Cal. .50 Machine Gun
M2 HB (flexible). . . .On pedestal, on turret
1 Cal. .50 Tripod Mount M3
1 Cal. .30 Tripod Mount M2
Provision for:
4 Cal. .30 carbines
1 Grenade Launcher M8
Ammunition, Stowage
37-mm. . . . . .93 rounds
Cal. .50. . . . . .440 rounds
Cal. .30. . . . . .1,750 rounds
Smoke pots. 4
Grenades (hand, 12; rifle, 6). 18

Armor	Actual	Basis
Hull, front	⅜ in.	⅝ in. and 1½ in.
Sides and rear	⅜ in.	⁷⁄₁₆ in.
Top	¼ in.
Bottom, front 10 in.	⅜ in.
Remainder	¼ in.
Turret, front	½ in.	⅝ in.
Sides	⅜ in.	⁷⁄₁₆ in.
Rear	⅜ in.	⅜ in.
Top	Open

Performance
Maximum speed, on Level. . . . . .60 m.p.h.
On 3% grade. . . . . .35 m.p.h.
Maximum grade ability. 60%
Vertical obstacle ability. . . . . .24 in.

Trench crossing ability. . . . . .50 in.
Fording ability (slowest forward speed). .48 in.
Turning radius. . . . . .28 ft.
Fuel capacity. . . . . .51 gal.
Cruising range. . . . . .300 miles
Vision and Fire Control
Periscope M6 (for driver). 1
Telescope M70D, w/Instrument Light M39C. .1
Auxiliary knife-blade pointing sight. 1
Provision for:
Observation Telescope M49
Tripod M15
Communications
Radio. . . . . .SCR-506 and 528 or 510
Interphone stations. 4
Battery, Voltage, total. 12
Fire Protection and Decontamination
Fire Extinguisher, CO₂—4 lb. (hand). 1
Engine, Make and model. . . . . .Cadillac 42
Type. . . . . .V-8, L.C.
Displacement. . . . . .346 cu. in.
Fuel (gasoline). . . . . .80 octane
Gross hp. . . . . .148 at 3,200 r.p.m.
Max. torque. . . . . . .280 lb.-ft. at 1,200 r.p.m.
Transmission, Type. . . . . .Hydra-Matic
Gear ratios
First speed. 3.92:1
Second speed. 2.53:1
Third speed. 1.55:1
Fourth speed. 1.00:1
Reverse. 4.167:1
Transfer Case, Gear ratios. . .3.441:1; 1.392:1
Differential, Gear ratio. 6.667:1
Suspension, Type. Independent, swing arm, 6x6
Clutch, Type. . . . . .Fluid coupling
Radiator, Capacity of system. . . . . .38 qt.
Brakes, Type. . . . . .Vacuum

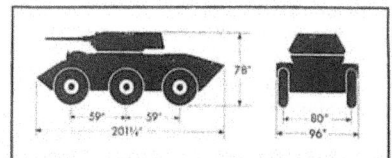

UNIVERSAL CARRIERS T16, T16E2—LIMITED PROCUREMENT

UNIVERSAL CARRIER T16 IS MODIFICATION OF BRITISH BREN GUN CARRIER

TYPICAL CHARACTERISTICS

(UNIVERSAL CARRIER T16)

Crew. 4

Physical Characteristics
Weight (gross w/payload, approx.).10,500 lb.
   Net (unserviced). . . . . .8,194 lb.
Length. . . . . .12 ft., 11⅛ in.
Width. . . . . .6 ft., 11½ in.
Height. . . . . .5 ft., 1 in.
Ground clearance. . . . . .10½ in.
Tread (center to center of tracks). . . .61½ in.
Ground contact length. . . . . .71 in.
Ground pressure (gross weight). . .7.4 lb./sq. in.

Armament
Provision for:
1 Infantry antitank projector (PIAT)
2 Bren machine guns
1 2-inch smoke mortar
2 Service rifles

Ammunition. . . . . .Supplied by British

Armor	Actual
Hull, front, upper.	$\frac{7}{32}$ in.
Lower.	$\frac{9}{32}$ in.
Sides, rear, and bottom.	$\frac{9}{32}$ in.

Performance
Maximum speed on level. . . . . .30 m.p.h.
Maximum grade ability. 60%
Trench crossing ability. . . . . .30 in.
Vertical obstacle ability. . . . . .18 in.
Fording depth (slowest forward speed). .Floats
Turning diameter. . . . . .32 ft.
Fuel capacity. . . . . .23.6 gal.
Cruising range (approx.). . . . . . . .100-150 miles
Payload. . . . . .1,200 lb.

Vision. . . . . .3 vision slots

Communications
Provision for British Wireless
   Set No. 19. 1

Battery, Voltage, total. 12

Fire Protection
Fire Extinguisher, Carbon Tetrachloride,
   1 qt.. 3

Engine, Make and model. . . . .Ford V-8, GAU
Type. . . . . .90°, L-head
No. of cylinders. 8
Fuel (gasoline). . . . . .70 octane
Displacement. . . . . .239 cu. in.
Max. governed speed. . . . . .3,300 r.p.m.
Net hp. . . . . .102.5 at 4,000 r.p.m.
Max. torque. . . . . . .176 lb.-ft., at 2,000 r.p.m.

Transmission, Type. . . . . .Spur gear
Gear ratios
   First speed. 6.40:1
   Second speed. 3.09:1
   Third speed. 1.69:1
   Fourth speed. 1.00:1
   Reverse. 7.82:1

Differential, Type. . . . . .Controlled
Gear ratio (ring gear to pinion). 5.83:1
Steering ratio. 1.8:1

Final Drive
No. of teeth in sprocket. 35
Pitch diameter of sprocket. . . . . .19.4 in.

Suspension, Type. . . . . .Coil spring

Idler, Type. . . . . .Fixed, front-mounted

Track, Type. . . . . .T79, cast steel
Width. . . . . .10 in.
Pitch. . . . . .1.75 in.
No. of shoes per vehicle. 348

Clutch, Type. . . . . .Dry, single-plate

UNIVERSAL CARRIER T16E2

Characteristics same as for Universal Carrier T16 except:

Length. .13 ft., 6 in.
Ground contact length. . . . . .77 in.
Ground pressure (gross weight). . . .6.8 lb./sq. in.
Armor, hull, front. . . . .$\frac{9}{32}$ and $\frac{25}{64}$ in.
Fuel capacity. . . . . .27.8 gal.

These are full-track, high-speed cargo carriers, designed to transport personnel, ammunition, and accessories. They are produced for the British only.

Universal Carrier T16 is a modification of the so-called Bren gun carrier, widely used by the British. The principal changes in design provide for the use of the controlled differential steering system, Ford Mercury engine, two two-wheeled bogies on each side, a redesigned and simplified welded hull structure, and for refinement of the track and suspension.

The original vehicle was designated Cargo Carrier T16, but was redesignated Universal Carrier T16 for the sake of uniformity with British nomenclature. Production of 30,000 for the British was authorized by agreement of the Joint British Tank Mission and the U. S. Tank Committee.

Universal Carrier T16E2, authorized to replace the T16 in production in 1945, is an elongated vehicle designed for improved stability and better bogie loading without major change in the spare parts required. The front bogie was moved back 6 in., the rear bogie was moved back 9 in. and reversed, and the drive axle was moved back 8 in.

Each vehicle has accommodations for a crew of four men, including the driver, and is armored at the front, sides, rear, and bottom, but is open at the top.

Sustained speed on improved level roads is 30 m.p.h. The vehicles will float with a partial load, propelling themselves by the action of the tracks in the water.

REFERENCES—TM 9-746, 9-1746A, 9-1746B; OCM 16635, 16727, 18229, 18434, 18598, 19782, 20576, 23959, 24491, 25361, 26380; SNL G-166.

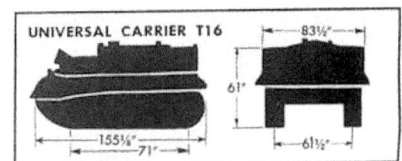

CARGO CARRIERS M28—LIMITED STANDARD; M29, M29C—STANDARD

Designed originally for use over snow and ice, Cargo Carriers M28 and M29 have proved useful wherever small, speedy vehicles with very low ground pressures have been required. Cargo Carrier M29C is an amphibian vehicle.

Power is supplied by a liquid-cooled, six-cylinder engine. The flywheel end of the engine is connected by means of a single-plate clutch, a conventional transmission, a propeller shaft, and two needle-bearing type universal joints to a controlled differential and the driving axle. The axle is of the planetary, two-speed type.

Vehicles are fully suppressed for radio installation. Except for various covers which are removable to facilitate maintenance and inspection operations, the hulls are of welded sheet steel. Plugs and a plate are provided for draining purposes.

CARGO CARRIER M28—LIMITED STANDARD—This vehicle has accommodations for a crew of two and for 800 pounds of equipment, including skis, ski poles, snowshoes, rucksacks, mountain-climbing axes, and other items essential for operations in snowy country. It was classified as Limited Standard by Ordnance Committee action in September 1943.

The engine is at the rear of the hull, and the driving axle at the front of the vehicle. The rear and side walls of the rear air duct and the front wall of the cargo boxes are of armor plate.

The track, designed especially for use on snow, is 18 inches wide. The track shoes are rubber covered.

There are two sets of bogie suspensions on each track, each with a semielliptic, three-section spring. Two rubber-tired bogie wheels are at each end of the spring, one riding each belt band. Two guide wheels on each side support and guide the track. Proper tension on the track is maintained by the spring-loaded rear idler.

A windshield defroster with an electric heating element is supplied. A pump-type primer aids in starting the engine when cold.

Towing eyes are mounted at the front of the vehicle and a pintle at the rear. Provision is made for carrying the armament of the crew members and the necessary ammunition.

REFERENCES—TM 9–893; OCM 18436, 19138, 19819, 19820, 19989, 20976, 21397, 21627, 23957; SNL G–154.

CARGO CARRIER M29—STANDARD—This vehicle, standardized in September 1943, is basically similar to Cargo Carrier M28, but has a rear drive. The change in design moved the center of gravity forward and also resulted in a more desirable arrangement of engine, crew, and cargo. The revised suspension,

CARGO CARRIER M28 HAS ENGINE AT REAR AND DRIVING AXLE AT FRONT

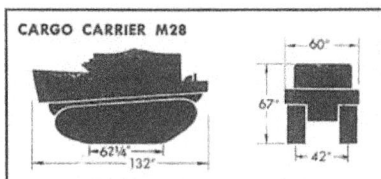

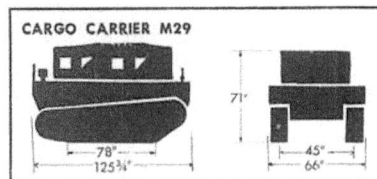

CARGO CARRIER M28

60″
67″
62¼″
132″
42″

CARGO CARRIER M29

71″
78″
125¾″
45″
66″

CARGO CARRIER M29 HAS DRIVING AXLE AT REAR, USES MORE BOGIES

which has transverse springs and twice the number of bogie wheels, provides improved riding characteristics.

The engine, engine accessories, fuel tank, driver's seat, vehicle controls, etc., are in the front of the vehicle. The rear houses the radio equipment and has seating capacity for the assistant driver and two extra passengers, or space for approximately 1,000 pounds of miscellaneous equipment. A track guard and step plates are on each side of the vehicle. An A-frame towing hitch permits use of the vehicles in tandem.

The transmission has three speeds forward and one reverse. A transfer unit provides a total of six speeds forward and two reverse.

First production vehicles were provided with 15-inch tracks, but later models have 20-inch tracks. A 40-ampere generator is furnished. When the vehicle uses a radio set with a drain in excess of 40 amperes, a 55-ampere generator can be installed by means of a conversion kit.

REFERENCES—TM 9–772; OCM 20976, 21397, 21627, 22590, 22704, 22753, 22851, 23077, 23652, 23956, 24274, 25472, 25697; SNL G–179.

CARGO CARRIER M29C—STANDARD—This is a modification of Cargo Carrier M29 adapted for amphibious operation. Watertight cells are added at the front and rear of the vehicle for buoyancy. Openings in the top of these cells permit bilge water to be pumped out. A surf guard on the forward edge of the front cell reduces the amount of water that is shipped.

The vehicle is propelled by its tracks, in water as well as on land.

Aprons fastened over the upper portion of the tracks facilitate the forward motion of the vehicle in water. Twin rudders are provided at the stern. Special equipment includes a fixed mounted driving light on the front deck, a signal spotlight and reel, and a capstan on the front deck.

The basic Cargo Carrier M29 is so designed that it can be converted in the field for amphibious use if required.

REFERENCES—TM 9–772; OCM 22590, 22851, 23331, 23574, 23652, 23956; SNL G–179.

CARGO CARRIER M29C, SHOWING SEATING ARRANGEMENT

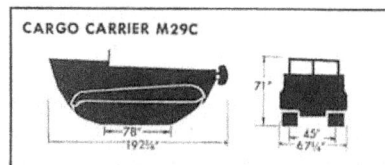

CARGO CARRIER M29C

TYPICAL CHARACTERISTICS

	Cargo Carrier M28	Cargo Carrier M29	Cargo Carrier M29C
Crew	2	2 to 4	2 to 4
Physical Characteristics			
Weight (gross)	4,650 lb.	5,425 lb.	6,000 lb.
Length (overall)	11 ft.	10 ft., 5¾ in.	16 ft., ⅛ in.
Width, With 15-in. track	5 ft.	5 ft.	
With 20-in. track		5 ft., 6 in.	5 ft., 7¼ in.
Height (overall)	5 ft., 7 in.	5 ft., 11 in.	5 ft., 11 in.
Top & windshield folded	4 ft., 8 in.	4 ft., 5¾ in.	4 ft., 7⅝ in.
Ground clearance	11 in.	11 in.	11 in.
Tread (center to center of tracks)	42 in.	45 in.*	45 in.*
Center of gravity, From front	62¾ in.	64 in.	83 in.
Below deck line	22 in.	19 in.	21⅜ in.
Ground contact length at 0 penetration	62¼ in.	78 in.	78 in.
Ground pressure at 0 penetration, With 15-in. track	2.15 lb./sq. in.	2.3 lb./sq. in.	
With 20-in. track		1.7 lb./sq. in.	1.9 lb./sq. in.
Freeboard in deep water			8–10 in.
Performance			
Maximum speed on hard-surfaced road, at 3,000 ft. altitude	35 m.p.h.	36 m.p.h.	36 m.p.h.
Maximum speed in water			4 m.p.h.
Maximum grade ability on hard surface	100%	100%	100%
Trench crossing ability	3 ft.	3 ft.	3 ft.
Angle of approach		90°	47°
Angle of departure		60°	36°
Turning diameter	24 ft.	24 ft.	24 ft.
Fuel capacity	25 gal.	35 gal.	35 gal.
Cruising range (approx.)	115 miles	175 miles	175 miles
Maximum drawbar pull		3,800 lb.	4,200 lb.
Payload	1,260 lb.	1,200 lb.	1,200 lb.

	Cargo Carrier M28	Cargo Carriers M29, M29C
Communications		
Radio	As specified	As specified
Battery, Voltage, total	12	12
Fire Protection and Decontamination		
Fire Extinguisher, CCl₄, 1 qt.	1	1
Engine, Make and model	Studebaker 6–170	Studebaker 6–170
Type	L-head, In-line, L.C.	L-head, In-line, L.C.
No. of cylinders	6	6
Fuel (gasoline)	80 octane at sea level 70 octane at 3,000 ft.	80 octane at sea level 70 octane at 3,000 ft.
Displacement	169.6 cu. in.	169.6 cu. in.
Compression ratio	7:1	7:1
Net hp.	65 at 3,600 r.p.m.	65 at 3,600 r.p.m.
Max. torque	125 lb.-ft. at 1,600 r.p.m.	125 lb.-ft. at 1,600 r.p.m.
Transmission		
Gear ratios		
First speed	2.66:1	2.66:1
Second speed	1.49:1	1.56:1
Third speed	1.00:1	1.00:1
Reverse	3.55:1	3.55:1
Transfer Case		
Gear ratios	1.154:1; 2.294:1	0.866:1; 2.74:1
Differential, Type	Controlled	Controlled
Gear ratio	5.857:1	4.87:1
Steering ratio	1.73:1	1.73:1
Final Drive		
Sprocket, No. of teeth	9	9
Suspension, Type	Semielliptic	Transverse, leaf spring
Idler		
Wheel or tire size	17x7¼	11¾x7
Track, Type	T77	T76E1
Width	18 in.	20 in.
Pitch	6 in.	4½ in.
No. of shoes per vehicle	82	112

*With 20-in. track.

SNOW TRACTOR M7—LIMITED STANDARD
1-TON SNOW TRAILER M19—LIMITED STANDARD

SNOW TRACTOR M7, SHOWN WITH WHEELS ON FRONT AND TOP REMOVED

TRAILER, ON SKIS, CARRYING TWO LITTERS

Designed to provide a light vehicle and trailer for transportation on snow, Snow Tractor M7 and 1-Ton Snow Trailer M19 are characterized by the fact that their wheels may be replaced by skis for use in deep snow. Standardized in August 1943, they were reclassified as Limited Standard in November 1944.

The pilot tractors and trailers were built by the Allis-Chalmers Manufacturing Co.

REFERENCES—OCM 18480, 19138, 19632, 20202, 20772, 21003, 21395, 21629, 24606, 25473, 25642; SNL G-194, G-195.

SNOW TRACTOR M7 is a half-track type high-speed vehicle. For negotiating deep snow, the front wheels may be replaced with skis. When not in use, the skis are carried at the side of the hood, serving as mudguards. The crew consists of two men, including the driver, one seated behind the other.

Grade ability is dependent upon shear strength of the snow; however, under extremely soft snow conditions the vehicle has negotiated a 38% grade with the driver only. It will climb a 60% grade if traction is available.

Power is supplied by a Willys MB four-cylinder liquid-cooled engine, similar to that used on the ¼-Ton, 4x4, Truck.

The transmission has three speeds forward and one reverse speed.

The steering mechanism is of the roller and segment type.

A six-volt ignition system suppressed for 30 meters is provided.

The vehicle has a towing pintle on the rear. Standard ¼-Ton, 4x4, Truck cold starting equipment is installed. Other equipment includes a removable canopy top and side curtains, a ten-foot tow chain, and a set of tools. Two spare skis are carried on each tractor.

1-TON SNOW TRAILER M19 is an unsprung light-weight trailer for use in towing equipment and supplies behind the Snow Tractor M7 or other suitable prime mover either on snow or over ground for limited distances.

For operation in deep snow, the wheels may be replaced by skis. A drop pole is provided for balancing the trailer when separated from the tractor.

Space is provided for carrying two litters, one above the other. When desired, the litters may be removed, and the trailer used to carry one C13 gasoline-electric generator set and cold starting equipment designed in accordance with Army Air Forces specifications. A pintle is provided on the rear of the trailer to permit towing of trailers in tandem.

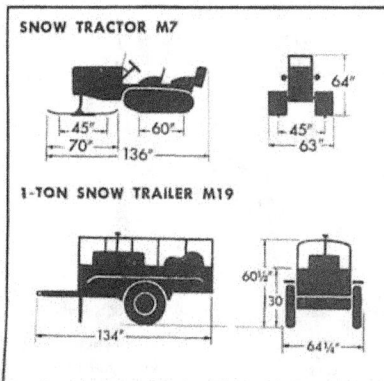

TYPICAL CHARACTERISTICS
SNOW TRACTOR M7

Crew...2
Physical Characteristics
  Weight (gross).....................3,049 lb.
  Length (overall from tip of skis to end
    of pintle hook—approx.).......11 ft., 4 in.
  Width............................5 ft., 3 in.
  Height (to top of windshield)......5 ft., 4 in.
    (to top of windshield lowered)...3 ft., 7 in.
  Ground clearance (approx.).........12¾ in.
  Tread (center to center of tracks)....45 in.
  Ground contact length at 3-in.
    penetration—track..................60 in.
      —skis..................45 in.
  Ground pressure............0.75 lb./sq. in.
  Tire equipment.....................4.00x15
Performance
  Maximum speed at 2,400 r.p.m......40 m.p.h.
  Maximum grade ability (with driver only) 60%
    —in deep soft snow.................38%
  Fording depth (slowest forward speed)..30 in.
  Turning radius (approx.)............15 ft.
  Angle of approach, w/skis............40°
    w/wheels..........60°
  Angle of departure..................60°
  Fuel capacity..................10½ gal.
  Cruising range (approx.)...........160 miles
  Normal towed load......2,000 lb. plus trailer
  Payload...........................500 lb.
Battery, Voltage, total.................6
Suspension, Type,
  Rear............Unsprung walking beam
  No. of wheels.......................10
  Wheel size...................8x1¼ in.
Track, Type..................Endless band
  Width............................18 in.
  Pitch..............................3 in.
  No. of shoes per vehicle.............66
Skis...........Interchangeable with front wheels
  Width.............................9 in.
  Length, overall....................70 in.

1-TON SNOW TRAILER M19
Physical Characteristics
  Weight (net with skis)..............640 lb.
  Length (overall—approx.).......11 ft., 2 in.
  Width—with wheels...........5 ft., 4¼ in.
    —with skis..............5 ft., 4¼ in.
  Ground clearance...................16 in.
  Tread..............................58 in.
  Payload (maximum)...............2,000 lb.
Skis.....Same as provided on Snow Tractor M7

SCOUT CAR M3A1—STANDARD

This vehicle, designed for high-speed scouting duty, consists of a specially designed, commercial type, 4-wheel truck chassis, surmounted by an armored body mounted on a double-drop type, channel section frame. It can attain a maximum road speed of 55 m.p.h. It was standardized in June 1939.

Seats are provided in the driver's compartment for the driver and the observation commander, and in the personnel compartment for six additional riders.

Armament consists of a cal. .50 and a cal. .30 machine gun. These can be fired from the skate rail which encircles the body interior and permits the gunners to aim in any direction, or on tripod mounts independently of the vehicle.

The body is protected by ¼-inch armor on the sides and rear. Top and side protection for the engine is provided by the armored hood. Armored shutters, controlled from within the driver's compartment, protect the radiator.

The windshield is of shatter-proof glass. An armor plate windshield shield, ½-inch thick, with direct-vision slots, is hinged above the windshield, and other armor plate shields are hinged above the doors. These can be swung into position to provide additional protection in combat areas.

The detachable canvas top is supported by three removable bows and the wind-

SCOUT CAR M3A1 WITH TOP UP AND RADIATOR SHUTTERS CLOSED

shield frame. Side curtains are of canvas with pyralin windows.

Ammunition racks are located at both sides of the personnel compartment, and space is provided between the front seats for additional ammunition or a radio set. The radio mast is mounted inside the body. Smaller sections for ammunition and water chests and a tool box are behind the front seats.

The vehicle is powered by a 6-cylinder Hercules 110 hp. gasoline engine. The pilot vehicle was built by the White Motor Co.

REFERENCES — TM 9-705, 9-1706, 9-1709; OCM 13253, 13578, 13997, 14321, 14386, 14965, 15064, 15948, 17919, 17952, 18312, 20483, 20680, 20723, 21002; SNL G-67.

TYPICAL CHARACTERISTICS

Crew 8
Physical Characteristics
Weight (gross) . . . . 12,400 lb.
Length . . . . 18 ft., 5½ in.
Width . . . . 6 ft., 8 in.
Height . . . . 6 ft., 6½ in.
Ground clearance . . . . 15¾ in.
Center of gravity, Above ground . . . . . . 33.9 in.
   Rear of center line of front axle . . . . . . 81 in.
Tread (center to center, rear) . . . . 65¼ in.
Wheelbase . . . . 131 in.
Ground pressure . . . . 60 lb./sq. in.
Tire equipment . . . . 8.25x20, combat
Armament
1 Cal. .50 Browning Machine Gun M2
  HB (flexible) . . . . Skate rail mount
1 Cal. .30 Browning Machine Gun
  M1919A4 (flexible) . . . . . . Skate rail mount
1 Cal. .30 Tripod Mount M2
1 Cal. .50 Tripod Mount M3
2 Cal. .30 or cal. .50 carriage assemblies
1 Cal. .50 cradle assembly
Provision for:
1 Cal. .45 submachine gun
Ammunition, Stowage
Cal. .50 . . . . 750 rounds
Cal. .45 . . . . 540 rounds
Cal. .30 . . . . 8,000 rounds

Armor	Actual
Windshield shield	½ in.
Engine compartment	¼ in.
Sides and rear	¼ in.

Performance
Maximum speed on level . . . . 50 m.p.h.
Maximum grade ability 60%
Vertical obstacle ability . . . . 12 in.
Fording depth (slowest forward speed) . . 28 in.
Angle of approach . . . . 37°
Angle of departure . . . . 35°
Turning diameter . . . . 28½ ft.
Fuel capacity . . . . 30 gal.
Cruising range . . . . 250 miles
Maximum drawbar pull . . . . 6,155 lb.
Vision—Direct . . . . Slits in shields
Communications
Radio . . . . SCR-506, 508, or 510
Battery, Voltage, total 12
Fire Protection and Decontamination
Fire Extinguisher, CO$_2$-2 lb. (hand) 1
Decontaminating Apparatus M2, 1½ qt. . . . 1
Engine, Make and model . . . . . . Hercules JXD
Type . . . . In-line, L.C.
No. of cylinders 6
Displacement . . . . 320 cu. in.
Fuel (gasoline) . . . . 70-80 octane
Net hp. . . . . 87 at 2,400 r.p.m.
Max. torque . . . . . . 220 lb.-ft. at 1,150 r.p.m.
Transmission, Type . . . Combination sliding and
                                 constant mesh
  Gear ratios
  First speed 5.00:1
  Second speed 3.07:1
  Third speed 1.71:1
  Fourth speed 1.00:1
  Reverse 5.83:1

Transfer Case, Gear ratios 1.00:1; 1.87:1
Steering, Type . . . . Cam and twin lever
Differential, Gear ratio 5.14:1
Suspension, Type . . . . . Semi-elliptic leaf springs
Clutch, Type . . . . Dry, single-plate
Fan, Type 6-blade
Radiator, Type . . . . Fin and tube
  Capacity of system . . . . 19 qt.
Brakes, Type . . . . Internal-expanding
  Operation . . . . Hydraulic
Brakes, Parking, Type . . . . Disk
  Location . . . . Rear of transfer case

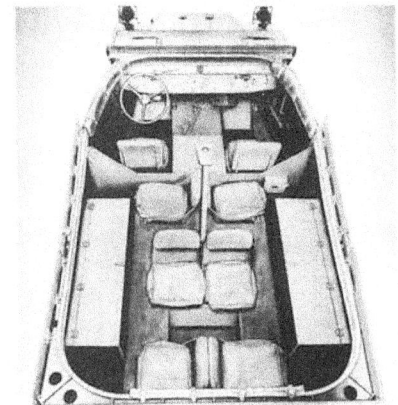

OVERHEAD VIEW, SHOWING SEATING

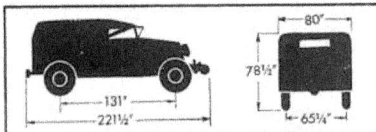

HALF-TRACK CARS M2, M2A1—LIMITED STANDARD
HALF-TRACK PERSONNEL CARRIERS M3, M3A1—LIMITED STANDARD
HALF-TRACK CAR M3A2—STANDARD

Half-Track Car M2 and Half-Track Personnel Carrier M3, the basic half-track vehicles, were standardized in 1940 and used throughout 1941 and 1942. With the addition of ring mounts for antiaircraft use and with other modifications, their designations were changed to M2A1 and M3A1 respectively. All of these vehicles are now classified as Limited Standard and will be replaced in production by Half-Track Car M3A2.

Consisting of a specially designed, commercial-type, front-and-rear drive truck chassis with an armored hull, the half-track vehicle can attain a maximum road speed of 40 m.p.h. Because of its endless-band track-laying rear drive, however, it can be used over rough terrain. It will cross ditches which are not sufficiently deep to cause the front or rear to become embedded. Some models are provided with a roller at the front to assist in climbing out of ditches. On other models, the roller is replaced by a winch for use in towing the vehicle out of soft terrain.

The body is protected by ¼-in. armor at the sides and rear. Top and side protection is given the engine by the armored hood. The radiator is protected by armored shutters which can be opened or closed or set in three intermediate positions from within the driver's compartment. The windshield is of shatterproof glass.

For further protection, a ½-in. armored shield is hinged above the windshield frame, held open by three supports, and additional armored shields are hinged to the doors. In combat zones, the windshield can be removed and these shields swung into place. They are provided with direct-vision slots.

The detachable top is of canvas and is supported by three removable bows and the windshield frame. Removable side curtains with transparent windows also are provided. Mine racks are mounted on the sides of late production models.

Power is supplied by a White 160AX gasoline engine.

HALF-TRACK CAR M2—LIMITED STANDARD, has seats for a crew of ten. A skate rail surrounds the interior of the vehicle. By the use of two carriage mounts, a cal. .30 and a cal. .50 machine gun can be moved along this rail and fired in any direction.

This vehicle can be used as a prime mover for the 105-mm howitzer.

HALF-TRACK CAR M2 HAS GUN RAIL AROUND INTERIOR

HALF-TRACK CAR M2A1 HAS RING MOUNT FOR MACHINE GUN

HALF-TRACK PERSONNEL CARRIER M3 HAS PEDESTAL MOUNT

HALF-TRACK PERSONNEL CARRIER M3A1 WITH WINCH AT FRONT

HALF-TRACK CAR M2A1—LIMITED STANDARD, is similar to the M2 but has an M49 ring mount for cal. .50 machine gun over the assistant driver's seat. By use of this mount the cal. .50 HB machine gun can be traversed 360° from a single position, permitting rapid fire against low-flying aircraft as well as against ground targets. It can be elevated from −15° to +85°.

Three fixed pintle sockets are mounted, one on each side and one on the rear of the body, permitting the use of a cal. .30 machine gun.

HALF-TRACK PERSONNEL CARRIER M3—LIMITED STANDARD, is generally similar to the M2 but has seating accommodations for 13 men. The body is about 10 inches longer than on the M2 and has a door at the rear. Instead of a skate rail, the vehicle has an M25 pedestal mount for a cal. .30 machine gun, which is secured to the floor of the personnel compartment.

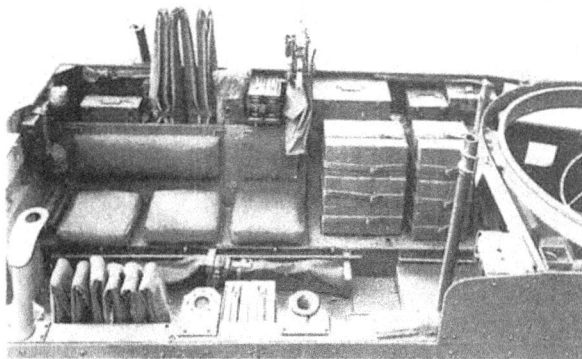

TYPICAL STOWAGE ARRANGEMENT OF HALF-TRACK CAR M3A2

This half-track, with modifications, is used as the chassis for several gun motor carriages.

HALF-TRACK PERSONNEL CARRIER M3A1—LIMITED STANDARD, is similar to the M3 but has an M49 ring mount for a cal. .50 machine gun over the assistant driver's seat.

Three pintle sockets are mounted, one on each side and one on the rear of the body.

HALF-TRACK CAR M3A2—STANDARD, is a modification of the Half-Track Personnel Carrier M3A1 designed to take the place of Half-Track Personnel Carriers M3 and M3A1, and Half-Track Cars M2 and M2A1.

Variations in stowage arrangements, through the use of suitable boxes, give the vehicle a variety of uses. Crews range from 5 to 12 men, depending on the amount of stowage carried and the tactical purpose intended.

Normally the vehicle mounts one cal. .50 machine gun or one cal. .30 machine gun, together with the required vehicular accessories, tools, spare parts, and equipment which are provided for all half-tracks. Under such circumstances, a crew of 12 can be carried. Three pintle sockets are provided to accommodate additional machine guns when authorized.

When the vehicles carry special loadings or have radios installed, personnel are displaced. As an example, if an SCR-508 radio is installed, the crew is reduced by two men.

The basic vehicle is equipped to stow and carry 330 rounds of cal. .50 ammunition and 2,000 rounds of cal. .30 ammunition. When used as a machine gun squad carrier, however, additional ammunition is carried in place of two of the seat positions. When used by a heavy machine gun squad armed with water-cooled machine guns, these guns and their accessories are substituted for the air-cooled cal. .30 machine gun.

HALF-TRACK CAR M3A2 WITH FRONT ROLLER. VEHICLE HAS RING MOUNT AND THREE PINTLE MOUNTS FOR MACHINE GUNS. IT SEATS 5 TO 12 MEN

Miscellaneous equipment boxes are provided for carrying additional stowage items pertaining to special loading of different organizations. When the vehicle is used to carry cargo in considerable quantity, fewer personnel are carried.

Half-Track Car M3A2 is intended for manufacture by the Autocar Co., the Diamond T Motor Co., and the White Motor Co.

A Ring Mount M49, for a cal. .50 machine gun, is erected above the assistant driver's seat, for use against low-flying aircraft. A one-piece armor shield protects the machine gunner.

REFERENCES—TM 9-710, 9-710A; OCM 16112, 16187, 16410, 16679, 17952, 18312, 18394, 20070, 20368, 20438, 20680, 21002, 21501, 21782; SNL G-102, Vols. 1, 2, 3, 4.

TYPICAL CHARACTERISTICS

	M2	M2A1	M3	M3A1	M3A2
Crew	10	10	13	13	5 to 12
Physical Characteristics					
Weight (gross)	19,800 lb.	19,600 lb.	20,000 lb.	20,500 lb.	21,200 lb.
Length—with roller	19 ft., 6¾ in.	19 ft., 6¾ in.	20 ft., 3½ in.	20 ft., 3½ in.	20 ft., 3½ in.
with winch	20 ft., 1⅝ in.	20 ft., 1⅝ in.	20 ft., 9⅝ in.	20 ft., 9⅝ in.	20 ft., 9⅝ in.
Width—without mine racks	6 ft., 5¼ in.	6 ft., 5¼ in.	6 ft., 5¼ in.	6 ft., 5¼ in.	6 ft., 5¼ in.
with mine racks	7 ft., 3½ in.	7 ft., 3½ in.	7 ft., 3½ in.	7 ft., 3½ in.	7 ft., 3½ in.
Height—overall	7 ft., 5 in.	8 ft., 10 in.	7 ft., 5 in.	8 ft., 10 in.	8 ft., 10 in.
Ground clearance	11³⁄₁₆ in.	11³⁄₁₆ in.	11³⁄₁₆ in.	11³⁄₁₆ in.	11³⁄₁₆ in.
Tread—front	64½ in.	64½ in.	64½ in.	64½ in.	64½ in.
rear	63¹³⁄₁₆ in.	63¹³⁄₁₆ in.	63¹³⁄₁₆ in.	63¹³⁄₁₆ in.	63¹³⁄₁₆ in.
Wheelbase	135½ in.	135½ in.	135½ in.	135½ in.	135½ in.
Ground contact length	46¾ in.	46¾ in.	46¾ in.	46¾ in.	46¾ in.
Tire equipment (combat, 12-ply)	8.25 x 20	8.25 x 20	8.25 x 20	8.25 x 20	8.25 x 20
Armament					
Cal. .50 Machine Gun M2, HB (flexible)	1	1		1	1
Cal. .30 Browning Machine Gun M1919A4 (flexible)	1	1	1	1	1
Pedestal Mount M25			1		
Ring Mount M49 for cal. .30 or cal. .50 Machine Gun		1		1	
Carriage assembly		1		1	
Cradle assemblies		2		2	
Cal. .50 Tripod Mount M3	1	1		1	1
Cal. .30 Tripod Mount M2	1	1	1	1	1
Machine Gun Mounts M35	2				
Provision for:					
Rocket Launcher, AT, 2.36-in., M9 or M1A1					1
Cal. .45 Submachine Gun M3 or M1928A1	1	1	1	1	1
Cal. .30 Rifles M1 or Carbines M1			12	12	12
Ammunition, Stowage					
Cal. .50	700 rounds	700 rounds	700 rounds	700 rounds	330 rounds*
Cal. .30	7,750 rounds	7,750 rounds	4,000 rounds	7,750 rounds	2,000 rounds*
Cal. .45	540 rounds	540 rounds	540 rounds	540 rounds	180 rounds
Rockets, Grenade, AT, 2.36-in., M6					6
Grenades, Hand (Fragmentation, Mk. II; Smoke, WP, M15; Smoke, Colored, M6 or M18)	10	10	22	22	24
Mines, AT, H.E., w/Fuze M1	14	14	24	24	24

Armor—Front .... ¼ in.
Sides and rear .... ¼ in., F.H.
Windshield protective plate .... ½ in.

Performance
Maximum speed on level .... 40 m.p.h.
Maximum grade ability 60%
Vertical obstacle ability .... 12 in.
Fording depth (slowest forward speed) .... 32 in.
Turning radius .... 30 ft.
Fuel capacity .... 60 gal.
Cruising range (approx.) .... 175 miles

Vision
Driver .... Slits in windshield and wingshield

Communications
Radio ..... SCR-193 or 506, and 508 and 593; 284 and 508 and 593; 193 or 506, and 508 or 528 or 510 or 608 or 610 or 628. (Or any of these individually)

Battery, Voltage, total 12

Fire Protection and Decontamination
Fire Extinguisher, CO₂-4 lb. (hand) 1
Decontaminating Apparatus M2, 1½ qt. 3

Engine, Make and model .... White 160AX
Type .... In-line, "L"
No. of cylinders 6

Cycle 4
Fuel (gasoline) .... 80 octane
Bore and stroke .... 4 x 5⅛ in.
Displacement .... 386 cu. in.
Compression 6.3:1
Net hp. .... 128 at 2,800 r.p.m.
Max. torque .... 300 lb.-ft. at 1,200 r.p.m.
Crankshaft rotation .... C'Clockwise
Length .... 52¼ in.
Width .... 26 in.
Height .... 37 in.
Ignition .... Battery
Weight, dry .... 1,015 lb.
Weight, installed .... 1,207 lb.

Transmission, Gear ratios
First speed 4.92:1
Second speed 2.60:1
Third speed 1.74:1
Fourth speed 1.00:1
Reverse 4.37:1

Transfer Case
Gear ratios 1.00:1; 2.48:1

Differential, Track Drive, Gear ratio . 4.444:1
Ring gear, No. of teeth 40
Pinion, No. of teeth 9

Differential, Front Axle, Gear ratio ... 6.8:1
Ring gear, No. of teeth 34

Pinion, No. of teeth 5
Steering ratio 23.4; 19.5; 23.4:1

Final Drive
Sprocket, No. of teeth 18
Pitch diameter .... 22.918 in.

Suspension, Track, Type .... Volute spring
Wheel or tire size .... 12 x 4⅛ dual

Suspension, Front
Type (longitudinal leaf) .... Semi-elliptic
Wheel or tire size .... 8.25 x 20
Wheel construction .... Ventilated disk

Idler, Wheel size .... 12½ x 9⅜

Track, Type .... Endless band
Width .... 12 in.
Pitch .... 4 in.

Master Clutch, Type .... Dry, single plate

Radiator, Type .... Fin and tube
Capacity of system .... 26 qt.

Brakes, Type .... Internal expanding
Operation .... Hydraulic

Brakes, Parking, Type .... Disk

*When organizational use of vehicle requires it, 600 rounds of additional cal. .50 ammunition or 6,000 rounds of additional cal. .30 ammunition are carried, and personnel capacity is reduced by two men.

HALF-TRACK CAR **M9A1**—LIMITED STANDARD
HALF-TRACK PERSONNEL CARRIERS **M5, M5A1**—LIMITED STANDARD
HALF-TRACK CAR **M5A2**—SUBSTITUTE STANDARD

These vehicles are generally similar to Half-Track Car M2A1, Half-Track Personnel Carriers M3 and M3A1, and Half-Track Car M3A2, respectively, but they were manufactured by the International Harvester Co., and contain that company's component parts.

Each is powered by an International RED 450B 6-cylinder, 4-cycle, in-line gasoline engine. Body armor is of homogeneous armor plate. The windshield protective plate is ⅝ in. thick and the other armor ⁵⁄₁₆ in.

References—TM 9-707; OCM 18370, 18509, 20070, 20368, 21501, 21782, 21847; SNL G-147.

HALF-TRACK CAR M9A1—This corresponds to Half-Track Car M2A1, and has seats for ten men. It is provided with a Ring Mount M49 for a cal. .50 antiaircraft machine gun and has three fixed pintle sockets, permitting the use of a cal. .30 machine gun.

HALF-TRACK PERSONNEL CARRIER M5A1—This corresponds to Half-Track Personnel Carrier M3A1 with seats for 13. It has a Ring Mount M49 for a cal. .50 antiaircraft machine gun and three fixed pintle sockets, permitting the use of a cal. .30 machine gun.

HALF-TRACK CAR M5A2—This corresponds to Half-Track Car M3A2, with the same stowage arrangements and with accommodations for crews varying from 5 to 12 men. It has a Ring Mount M49 and three pintle sockets. It is intended for International Aid Requirements only.

HALF-TRACK CAR M9A1 FROM ABOVE, SHOWING RING MOUNT AND PINTLE MOUNTS

HALF-TRACK CAR M5A2 SHOWING STOWAGE ON LEFT SIDE AND ON REAR

TYPICAL CHARACTERISTICS

Physical Characteristics

Weight (gross)—M9A1	21,200 lb.
M5	20,500 lb.
M5A1	21,500 lb.
M5A2	22,500 lb.
Length—with roller	20 ft., 2³⁄₁₆ in.
with winch	20 ft., 9¹⁄₁₆ in.
Width—over mine racks	7 ft., 2⅞ in.
Height—over bows	7 ft., 7 in.
Top of A.A. gun (M49 Mount)	9 ft.
Ground clearance	11³⁄₁₆ in.
Tread—front	66½ in.
rear	63¹³⁄₁₆ in.
Wheelbase	135½ in.
Tire equipment	9.00 x 20 (combat)
Armor—Front, sides, and rear	⁵⁄₁₆ in. homo.
Floor	⁵⁄₁₆ in.
Windshield protective plate	⅝ in.

Performance

Maximum speed on level	38 m.p.h.
Maximum grade ability	60%
Vertical obstacle ability	12 in.
Fording depth	32 in.
Angle of approach—with roller	40°
with winch	36°
Angle of departure	32°
Fuel capacity	60 gal.
Cruising range (approx.)	125 miles
Normal towed load	4,500 lb.

Engine, Make | International
Model	RED 450B
Type	In-line, L.C.
Number of cylinders	6
Cycle	4
Fuel (gasoline)	80 octane
Max. governed speed	2,700 r.p.m.
Net hp.	143 at 2,700 r.p.m.
Max. torque	348 lb.-ft. at 800 r.p.m.

Radiator, Capacity | 31 qt.

Other characteristics same as for corresponding models in Half Track M2 and M3 series.

ARMORED UTILITY VEHICLE T41—LIMITED PROCUREMENT

This vehicle is a modification of the 76-mm Gun Motor Carriage M18 designed in order to provide a prime mover equal to the M18 in performance.

As compared to the gun motor carriage, the turret is omitted and certain components are rearranged to provide better stowage. Limited procurement of the vehicles was authorized in June 1944.

The vehicle has stowage and accessory equipment for use as a prime mover for the 3-Inch Gun Carriage M6. It is capable of carrying the crew members and initial rounds of ammunition for the gun.

The vehicle is of the full track-laying type, using an independently sprung torsion bar suspension, driven from the front sprocket. It will accommodate a crew of nine men, including the driver and assistant driver.

Armament consists of a Cal. .50 Machine Gun M2 HB (flexible), mounted on a concentric ring in the forward part of the crew compartment, and a Cal. .50 Tripod Mount M3. Provision is made for carrying two Cal. .30 Carbines M1, and additional carbines may be carried by crew members.

Armor at the front, sides, and rear is ½ inch, with additional ⅝-inch armor applied locally at the front. Top armor is ⁵⁄₁₆ inch, and bottom armor ¼ inch.

The vehicle will attain a speed of 50 miles per hour or better, and will climb grades up to 60%.

Power is supplied by a Continental R-975-C1 or C4 engine.

Hatches for the driver and assistant driver are provided with periscopes for vision in combat areas. An additional escape hatch is in the floor of the hull. The crew compartment is open at the top but has a detachable canvas cover for protection against inclement weather. The vehicle is equipped with a two-way radio.

REFERENCES—OCM 24056, 24262.

TYPICAL CHARACTERISTICS

Crew.................................9

Physical Characteristics
Weight (gross)................35,000 lb.
Length.........................17 ft., 4 in.
Width..........................9 ft., ½ in.
Height—over antiaircraft gun.......6 ft., 7 in.
over crew compartment ...5 ft., 11 in.
Ground clearance...................14 in.
Tread (center to center of tracks).....94¼ in.
Ground contact length..............116 in.

Armament
1 Cal. .50 Machine Gun M2 HB
(flexible) on ring mount, antiaircraft
1 Tripod Mount, Cal. .50, M3
Provision for:
2 Cal. .30 Carbines M1

Ammunition, Stowage
3-in...........................42 rounds
Cal. .50.....................900 rounds
Cal. .30 Carbine............1,620 rounds
Grenades, Hand (Fragmentation,
Mk. II, 6; Smoke, W.P., 6).............12
Smoke Pots...........................4

Armor   Actual
Hull, Front.........................½ in.
Sides and rear....................½ in.
additional, frontal, local.........⅝ in.
Top..............................⁵⁄₁₆ in.
Bottom............................¼ in.

Performance
Maximum speed on level...........50 m.p.h.
Speed on 10% grade.............15 m.p.h.
Maximum grade ability................60%
Trench crossing ability............6 ft., 2 in.
Vertical obstacle ability...............36 in.
Fording depth (slowest forward speed)...48 in.
Cruising range (approx.)............150 miles

Vision and Fire Control
Periscopes M6 2

Communications
Radio............................SCR-610

Battery, Voltage, total....................24

Fire Protection and Decontamination
Fire Extinguisher, CO₂-10 lb. (fixed)........2
CO₂-4 lb. (hand)....................1
Decontaminating Apparatus M2, 1½ qts....1

Other characteristics same as 76-mm Gun Motor Carriage M18.

ARMORED UTILITY VEHICLE T41 IS PRIME MOVER FOR 3-INCH GUN CARRIAGE

VEHICLE ALSO CARRIES CREW MEMBERS AND AMMUNITION FOR TOWED GUN

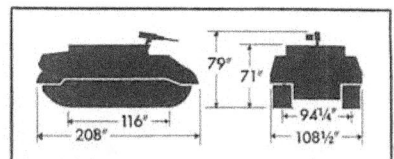

79" 71"

116"
208"

94¼"
108½"

FULL-TRACK PRIME MOVERS M33, M34, M35—SUBSTITUTE STANDARD

These prime movers for 240-mm howitzer and 8-in. gun materiel were designed as expedients pending production in quantity of the 38-ton High Speed Tractor M6. They are Substitute Standard.

REFERENCES—OCM 23183, 23571.

FULL-TRACK PRIME MOVER M33 is a modification of Tank Recovery Vehicle M31 and has a riveted hull. The turret, turret ring, and boom assembly, and certain other parts peculiar to the tank recovery vehicle, were removed, as were also the cal. .30 bow and turret machine guns and the cal. .30 machine gun tripod mount. An air compressor and rear outlet lines for operation of brakes on the towed load were added, as well as an electric outlet for stop and tail lights on the trailed load. A cal. .50 machine gun mount for anti-aircraft use was supplied. Canvas covers are furnished for the turret and machine gun mount openings.

FULL-TRACK PRIME MOVER M34 is a conversion of Tank Recovery Vehicle M32B1 and has a cast hull. The 81-mm mortar and mount, the cal. .50 machine gun, and the cal. .30 machine gun and tripod mount were removed, as were also the boom assembly and miscellaneous stowage items and accessories. An air compressor and lines for operation of towed load brakes were added, with outlets front and rear, together with an electric outlet for stop and tail lights on the trailed load, and necessary stowage.

FULL-TRACK PRIME MOVER M35 is a modification of 3-in. Gun Motor Carriage M10A1 with a welded hull. The turret, including the 3-in. Gun M7 and cal. .50 machine gun, and the cal. .50 tripod mount were removed, as were also the rear pintle, the pioneer compass, and miscellaneous stowage items. An air compressor unit and lines, with outlets front and rear, were added. Pintle assemblies, similar to those on the Tank Recovery Vehicle M32 series, were supplied at front and rear. Four seats were installed in the crew compartment. An electric outlet for the towed load stop and tail lights and various stowage items were added.

FULL-TRACK PRIME MOVER M33 HAS RIVETED HULL

FULL-TRACK PRIME MOVER M34 HAS CAST HULL

TYPICAL CHARACTERISTICS

	Prime Mover M33	Prime Mover M34	Prime Mover M35
Crew	6	6	6
Physical Characteristics			
Weight (gross)	60,000 lb.	63,000 lb.	55,000 lb.
Length	18 ft., 6 in.	19 ft., 1¼ in.	19 ft., 7 in.
Width	8 ft., 11 in.	8 ft., 7 in.	10 ft.
Height	7 ft., 3 in.	8 ft., 8³⁄₁₆ in.	5 ft., 10 in.
Ground clearance	17⅛ in.	17⅛ in.	17⅛ in.
Tread (center to center of tracks)	83 in.	83 in.	83 in.
Ground contact length	147 in.	147 in.	147 in.
Ground pressure	12.3 lb./sq. in.	13.0 lb./sq. in.	11.3 lb./sq. in
Armor, Actual			
Hull, Front, Upper	2 in.	2 in.	½-2 in.
Lower	1½-2 in.	1½-2 in.	1 in.
Sides	1½ in.	1½ in.	¾-1 in.
Rear	1-1½ in.	1-1½ in.	1-1½ in.
Top	½ in.	¾ in.	⅜-¾ in.
Bottom	½-1 in.	½-1 in.	¼ in.
Performance			
Maximum speed on level	25 m.p.h.	24 m.p.h.	30 m.p.h.
Maximum grade ability	60%	60%	60%
Trench crossing ability	7 ft., 5 in.	6 ft., 2 in.	7 ft., 6 in.
Vertical obstacle ability	24 in.	24 in.	24 in.
Fording depth (slowest forward speed)	42 in.	48 in.	36 in.
Turning radius	35 ft.	31 ft.	31 ft.
Fuel capacity	185 gal.	175 gal.	192 gal.
Cruising range (approx.)	150 miles	120 miles	160 miles
Vision and Fire Control			
Periscope M6		5	3
Protectoscopes and direct vision slots	4		

Other characteristics same as for Medium Tank M3, Medium Tank M4A1, Gun Motor Carriage M10A1.

FULL-TRACK PRIME MOVER M35 HAS WELDED HULL

TRUCK MOUNTED CRANE M2; CLAMSHELL TRAILER M16—STANDARD

TRUCK MOUNTED CRANE, M2, WITH BOOM IN TRAVELING POSITION, TOWING CLAMSHELL TRAILER, M16, CARRYING 5/8 YARD CLAMSHELL BUCKET

TRUCK MOUNTED CRANE, M2, is designed to handle 240 mm howitzer matériel and 8 inch gun matériel in the field. It was developed in connection with design and development of the 240 mm howitzer matériel, M1918A2 and M1, to handle components of the matériel when changing from traveling to firing position and vice versa. It was standardized in September, 1942.

The cradle recoil mechanism and tube (approximately 36,000 pounds for the heaviest weapon) are carried as one load and the carriage (approximately 33,000 pounds for the heaviest weapon) as another load on transport wagons. Truck Mounted Crane, M2, is used to remove the matériel from the transport wagons and to set it up in firing position.

Basis of issue is one per firing battery armed with 240 mm Howitzer, M1918M1, on 240 mm Howitzer Carriage, M1918A2; 240 mm Howitzer and Carriage, M1; and 8 inch Gun, M1, on 8 inch Gun Carriage, M2.

The crane is capable of accompanying the transport wagons in convoy at a maximum speed of about 30 miles per hour, with road ability and cross country ability comparable to the prime mover towing the trailed loads. The crew consists of the chassis operator and the crane operator. In addition to these particular uses, the crane may be employed for many other purposes by field maintenance and depot organizations.

The chassis is of special construction for full revolving crane service, and is equipped with screw type extension outrigger beams and floats.

It is of the six-wheeled type, with power supplied to all six wheels. Four of the wheels are dual tired. A 5/8 yard clamshell bucket is provided with each

TYPICAL CHARACTERISTICS

TRUCK MOUNTED CRANE, M2

Crew 2

Physical Characteristics

Weight (gross)	54,760 lb.
Length, over-all (boom in traveling position)	33 ft., 7 ins.
Length of truck	25 ft., 7 ins.
Width	9 ft., 1/2 in.
Height	11 ft., 8 ins.
Ground clearance	17 1/2 ins.
Tread (center to center, rear)	78 ins.
Wheelbase	168 3/4 ins.
Tire equipment	12.00 x 20
	(mud and snow type)
Ground contact at 4 in. penetration	3,100 sq. ins.
Ground pressure	17.6 lb./sq. in.

Performance

Lifting capacities with 22 ft. boom at 11 ft. radius

—with outriggers set	40,000 lb.*
—over back without outriggers	24,500 lb.*
—over side without outriggers	21,850 lb.*
Maximum speed on level	30 m.p.h.
Cross country speed	5 m.p.h.
Maximum grade ability	40%
Trench crossing ability	3 ft.
Turning radius	47 ft., 2 ins.
Fuel capacity	100 gals.
Cruising range	150 miles
Maximum drawbar pull	29,000 lb.

*Includes weight of hooks, blocks, slings, etc.

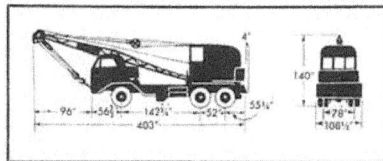

crane. The entire crane cab may be closed and locked. Windows are provided with shatterproof glass. Tow hooks are provided at the front and a pintle at the rear. The vehicle is manufactured by the Thew Shovel Co.

REFERENCES — OCM 16600, 17111, 17178, 17240, 18648, 18863.

Battery, Voltage, total	12
Engine, Make and Model (Crane Carrier)	Hercules HXC
Type	L head
No. of cylinders	6
Fuel (gasoline)	70 octane
Displacement	779 cu. ins.
Rated hp.	179 at 2,200 r.p.m.
Max. torque	555 lb.-ft. at 900 r.p.m.
Engine, Make and Model (Crane)	Waukesha 6 MZR
Type	L head
No. of cylinders	6
Fuel (gasoline)	70 octane
Displacement	404 cu. ins.
Rated hp.	82 at 1,600 r.p.m.
Weight without accessories	920 lb.
Transmission, Type	Constant mesh
Gear ratios	
First speed	6.54:1
Second speed	3.27:1
Third speed	1.76:1
Fourth speed	1.00:1
Reverse	7.24:1
Suspension, Type, Front	Semi-elliptic
Rear	Steel beams
Master Clutch, Type	Single plate
Radiator, Type	Fin and tube
Capacity of system	14 gals.
Brakes, Type	Internal-expanding, air
Brakes, Parking	Ventilated disk

CLAMSHELL TRAILER, M16

Physical Characteristics

Weight—empty (approx.)	2,425 lb.
loaded (approx.)	8,240 lb.
Length—empty	13 ft., 3 ins.
loaded	14 ft., 3 ins.
Width	9 ft.
Height—empty	4 ft., 1 1/2 ins.
loaded	10 ft., 4 ins.
Ground clearance	20 ins.
Tread (center to center)	96 ins.
Tire equipment	12.00 x 20 (highway)

CLAMSHELL TRAILER, M16, is designed to be towed by the Truck Mounted Crane, M2, to carry the clamshell bucket, and the ten 3"x24"x10' timbers required for use where operations are on soft or marshy ground. It was standardized July, 1943.

7-TON HIGH-SPEED TRACTOR M2—STANDARD

7-TON HIGH-SPEED TRACTOR, M2, IS USED TO TOW HEAVY AIRCRAFT

The 7-Ton High-Speed Tractor, M2, is the first of several tractors, built to Ordnance specifications, and combining speed with great pulling power. It was standardized in February, 1941, as Medium Tractor, M2.

Based on a commercial tractor, modified in accordance with military requirements, it is used for towing aircraft of the heavy bombardment type and for general utility use on flying fields.

Low enough to drive under the wings of a big plane, the tractor can be used as a platform for servicing operations.

Special equipment includes a three-stage air compressor driven by the tractor engine for inflation of landing-gear shock struts. The compressor operates at 16.7 cubic feet per minute, with a maximum pressure of 2,000 pounds per square inch. It is equipped with pressure outlets reducible to 100 pounds per square inch. A 3KW, 100-volt, DC auxiliary generator is driven by a V-belt from the tractor engine.

Power is supplied by a Hercules WXLC3 in-line, L-type, 6-cylinder gasoline engine. The selective type transmission provides four speeds forward, ranging from 2½ to 22 m.p.h., and a reverse. Normal high speed is 15 m.p.h. Steering is by a controlled differential. Drive sprockets are at the rear to provide steering characteristics desired for handling airplanes.

The vehicle is capable of starting and turning without jerking, of negotiating marshy terrain and of starting from a dead stop in the same terrain. It is designed to turn on a radius of 11 feet without excessive disturbance of turf, and to maneuver easily in close quarters. Continuous rubber track, with detachable rubber blocks, is used.

Upholstered seats are provided for a crew of three. The front-mounted winch, which is operated from the side of the tractor, has a pull of 10,000 pounds on the first layer, and a line speed of approximately 65 feet per minute. The winch drum has a capacity of 300 feet of ⅜ inch cable.

A quickly detachable, spring-type swinging hitch is supplied, together with a standard Ordnance pintle. An extra set of steel-backed rubber blocks, and an extra set of steel grousers, are furnished with each tractor. Special equipment includes a channel type front bumper with wood filler, an air cleaner, and an oil filter.

The vehicle is manufactured by the Cleveland Tractor Co.

REFERENCES — OCM 16409, 16521, 21220.

TYPICAL CHARACTERISTICS

Crew 3

Physical Characteristics
Weight (gross) . . . . 15,000 lb.
Length . . . . 13 ft., 10 ins.
Width . . . . 5 ft., 10 ins.
Height . . . . 5 ft., 8 ins.
Height of hitch . . . . 20 ins.
Ground clearance . . . . 19 ins.
Center of gravity above ground . . . . 31 ins.
Tread (center to center of tracks) . . . . . . 52 ins.
Ground contact length . . . . 63 ins.
Ground pressure . . . . 8.5 lb./sq. in.

Performance
Maximum speed on level . . . . 22 m.p.h.
Maximum grade ability 60%
Trench crossing ability . . . . 5 ft.
Vertical obstacle ability . . . . 20 ins.
Fording depth (slowest forward speed) . 32 ins.
Angle of approach . . . . 45°
Angle of departure . . . . 41°
Turning radius . . . . 10½ ft.
Fuel capacity . . . . 33 gals.
Cruising range (approx.) . . . . 100 miles
Maximum drawbar pull . . . . 9,000 lb.
Normal towed load . . . . Heavy aircraft
Winch capacity . . . . 10,000 lb.

Vision . . . . Open vehicle

Battery, Voltage, total 12

Fire Protection and Decontamination
Fire Extinguisher, CO₂—15 lb. (hand) 1
Decontaminating Apparatus, M2, 1½ qts. . . . 1

Engine, Make and Model . . . . Hercules WXLC3
Type . . . . In-line "L"
No. of cylinders 6
Fuel (gasoline) . . . . 70 octane
Max. governed speeds. 2,500 and 3,280 r.p.m.
Net hp . . . . 150 at 3,000 r.p.m.
Max. torque . . . . . . 312 lb.-ft. at 1,200 r.p.m.

Transmission, Type . . . . Selective
Gear ratios
First speed 2.37:1
Second speed 1.16:1
Third speed 80:1
Fourth speed 49:1
Reverse 1.92:1

Differential, Type . . . . Controlled
Gear ratio 3.5:1
Steering ratio 1.8:1

Final Drive, Type . . . . Spur Gear
Gear ratio 6.61:1
Sprocket, no. of teeth 20
Pitch diameter . . . . 25.468 ins.

Suspension, Type . . . . Volute spring
Wheel or tire size . . . . 14 x 4⅛ ins.

Track, Type . . . . Band block
Width . . . . 13⅝ ins.
Pitch . . . . 4 ins.
No. of shoes per vehicle 148

Master Clutch, Type . . . . Double plate

Radiator, Type . . . . Tube and fin
Capacity of system . . . . 37 qts.

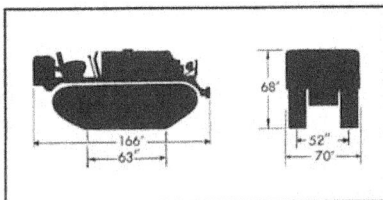

18-TON HIGH-SPEED TRACTOR M4—STANDARD

This prime mover is designed for artillery loads of from 18,000 to 30,000 pounds weight, and is capable of transporting personnel, ammunition, and accessories pertaining to the section.

It can be used for the following types of matériel:

3 inch A.A. Gun Mount, M2A2
90 mm A.A. Gun Mounts, M1A1, M2
155 mm Gun Carriages, M1, M2 and M3
8 inch Howitzer Carriage, M1
240 mm Howitzer Carriage, M1918

It is designated Class A when carrying an ammunition box with shell racks for 3 inch and 90 mm ammunition, and Class B when carrying a cargo box, with shell racks and hold-down plates suitable for 155 mm howitzer, 8 inch howitzer, and 240 mm gun ammunition. A special swing crane with trolley hoist is provided with each cargo box for hoisting shells into the box.

The cab is divided into two compartments, with seating room for the driver and two men in the front compartment, and double seats accommodating eight additional men in the rear compartment. Back cushions are leather covered, and canvas zipper bags padded with blankets serve as seat cushions.

The winch, equipped with 300 feet of ¾ inch wire cable, has a maximum pull of 30,000 pounds.

A Ring Mount, M49C, for a cal. .50 Machine Gun, M2, HB, is provided for protection against aircraft. The gun has an elevation from −20° to +80°. However, full depression is not obtainable to the front and rear.

The tractor is equipped with complete controls and operating mechanism for both air brakes and electric brakes for the trailer. A tire inflation hose is part of the equipment.

The vehicle is powered by a Waukesha, 145GZ, in-line, 6 cylinder, 4 cycle gasoline engine.

The tractor is manufactured by the Allis-Chalmers Manufacturing Co.

References—TM 9–785; OCM 16726, 16806, 17816, 17925, 18583, 18730, 19365, 19458, 20208, 21220.

18-TON HIGH-SPEED TRACTOR, M4, HAS RING MOUNT FOR MACHINE GUN ON TOP

TYPICAL CHARACTERISTICS

Crew 11

Physical Characteristics

Weight (gross) . . . . 31,500 lb.
Length—Class A . . . . 17 ft., 2 ins.
            Class B . . . . 16 ft., 11 in.
Width . . . . 8 ft., 1 in.
Height, to top of cab . . . . 7 ft., 10 ins.
        to top of gun mount . . . . 8 ft., 3 ins.
Turret ring diameter (inside) . . . . 42 ins.
Height of pintle . . . . 29 ins.
Ground clearance . . . . 20 ins.
Tread (center to center of tracks) . . . . . . 80 ins.
Ground contact length . . . . 124 ins.
Ground pressure (with 90 mm gun)
                                 7.6 lb./sq. in.

Armament

Ring Mount, M49C, for cal. .50 machine gun
1 Tripod Mount, cal. .50, M3
1 Carriage assembly
1 Cradle assembly
Provision for:
1 cal. .50 Machine Gun, M2, HB (flexible)

Ammunition

Cal. .50 . . . . 500 rounds
One of the following, depending on
artillery towed:
90 mm A.A. . . . . 54 rounds
3 inch A.A. . . . . 54 rounds
155 mm Gun . . . . 30 rounds
8 inch Howitzer . . . . 20 rounds
240 mm Howitzer . . . . 12 rounds

Performance

Maximum speed towing 90 mm A.A. gun
    On level . . . . 33 m.p.h.
    On 3% grade . . . . 20 m.p.h.
Maximum grade ability 60%
Trench crossing ability . . . . 5 ft.
Vertical obstacle ability . . . . 29 ins.
Fording depth (slowest forward speed) . . 41 ins.
Turning radius . . . . 18 ft., 6 ins.
Fuel capacity . . . . 125 gals.
Cruising range (approx.) . . . . 180 miles
Maximum drawbar pull . . . . 38,700 lb. at stall
                   13,000 lb. at 4 m.p.h.
Winch capacity . . . . 30,000 lb.

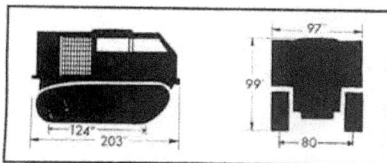

Battery, Voltage, Total 12

Fire Protection and Decontamination

Fire Extinguisher, CO₂—4 lb. (hand) 2
Decontaminating Apparatus, M2, 1½ qts. . . 2

Engine, Make and Model . . . Waukesha 145GZ
Type . . . . In-line
No. of cylinders 6
Fuel (gasoline) . . . . 70 octane
Max. governed speed . . . . 2,100 r.p.m.
Net hp. . . . . 210 at 2,100 r.p.m.
Max. torque . . . . . 528 lb.-ft. at 1,680 r.p.m.

Transmission, Type . . . . Selective
Gear ratios—First speed 2.166:1
      Second speed 1.555:1
      Third speed 0.437:1
      Reverse 1.822:1

Torque Converter, Gear ratio 1.372:1

Differential, Type . . . . Controlled
Gear ratio 2.666:1
Steering ratio 1.747:1

Suspension, Type . . . . . Horizontal volute spring
Wheel or tire size . . . . 20 x 9

Idler, Type . . . . Trailing
Wheel or tire size . . . . 32 x 9

Track, Type . . . . . . Steel Block, Rubber Bushed
Width . . . . 16⁹⁄₁₆ ins.
Pitch . . . . 6 ins.
No. of shoes per vehicle 130

Master Clutch, Type . . . Spring loaded, dry disk

Final Drive, Type . . . . Spur gear
Sprocket, no. of teeth 13
Pitch diameter . . . . 25.038 ins.
Gear ratio 2.764:1

Radiator, Type . . . . Fin and tube
Capacity of system . . . . 72 qts.

Brakes, Type . . . . Mechanical on controlled differential

Brakes, Trailer, Type . . . . Air and/or electrical

13-TON HIGH-SPEED TRACTOR M5—STANDARD

13-TON HIGH-SPEED TRACTOR, M5, WITH RING MOUNT, M49C, FOR CAL. .50 MACHINE GUN

TYPICAL CHARACTERISTICS

Crew 9

Physical Characteristics
Weight (gross) . . . . 28,300 lb.
Length . . . . 15 ft., 11 ins.
Width . . . . 8 ft., 4 ins.
Height
  Top of windshield lowered . . . . . . 6 ft., 8 ins.
  Top of canopy top . . . . 8 ft., 8 ins.
Height of pintle . . . . 28¼ ins.
Ground clearance . . . . 20 ins.
Tread (center to center of tracks) . . . . . . 83 ins.
Ground contact length . . . . 108½ ins.
Ground pressure . . . . 11.1 lb./sq. in.

Armament
Ring Mount, M49C, for Cal. .50 Machine Gun
1 Tripod Mount, Cal. .50, M3
1 Elevator Cradle, M1

Provision for:
1 Cal. .50 Machine Gun, HB, M2
  (flexible)
9 cal. .30 rifles or   ⎫
9 cal. .30 carbines ⎬ . . . . Equipment of crew

Ammunition, Stowage
Cal. .50 . . . . 400 rounds
One of the following:
  105 mm Howitzer . . . . 56 rounds
  4.5 inch Gun . . . . 38 rounds
  155 mm Howitzer . . . . 24 rounds

Performance
Maximum speed towing 155 mm howitzer
  carriage, on level . . . . 35 m.p.h.
Speed on 3% grade . . . . 20 m.p.h.
Maximum grade ability, with towed load. 50%
                 without towed load. 72%
Trench crossing ability . . . . 5 ft., 6 ins.
Vertical obstacle ability . . . . 18 ins.
Fording depth (slowest forward speed) . . 53 ins.
Turning radius . . . . 18 ft.
Fuel capacity . . . . 100 gals.
Cruising range (approx.) . . . . 125 miles

Maximum drawbar pull . . . . 20,300 lb.
Payload . . . . 5,000 lb.
Winch capacity . . . . 17,000 lb.

Battery, Voltage, total 12

Fire Protection and Decontamination
Fire Extinguisher, CO₂—4 lb. (hand) 1
Decontaminating Apparatus, M2, 1½ qts. 1

Engine, Make and Model . . Continental, R6572
Type . . . . In-line
No. of cylinders 6
Fuel (gasoline) . . . . 70 octane
Displacement . . . . 572 cu. ins.
Max. governed speed . . . . 2,900 r.p.m.
Net hp. . . . . 235 at 2,900 r.p.m.
Max. torque . . . . . 475 lb.-ft. at 1,600 r.p.m.

Transmission, Type . . . . Constant mesh
Gear ratios
  First speed 5.43:1
  Second speed 3.20:1
  Third speed 1.71:1
  Fourth speed 1.00:1
  Reverse 5.36:1

Transfer Case, Gear ratios . . 1.00:1 and 1.71:1

Differential, Type . . . . Controlled
Gear ratio 2.60:1
Steering ratio 1.844:1

Final Drive, Type . . . . Spur gear
Sprocket, no. of teeth 14
Pitch diameter . . . . 24.56 ins.
Gear ratio 2.35:1

Suspension, Type . . . . Volute spring
Wheel or tire size 20x6

Track, Type . . . . Same as Light Tank, M3

Idler, Type . . . . Trailing
Wheel or tire size 28x6

The 13-Ton High-Speed Tractor, M5, is a prime mover for artillery loads weighing up to 16,000 pounds, and for transporting the personnel, ammunition, and accessories pertaining to the section. It was standardized in October, 1942, as Medium Tractor, M5.

It is used as a prime mover for:
  105 mm Howitzer Carriage, M2;
  4.5 inch Gun Carriage, M1;
  155 mm Howitzer Carriages, M1, M1917A4, or M1918A3.

The vehicle uses Light Tank, M3, tracks, and modified suspension.

Power is supplied by a Continental R6572, in-line, 6-cylinder, 4-cycle gasoline engine. Eight forward speeds and two reverse speeds are provided through the transmission, in conjunction with a dual-range clutch and gear reduction unit.

While towing a 155 mm Howitzer Carriage, the tractor can attain a maximum speed of 35 m.p.h. on level roads and 20 m.p.h. on a 3% grade. It has a cruising range of approximately 125 miles.

The dual-range clutch is operated by air pressure or by hand and permits changing the drive one full gear ratio by pushing the service clutch pedal to the toeboard, past the neutral position.

The front-mounted winch has two wind and two unwind speeds, which are controlled by a lever below the driver's seat and the dual-range engine clutch. A roller located below the winch permits pulling from the rear of the tractor, if required.

The vehicle is equipped with air couplers at the front and rear, and an electric brake connection for the towed load. A folding top with side curtains is provided.

Ordnance Committee action in February, 1944, approved the inclusion of a Ring Mount, M49C, for a cal. .50 machine gun.

The vehicle is manufactured by the International Harvester Co.

REFERENCES—OCM 17512, 17538, 18887, 19038, 19874, 21220, 21524, 22663, 22803.

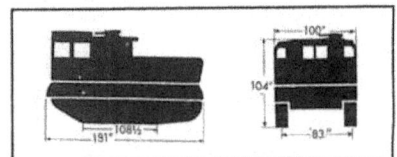

38-TON HIGH-SPEED TRACTOR M6—STANDARD

Development of high-speed fulltrack prime movers for the 240 mm Howitzer, M1, 8 inch Gun, M1, and 4.7 inch Antiaircraft Gun, T1, was authorized by Ordnance Committee action in February, 1942. Heavy Tractor, T22, was developed as the prime mover for the 240 mm Howitzer, M1, and 8 inch Gun, M1, matériel, and Heavy Tractor, T23, for the 4.7 inch Antiaircraft Gun, T1.

Heavy Tractor, T22, was designed with a fifth wheel for semi-trailing the Trailers, T29, T30 and T31, and with heavy-duty pintles for full-trailing the transport wagons for this matériel. Heavy Tractor, T23, was identical, except that the fifth wheel was omitted, allowing the installation of a cargo box on the rear of the tractor for ammunition and equipment pertaining to the section.

Decision of the Field Artillery Board to carry the 240 mm Howitzer, M1, and 8 inch Gun, M1, matériel on full-trailed transport wagons, rather than on trailers, eliminated the necessity for a prime mover, with a fifth wheel arrangement.

38-Ton High-Speed Tractor, M6, standardized in June, 1943, as Heavy Tractor, M6, represents a combination of the two pilot models. It provides a track-type prime mover for artillery loads of approximately 30,000 to 60,000 pounds, and is capable of transporting personnel, ammunition and accessories pertaining to the section.

The tractor consists of a personnel compartment, accommodating eleven men in two rows of seats, an engine compartment, and a cargo compartment, mounted on a high-speed, fulltrack-laying hull and suspension.

Power is supplied by two Waukesha 145 GZ gasoline engines, through torque converters and a constant mesh transmission which provides two speeds forward and one reverse.

A Ring Mount, M49C, for a cal. .50 machine gun, is provided on the roof for antiaircraft and ground use. Stowage is provided for 600 rounds of cal. .50 ammunition, as well as for ammunition for the gun being towed.

The vehicle is provided with a 60,000 pound capacity winch. It is equipped with air and electric brake-controls for the towed loads.

The pilot vehicles were built by the Allis-Chalmers Co.

REFERENCES — OCM 17247, 17302, 17388, 17569, 17646, 17744, 17823, 18596, 18928, 20398, 20715, 21220.

38-TON HIGH-SPEED TRACTOR, M6, IS A PRIME MOVER FOR HEAVY ARTILLERY

TYPICAL CHARACTERISTICS

Crew 11
Physical Characteristics
Weight (gross) . . . . 75,000 lb.
Length . . . . 21 ft., 6 ins.
Width . . . . 10 ft., ½ in.
Height, to top of cab . . . . 8 ft., 1 in.
to top of gun mount . . . . 8 ft., 7 ins.
Ground clearance . . . . 20 ins.
Tread (center to center of tracks) . . . . 98½ ins.
Ground contact length . . . . 172 ins.
Ground pressure . . . . 9.9 lb./sq. in.

Armament
Cal. .50 Machine Gun, M2, HB
(flexible) . . . . On Ring Mount, M49C
Elevation . . . . −10° to +85°
Traverse . . . . 360°
Provision for:
1 cal. .30 Rifle, M1, for driver

Ammunition, Stowage
Cal. .50 . . . . 600 rounds
One of the following:
4.7 in. A.A. . . . . 24 rounds
240 mm Howitzer, M1 . . . . 20 rounds
8 in. Gun, M1 . . . . 24 rounds

Performance
Maximum speed on improved road towing
240 mm Howitzer, M1, tube
Level . . . . 20.5 m.p.h.
2½ grade . . . . 18 m.p.h.
5% grade . . . . 14 m.p.h.
20% grade . . . . 3½ m.p.h.
Maximum grade ability 60%
Trench crossing ability . . . . 8 ft.
Vertical obstacle ability . . . . 30 ins.
Fording depth (slowest forward speed) . 54 ins.
Angle of approach and departure . . . . 30°
Turning radius . . . . 14 ft.
Fuel capacity . . . . 250 gals.
Cruising range (approx.) . . . . 110 miles
Winch capacity . . . . 60,000 lb.

Battery, Voltage, Total 12
Fire Protection and Decontamination
Fire Extinguisher, CO_2-4 lb. (hand) 2
(Fixed engine compartment installation)

Engine, Make and
Model . . . . Waukesha 145 GZ (two)
Cycle 4
No. of cylinders 12
Fuel (gasoline) . . . . 80 octane
Net hp. . . . . 191 at 2,100 r.p.m.
Max. torque . . . . . . 539 lb.-ft. at 1,500 r.p.m.

Transmission, Type . Constant mesh ⎱ with
Gear ratios   ⎰ torque
First speed . . . . 2.12:1   ⎰ converters
Second speed . 1.05:1
Reverse 2.76:1

Torque Converter, Gear ratio 4.5:1
Differential, Type . . . . Controlled
Steering ratio 1.6:1

Final Drive, Type . . . . Herringbone
Sprocket, No. of teeth 13
Pitch diameter . . . . 25.04 ins.
Gear ratios 3.06:1

Suspension, Type . . . . Horizontal volute spring
Wheel or tire size . . . . 20 x 9

Idler, Type . . . . Trailing

Track, Type . . . . Center guide
Width . . . . 21⁹⁄₁₆ ins.
Pitch . . . . 6 ins.
No. of shoes per vehicle 336

Master Clutch, Type . . Dry disk, spring-loaded

Brakes, Type . . . . Self-energized
Operation . . . . Levers

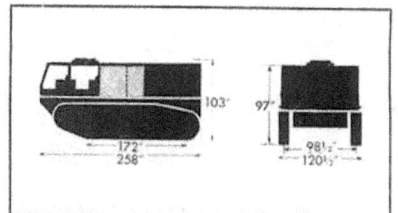

TRACKED LANDING VEHICLES

LVT (A) (1) IS ARMORED AND MOUNTS 37 MM GUN

LVT (2) WILL CARRY 30 MEN, FULLY EQUIPPED

Designed originally for rescue work in the Everglades, these vehicles have proved effective in landings on enemy beaches.

There are two general types which are supplied by the U. S. Navy and stored, issued, and maintained by the Chief of Ordnance.

The original type, nicknamed "the Alligator," represented by Landing Vehicle, Tracked (Unarmored), Mk. I, LVT (1), is now Limited Standard. It is powered by a Hercules WLXC3, 6-cylinder, in-line gasoline engine. An angle drive and right and left reverse transmissions transmit power from the main transmission to silent chains, which operate the final drive sprocket, which, in turn, operates the tracks. Steering is by clutches and brakes.

Present standard type is the so-called "Water Buffalo," represented by Landing Vehicles, Tracked (Armored), Mk. I, LVT (A) (1); Mk. II, LVT (A) (2); and Mk. IV, LVT (A) (4); and Landing Vehicles, Tracked (Unarmored), Mk. II, LVT (2); and Mk. IV, LVT (4).

These vehicles are longer and wider than the LVT (1) and incorporate a number of improvements. Power is supplied by a Continental W670-9A, 7-cylinder gasoline engine, this and the power train being the same as used in the Light Tank, M3, Series. Steering is by a controlled differential.

The vehicles employ a bogie system of an entirely new design, with eleven single-wheeled, rubber-tired bogie assemblies on each side. The torsional effect of a shaft floating in rubber is utilized to

cushion and support the vehicle. A hollow shaft, welded to the hull on a spring-end bracket, is placed inside another hollow shaft of larger diameter, to which is welded the bogie wheel arms and bogie wheel. Rubber is vulcanized between the shafts. Thus, as the vehicle negotiates irregular terrain, the outer shaft twists on the inner shaft. The natural resistance of the rubber serves to cushion the upward and downward movement of the bogie wheel, providing firm but flexible support.

These vehicles were originally designated as amphibian tractors. The nomenclature was changed to conform with designations of the U. S. Navy and the British.

The vehicles are manufactured by the Food Machinery Co.

REFERENCES — OCM 19108, 19367, 19992.

LANDING VEHICLE, TRACKED (UNARMORED), MK. I, LVT (1), LIMITED STANDARD—Formerly known as Amphibian Tractor, T33, this vehicle is now Limited Standard. It is shorter and narrower than later models, and has higher side pontoons, which cover the suspension except for the tracks. Track grousers are of a curved blade design. The cargo compartment provides space for 24 men with packs and rifles or 4,500 pounds of matériel. Machine gun rails are provided at the sides and rear of the cargo compartment.

The vehicle is of arc-welded sheet steel construction, without armor. The driver's cab has three front windows, the center of which may be opened for ventilation

or escape. It also has a sliding window on each side. Seats with safety belts are provided for a crew of three.

REFERENCE—TM 9–784.

LANDING VEHICLE, TRACKED (ARMORED), MK. I, LVT (A) (1)—STANDARD—This vehicle is, in effect, an amphibian tank, with a light tank turret mounted to the rear of the driver's cab.

Principal armament consists of a 37 mm Gun, M6, with a cal. .30 Machine Gun, M1919A5, in a Combination Gun Mount, M44. The guns may be elevated from —10° to +25°. A gyrostabilizer is provided. The turret may be traversed by a hydraulic apparatus or by hand. There are two entrance hatches in the roof of the turret. Two periscopes are provided for the commander. A gunner's periscope with telescopic sight is connected with the gun mount.

Two manholes in the rear of the turret are equipped with scarf mounts for cal. .30 machine guns.

A direct vision window in front of the driver is provided with an armored cover which may be kept closed in combat areas. There are two escape hatches in the top of the cab, each equipped with a rotating periscope.

REFERENCE—TM 9–775.

LANDING VEHICLE, TRACKED (UNARMORED), MK. II, LVT (2)—STANDARD—The basic hull design and major vehicular components of this vehicle are the same as on the LVT (A) (1). Construction is of sheet steel.

This vehicle has no turret. The space between the driver's cab and the engine

LVT (4) HAS RAMP AT REAR FOR LOADING VEHICLES

LVT (A) (4) MOUNTS 75 MM HOWITZER IN TURRET

compartment is used for transporting cargo and personnel. Propeller shafts, leading from the engine to the transmission, and connected at the center by a power take-off, are encased in a control tunnel which extends through the center of the cargo compartment.

Machine gun rails are provided at the front of the cargo compartment, and along the sides and rear, permitting fire in any direction.

The cab has two front escape windows, which hinge downward and may be opened for ventilation. There is also a small window on each side. All windows are constructed of safety glass.

REFERENCE—TM 9–775.

LANDING VEHICLE, TRACKED (ARMORED), MK. II, LVT (A) (2)—STANDARD—This vehicle is generally similar to the LVT (2), but is constructed of armor plate instead of sheet steel.

The cab is similar to that used on LVT (A) (1). The single window at the front is provided with a hinged armor plate cover. Two escape hatches, with rotating periscopes, are in the roof of the cab.

REFERENCE—TM 9–775.

LANDING VEHICLE, TRACKED (UNARMORED), MK. IV, LVT (4)—STANDARD—This vehicle is similar in general characteristics to the LVT (2) but is provided with a ramp at the rear. The engine compartment occupies a position directly in back of the driver's cab. The

cargo compartment is in the rear. The cab and the ramp are armored. The vehicle will transport a ¼-ton, 4x4, Truck with a 37 mm Gun Carriage, M4A1; or a 57 mm gun carriage or a 75 mm or 105 mm howitzer carriage. Two swinging mounts and two stationary mounts are provided for cal. .30 or cal. .50 machine guns.

LANDING VEHICLE, TRACKED, (ARMORED), MK. IV, LVT (A) (4)—STANDARD—This vehicle is generally similar to the LVT (A) (1) but is provided with an open-top turret similar to that on 75 mm Howitzer Motor Carriage, M8. Principal armament is a 75 mm Howitzer, M2 or M3. A cal. .50 Machine Gun, M2, HB, is mounted at the rear of the turret.

LANDING VEHICLE, TRACKED (ARMORED), MK. I, LVT (A) (1)

Crew 6
Physical Characteristics
  Weight (gross) . . . . 32,800 lb.*
  Length . . . . 26 ft., 1 in.
  Width . . . . 10 ft., 8 ins.
  Height . . . . 10 ft., 1 in.†
  Ground clearance . . . . 18 ins.
  Draft . . . . 4 ft., 2 ins.
  Tread (center to center of tracks) . . 113½ ins.
  Ground contact length . . . . 126½ ins.
  Ground pressure—at 4 in.
    penetration . . . . 8.7 lb./sq. in.

Armament
  37 mm Gun, M6, with
  1 cal. .30 Machine Gun, } In Combination
  M1919A5 . . . . } Gun Mount, M44
  2 cal. .30 Machine Guns,
  M1919A4 . . . . . . On Scarf Mounts, Mk. 21
  1 cal. .50 Machine Gun,
  M2, HB . . . . On Mount, M35

Ammunition, Stowage‡
  37 mm . . . . 104 rounds
  Cal. .30 . . . . 6,000 rounds

Armor, Actual
  Hull . . . . ¼ in.
  Cab, Front . . . . ½ in.
  Sides . . . . ¼ in.
  Turret, Side . . . . ½ in.
  Top . . . . ¼ in.

Performance
  Maximum speed on land . . . . 25 m.p.h.
  Maximum speed in water . . . . 6½ m.p.h.
  Maximum grade ability 60%
  Angle of approach . . . . 35°
  Angle of departure . . . . 30°
  Fuel capacity . . . . 106 gals.
  Cruising range—land . . . . 125 miles
    water . . . . 75 miles
  Maximum drawbar pull . . . . 18,000 lb.
  Payload . . . . 1,000 lb.

Vision and Fire Control
  Periscopes, M6 4
  Periscope, M4, w/ Telescope, M40 1
  Bore Sight 1

Communications—Radio . . . . TCS
  Interphone stations 6

Battery, Voltage, total 12

LVT (A) (1)

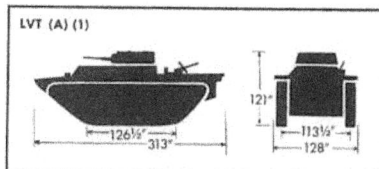

Fire Protection
  Fire Extinguisher, CO₂–10 lb. (fixed) 2
  CO₂–15 lb. (hand) 1

Engine, Make and Model . . . . Continental
                              W670-9A
  Type . . . . Radial AC
  No. of cylinders 7
  Fuel (gasoline) . . . . 80 octane
  Net hp. . . . . 250 at 2,400 r.p.m.
  Max. torque . . . . . . 584 lb.-ft. at 1,800 r.p.m.
  (See additional engine characteristics on page 27.)

Transmission, Type . . . . Syncromesh (Light Tank, M3)

Differential, Type . . . . Controlled (Light Tank, M3)

Final Drive, Type . . . . (Light Tank, M3)

Track, Type . . . . . . Steel, with extruded cleats
  Width . . . . 14¼ ins.
  No. of shoes per vehicle 146

*LVT (2), 30,900 lb., LVT (A) (2), 32,000 lb., LVT (4), 33,350 lb., LVT (A) (4), 40,000 lb.

†LVT (2), LVT (A) (2), LVT (4), 8 ft., 1 in.; LVT (A) (4), 10 ft., 5 ins.

‡LVT (2), LVT (A) (2), LVT (4), cal. .30, 2,000 rounds; cal. .50, 1,000 rounds; LVT (A) (4), 75 mm, 100 rounds; cal. .50, 400 rounds.

BOMB SERVICE TRUCK M6—STANDARD
BOMB LIFT TRUCK M1—STANDARD

BOMB SERVICE TRUCK, M6, SHOWING COLLAPSIBLE TOP AND BOMB HOIST

TYPICAL CHARACTERISTICS

BOMB SERVICE TRUCK, M6

Crew 5

Physical Characteristics

Weight (gross) . . . . 8,325 lb.
Length . . . . 18 ft., 5 ins.
Width . . . . 6 ft.
Height . . . . 7 ft., 7½ ins.
Ground clearance . . . . 9⅞ ins.
Wheelbase . . . . 125 ins.
Center of gravity above ground . . . . 31 ins.
Tread, front . . . . 60½ ins.
    rear . . . . 57¼ ins.
Ground contact . . . . 35 sq. ins.
Ground pressure . . . . 64 lb./sq. in.
Tire equipment . . 7.50x20, 8 ply (mud and snow)

Performance

Maximum speed on level . . . . 55 m.p.h.
Maximum grade ability 65%
Fording depth (slowest forward speed) . . 32 ins.
Angle of approach . . . . 45°
Angle of departure . . . . 38°
Turning radius . . . . 26 ft.
Fuel capacity . . . . 48 gals.
Cruising range (approx.) . . . . 250 miles
Payload . . . . 2,000 lb.

Vision . . . . Windshield
Battery, Voltage 6
Fire Protection . . . . CO_2, 2 lb.
(Other characteristics same as for 1½-ton, 4 x 4, Truck.)

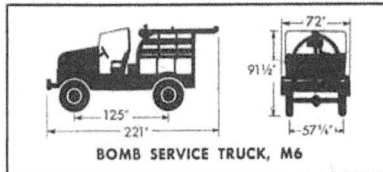

BOMB SERVICE TRUCK, M6

BOMB LIFT TRUCK, M1

Physical Characteristics

Weight . . . . 290 lb.
Length (handle extended) . . . . 7 ft., 1 in.
Width . . . . 2 ft., 9 ins.
Height (platform raised) . . . . 13 ins.
Height (platform lowered) . . . . 7 ins.
Tire equipment 5.00x4

BOMB LIFT TRUCK, M1, WITH PLATFORM LOWERED, AND HANDLE BACK

BOMB SERVICE TRUCK, M6, is used to load, unload, and tow bomb trailers.

It consists of a specially designed Chevrolet 1½-ton, 4x4, truck with an open body and a platform on which is mounted a hoist for loading and unloading the bomb trailer.

The hand-operated hoist has a capacity of 4,000 pounds.

The vehicle was designed for a low silhouette, short wheelbase and a short turning radius. Provision is made for the use of dual tires, front or rear, when required.

A removable top over the front seat provides protection during road marches in inclement weather or when the vehicle is stored in the open. Seats are provided in the front for two men, and in the rear for three additional men.

Power is supplied by a six-cylinder valve-in-head engine. A single plate dry disk clutch with a diaphragm spring is used. A selective sliding gear type transmission supplies four forward speeds and one reverse speed.

The truck is equipped with controls for electric brakes and a stop light on a trailer.

A pintle hook is provided at the rear and two pull hooks on the front of the vehicle.

The truck is manufactured by the Chevrolet Motor Division, General Motors Corporation.

REFERENCES—TM 9-765; OCM 15077, 15179, 16969, 17116.

BOMB LIFT TRUCK, M1, was designed to lift bombs weighing from 500 pounds to 2,000 pounds, with the bomb stand, from the ground and place them under the bomb bays of airplanes. From this point they can be loaded by the airplane hoisting gear.

It is a low three-wheeled, modified, standard shop lift truck, with a hydraulic-operated lifting platform and pneumatic tires.

The truck is used as an accessory to Bomb Service Truck, M6, and also is used separately in some branches.

REFERENCES—OCM 15970, 16969, 20517.

2½-TON, 6x6 (4DT), BOMB SERVICE TRUCK, M27—STANDARD

2½-TON, 6x6 (4DT), BOMB SERVICE TRUCK, M27, SHOWING BOMB ABOUT TO BE LOWERED TO DOLLY ON TRACK FOR TRANSFER TO AIRPLANE

This vehicle was designed at the request of Headquarters, Army Air Forces, for handling the 4,000 pound bomb.

It consists of a 2½-Ton, 6x6 (4dt), Cargo Truck, L.W.B. w/winch, less troop seats, on which is mounted a specially designed, power-operated bomb-lift mechanism, consisting of a steel superstructure built over the body, and independently controlling hoisting and traversing mechanisms driven from the vehicle power takeoff. This enables the unit to lift the bomb, carry it into the cargo body for transporting to position near an airplane, and lower it onto a dolly and track on which it may be pushed to a position beneath the bomb bay of the airplane.

A Dolly and Track Set, 2-Ton, consisting of two dollies and five track sections, is part of the equipment of the truck, and is carried inside the cargo body. During local operations, straight sections are carried on brackets on the sides of the body. The track, which has one curved section and a total length of 50 feet, provides considerable flexibility of operation and makes it possible to manhandle the bomb over soft and uneven terrain which would be impassable to the Bomb Lift Truck, M1. The dolly has dual, concave bomb cradles which provide adequate stability even though the track is not level, and operates with minimum rolling resistance.

The truck superstructure is constructed to permit its disassembly when necessary to conserve shipping space. Bows and tarpaulins are provided and give the vehicle an appearance similar to that of the standard 2½-ton cargo truck. The hoisting mechanism is equipped with an automatic overload slip clutch to prevent cable breakage. Bomb Service Kit, for 2½-Ton, 6x6, Cargo Truck contains all material necessary for field conversion of the standard truck to Bomb Service Truck, M27.

Basis of issue for the truck is one to each fighter squadron and fighter-bomber squadron, two to each bomber squadron, medium and heavy, and each Ordnance Am. Co. Aviation, and one to each Ordnance S. & M. Co.-Aviation. Basis of issue for the Dolly and Track Set is one to each Truck, Bomb Service, M27, and two additional to each Ordnance section of bombardment squadrons and Ordnance S. & M. Co.-Aviation.

REFERENCES — OCM 20964, 21256, 21499, 21787, 22150, 23148.

TYPICAL CHARACTERISTICS

Crew 2

Physical Characteristics
Weight (gross) . . . . 17,880 lb.*
Length (overall) . . . . 29 ft., 10 ins.
Length (frame and body only) . . 22 ft., 5⅜ ins.
Width . . . . 7 ft., 4 ins.
Height . . . . 10 ft., 6 ins.
Inside body length . . . . 12 ft.
Inside body width . . . . 6 ft., 8 ins.
Ground clearance . . . . 10 ins.
Tread (center to center, rear) . . . . 67¾ ins.
Wheelbase . . . . 164 ins.
Ground contact, front . . . . 90 sq. ins.
    rear . . . . 240 sq. ins.
Ground pressure, front . . . . 62 lb./sq. in.
    rear . . . . 52 lb./sq. in.
Tire equipment . . . . 7.50 x 20, 8 ply

Performance
Maximum speed on level . . . . 45 m.p.h.
Maximum grade ability 65%
Vertical obstacle ability . . . . 10 ins.
Fording depth (slowest forward speed) . 30 ins.†
Angle of approach . . . . 31°
Angle of departure . . . . 36°
Turning radius . . . . 35 ft.
Fuel capacity . . . . 40 gals.

Cruising range (approx.) . . . . 240 miles
Payload . . . . 4,000 lb.
Normal towed load . . . . 7,200 lb.
Winch capacity . . . . 10,000 lb.
(Other characteristics same as for 2½-ton, 6x6, Cargo Truck.)

Dolly, Type . . . . Welded Sheet Steel
Weight . . . . 85 lb.
Length . . . . 28 ins.
Width . . . . 25½ ins.
Height . . . . 6⅝ ins.
Wheelbase . . . . 21 ins.
Crosstie clearance—Dolly . . . . 1⅛ ins.
Rail Side Clearance . . . . 7/16 in.
Wheel type . . . . Cast Steel, Flanged
Wheel diameter . . . . 5 ins.

Track, Type . . . . All Steel
Gage (Ctr. to ctr. of rails) . . . . 21 ins.
Length—Straight rail . . . . 135½ ins.
Weight—Straight section . . . . 130 lb.
Curvature—Curved section . . . . 45°
Radius of curve—Inside rail . . . . 8 ft.
Weight—Curved section . . . . 85 lb.

*Including: Payload, 4,000 lb.; Dolly and Track Set, 780 lb.
†With fording equipment, 60 ins.

LIFT TRUCK M22—STANDARD
BOMB TRAILER M5—STANDARD

LIFT TRUCK, M22, IS USED IN HANDLING BOMBS AND TORPEDOES

TYPICAL CHARACTERISTICS

LIFT TRUCK, M22

Physical Characteristics

Weight (without cradle)	950 lb.
Weight (with cradle)	1,400 lb.
Length (excluding tongue)	10 ft., 3 ins.
Width	4 ft., 10 ins.
Height (cradle lowered)	18½ ins.
Height (cradle raised)	42 ins.
Over-all height (cradle lowered, with bomb adapter)	32 ins.
Over-all height (cradle raised, with bomb adapter)	56 ins.
Wheelbase	97 ins.
Tread (center to center) front	40 ins.
rear	50 ins.
Ground clearance	4 ins.
Tire equipment	5.50x18, 6 ply

Lift Characteristics

Range of lift (with cradle without adapter)	9 ins. to 33 ins.
Range of lift (with cradle with adapter)	25½ ins. to 49½ ins.
Angles of lift tilt	—15° to +15°

Performance

Angle of departure	24°
Turning radius	14 ft.
Payload	5,000 lb.

BOMB TRAILER, M5

Physical Characteristics

Weight empty	2,000 lb.
Weight loaded	7,000 lb.
Length overall	17 ft., 11 ins.
Length of deck	11 ft., 3 ins.
Width overall	7 ft., 4 ins.
Width of deck	5 ft., 9 ins.
Height	3 ft., 9 ins.
Height of deck loaded	21½ ins.
Wheelbase	102¾ ins.
Ground clearance	9 ins.
Tread (center to center, rear)	80½ ins.
Tire equipment, rear	7.50x18–8 ply
front	6.50x10–6 ply

Performance

Maximum speed on level	45 m.p.h.
Cross country speed	20 m.p.h.

Battery, Voltage | 6

LIFT TRUCK, M22, is used to carry the 4,000 lb. Bomb, AN-M56, and the 2,000 lb. Torpedo, Mk. XIII, Mod. 1 or 2, placing them in a position from which they can be loaded onto bombardment aircraft.

Two hand-operated, piston-type pumps are connected to the forward frame for raising and lowering the cradle.

The cradle assembly consists of a cradle body, folding jack legs and radius rods which can be raised by means of hydraulic jacks.

Normal range of lift is from 9 inches to 33 inches. A removable adapter is provided for lifting the 4,000 lb. bomb, by which the range of lift is changed from 25½ inches to 49½ inches.

A tongue on the front with lunette eye and handles permits towing behind a vehicle or pulling by the crew. Ball rollers on the truck bed facilitate shifting the position of the bomb or torpedo. Chock blocks and chain ties to position loads are provided. The truck is equipped with a pintle at the rear.

REFERENCES — TM 9–762; OCM 15970, 17947, 18019, 18819, 19428.

BOMB TRAILER, M5, is a castered third-wheel trailer for transporting bombs between munitions dumps and airfields, and is designed to meet requirements of low loading and ease of handling.

Trailers may be connected in trains behind a prime mover for operation at fairly high speed. The front caster unit permits a turning radius about equal to the wheelbase.

The front of the hitch yoke is provided with a reversible lunette which may be attached to the rear pintle of another trailer or a prime mover. The electric brakes and the lighting system are controlled by the driver of the prime mover by means of an electric connecting cable. A safety switch applies the brakes automatically in case the towing connection between the trailer and the prime mover is broken.

A stabilizer mechanism minimizes the tendency for the vehicle to "pitch" on rough roads.

Deck channels are provided to hold the bombs securely. A loading ramp and a supporting stand are furnished with each trailer to aid in loading. The ramp is equipped with hooks for engaging the pins on the side of the deck chamber.

REFERENCES—TM 9–760; OCM 13181, 13287, 14097, 15077, 15179, 16430.

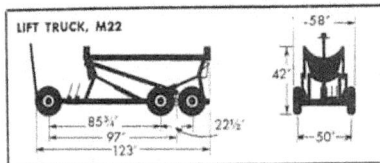

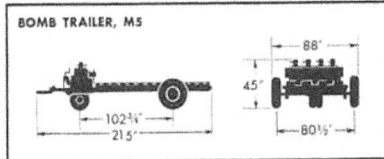

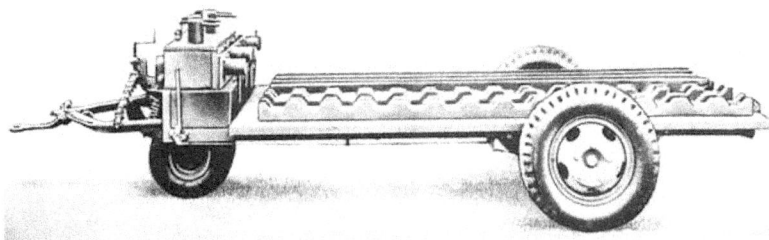

BOMB TRAILER, M5, TRANSPORTS BOMBS FROM DUMPS TO AIRFIELDS

GENERATOR TRAILER M7—STANDARD
DIRECTOR TRAILERS M13, M14—LIMITED STANDARD; M22—STANDARD
MOUNT TRAILER M17—STANDARD; TRAILER M18—STANDARD

These 4-wheel, short wheelbase vehicles use the same basic chassis, modified for particular purposes.

GENERATOR TRAILER M7, STANDARD, was designed specifically to transport an engine generator set and to give it a solid, level foundation when in use at a halt. It is now being used also by the Chemical Warfare Service for transporting smoke-generating equipment. Four built-in corner-lift jacks permit the lifting of body weight off springs and tires. The trailer, which has a welded-steel pick-up body and an adjustable tongue mounted in an A-frame, can be coupled quickly to any vehicle equipped with a pintle. Understructure is of the rocker-arm type, assuring 4-wheel ground contact.

DIRECTOR TRAILER M13, LIMITED STANDARD, is a modification of Generator Trailer M7. It is designed to transport Directors M9 and M10 and to give them a level operating foundation. It has a steel pick-up body that extends slightly higher than that of the basic trailer and is equipped with bows and a canvas top.

DIRECTOR TRAILER M14, LIMITED STANDARD, is a more durable modification of Generator Trailer M7 and also is designed for transporting Directors M9 and M10. It has a solid steel body with rigid top or superstructure. Double top and side walls are separated by insulation 1¾ inches thick. A gasoline heating system is mounted inside the trailer and an electric ventilating blower is installed in the superstructure. There are five windows, all equipped with sliding blackout panels.

DIRECTOR TRAILER M22, STANDARD, is a modification of Director Trailer M14 embodying improvements requested by the Antiaircraft Artillery Board.

MOUNT TRAILER M17, STANDARD, is the designation given to Generator Trailer M7 as modified to mount Multiple Cal. .50 Machine Gun Mount M45, the combination being designated Multiple Cal. .50 Machine Gun Carriage M51.

TRAILER M18, STANDARD, is Generator Trailer M7 modified by the addition of a winch. It is used in transporting generating units mounted on skids.

REFERENCES—TM 9-881, 9-881 (C1), 9-2800; OCM 16869, 19740, 19905, 20142, 20276, 21125, 21326, 21565, 22696, 23544, 23921, 24210; SNL G-221.

GENERATOR TRAILER M7 IS DESIGNED TO TRANSPORT AN ENGINE GENERATOR SET

DIRECTOR TRAILER M14, ON SAME CHASSIS, TRANSPORTS DIRECTORS M9, M10

TYPICAL CHARACTERISTICS

Physical Characteristics	Generator Trailer M7	Director Trailer M13	Director Trailers M14, M22
Weight (net)	4,500 lb.	4,800 lb.	5,800 lb.
Length (overall)	16 ft.	16 ft.	16 ft.
Width	8 ft.	8 ft.	8 ft.
Height	3 ft., 9 in.	8 ft.	8 ft., 2 in.
Ground clearance	4½ in.	4½ in.	4½ in.
Tread (center to center, rear)	83¾ in.	83¾ in.	83¾ in.
Wheelbase	40 in.	40 in.	40 in.
Ground pressure (empty)	28 lb./sq. in.	30 lb./sq. in.	36 lb./sq. in.
(loaded)	53 lb./sq. in.	51 lb./sq. in.	57 lb./sq. in.
Tire equipment	7.50 x 20, 8-ply	7.50 x 20, 8-ply	7.50 x 20, 8-ply
Performance—Payload	4,000 lb.	3,400 lb.	3,400 lb.
Brakes, Type	Electric	Electric	Electric

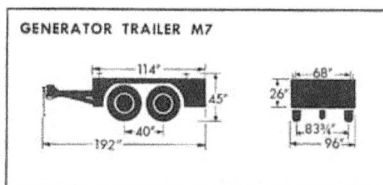

GENERATOR TRAILER M7

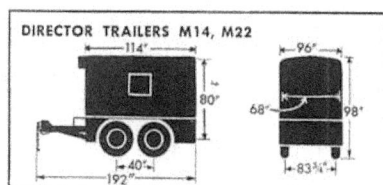

DIRECTOR TRAILERS M14, M22

4-TON, 2-WHEEL AMMUNITION TRAILER **M21**—STANDARD
1-TON, 2-WHEEL AMMUNITION TRAILER **M24**—STANDARD

4-TON, 2-WHEEL AMMUNITION TRAILER M21 CARRIES AMMUNITION, FUZES, AND PRIMERS

1-TON, 2-WHEEL AMMUNITION TRAILER M24

4-TON, 2-WHEEL AMMUNITION TRAILER M21, STANDARD, is a single-axle, sprung trailer, designed to transport 72 complete rounds of 155-mm howitzer ammunition or 108 complete rounds of 4.5-inch gun ammunition. A box is provided for fuzes and primers.

Brakes, operated by compressed air and controlled from the towing vehicle, are automatically applied if the trailer is accidentally disconnected. A hand brake is provided.

Brake parts and wheel bearings are interchangeable with those of the 4-Ton, 6x6, Truck. The lunette and the wheels, tires, and tubes are interchangeable with those of the 4.5-inch gun and the 155-mm Howitzer Carriage M1.

The body is built as an integral part of the trailer frame. A paulin, lashing hooks, hold-down straps for propelling charges, and ammunition racks are provided.

REFERENCES—OCM 18048, 20921, 21991, 22264.

1-TON, 2-WHEEL AMMUNITION TRAILER M24, STANDARD, is a modification of the 1-Ton, 2-Wheel Cargo Trailer designed to carry additional ammunition for Combination Gun Motor Carriage M15A1. The interior of the body is fitted with metal stowage boxes. Two lockers, each having two compartments, are bolted to the floor on the left side. The first three compartments (back to front) are each designed to carry nine Cal. .50 Ammunition Boxes M2, a total of 2,700 rounds, and the fourth compartment is intended to carry any articles desired. Outsides of the lockers are fitted with clamps to carry six machine gun barrels.

On the right side are five removable metal boxes fitted with spacers for carrying 350 rounds of 37-mm ammunition. Each box will carry seven clips of ten rounds each. The boxes are secured to the floor by spring clamps. A rainproof stowage compartment is at the front of the trailer.

REFERENCES—TM 9-883; OCM 24117, 24456.

TYPICAL CHARACTERISTICS

AMMUNITION TRAILER M21

Physical Characteristics

Weight (gross)	13,056 lb.
Length (over front lunette and rear towing hooks)	12 ft., 2½ in.
Width	8 ft., ¾ in.
Height	6 ft., 11⅛ in.
Ground clearance	13½ in.
Tread (center to center of tires)	82¾ in.
Tire equipment (may be changed to heavy-duty type)	14.00 x 20, highway

Body (inside dimensions)

Length	6 ft., 10½ in.
Width	7 ft., 2½ in.
Height	3 ft., 4⅞ in.
Brakes, Service	Air
Brakes, Parking	Hand

AMMUNITION TRAILER M24

Physical Characteristics

Weight (gross)	3,600 lb.
Length (overall)	12 ft., 1½ in.
Length (inside body)	8 ft.
Width (overall)	5 ft., 11⅛ in.
Width (inside body)	3 ft., 10¼ in.
Height (overall, top up)	6 ft., 1 in.
Height (inside body, top up)	3 ft., 7 in.
Ground clearance	16¼ in.
Tread (center to center of tires)	59 in.
Tire equipment	7.50 x 20, 8-ply, mud and snow
Desert	11.00 x 18, 10-ply

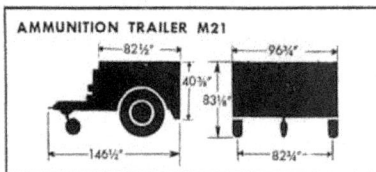

AMMUNITION TRAILER M21

AMMUNITION TRAILER M24

8-TON, 4-WHEEL, AMMUNITION TRAILER M23—STANDARD

8-TON, 4-WHEEL, AMMUNITION TRAILER M23, ¾ FRONT VIEW

OVERHEAD VIEW, SHOWING RACKS FOR POSITIONING AMMUNITION

This trailer, designed to transport 240-mm howitzer ammunition, 8-in. howitzer and gun ammunition, and 155-mm gun ammunition, was standardized in April 1944.

It is an 8-ton payload, 4-wheel trailer with walking beam axle. It can be used with Heavy Carriage Limber M5, which serves as a trailer dolly, as a trailed load for 18-Ton High-Speed Tractor M4 and 38-Ton High-Speed Tractor M6, or without limber as a trailed load behind the 7½-Ton, 6x6, Truck. In the latter case the trailer is attached by means of the universal pintle coupling installed on the truck.

The body, which is of steel construction, is an integral part of the trailer frame, and is provided with paulin, lashing hooks, hold-down straps for propelling charges, and ammunition racks. Stowage is provided for approximately 32 complete rounds of 240-mm howitzer ammunition, 60 complete rounds of 8-in. howitzer ammunition, 96 complete rounds of 155-mm ammunition, or 33 complete rounds of 8-in. gun ammunition up to the maximum payload of 16,000 lb.

The vehicle is capable of being towed at speeds up to 35 miles per hour on smooth concrete roadway and up to 20 miles per hour cross country.

Tire and wheel assemblies are interchangeable with those of the 155-mm Gun, 8-In. Howitzer Carriage M1, and Heavy Carriage Limber M5.

Air brakes, which operate on all four wheels of the walking beam axle, can be controlled from the towing vehicle. Hand-operated parking brakes located on the right and left sides of the trailer can be applied independently to a wheel on either side of the walking beam axle.

U.S. Army standard combat-zone lighting is provided, with current supplied from the towing vehicle. Reflectors conform to I.C.C. regulations. A retractable landing-wheel assembly is furnished.

The rear pintle is interchangeable with that on the 18-Ton High-Speed Tractor M4. The vehicle is equipped with towing hooks on the two rear corners and lifting eyes on the front and rear corners of the body.

REFERENCES—OCM 18048, 20921, 21741, 21944, 23262, 23569.

TYPICAL CHARACTERISTICS

8-TON, 4-WHEEL, AMMUNITION TRAILER M23

Physical Characteristics

Weight (gross)—Trailer only	26,000 lb.
Trailer and Limber	28,000 lb.
Weight (net)—Trailer only	10,460 lb.
Trailer and Limber	12,350 lb.
Length—center of bogie to center of lunette (coupling) eye	14 ft., 4½ in.
Length—overall	18 ft., 7 in.
Width	8 ft., 8½ in.
Height	6 ft., 11 in.
Ground clearance	16¾ in.
Tread (center to center of tires)	88¾ in.
Wheelbase—center of bogie to center of limber axle	170¼ in.
Tire equipment	11.00 x 20, 12-ply

Body—Inside dimensions

Propelling charge section Length	11 ft., 8 in.
Width	8 ft., 4 in.
Ammunition well Length	11 ft., 8 in.
Width	4 ft., 2 in.

Fuze Box—Inside dimensions

Length	4 ft., 11 in.
Depth	1 ft., 7½ in.
Width	1 ft., 4½ in.

Performance

Maximum speed on level	35 m.p.h.
Angle of departure	90°
Payload	16,000 lb.
Brakes, Type	Air
Brakes, Parking, Type	Hand

HEAVY CARRIAGE LIMBER M5

Physical Characteristics

Weight (net)	1,890 lb.
Length—overall	8 ft., 1½ in.
Ground clearance	11¾ in.
Tread (center to center of tires)	82 in.
Tire equipment	11.00 x 20, 12-ply

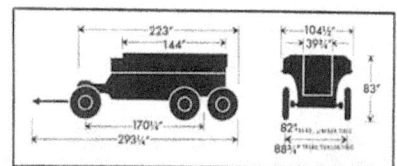

AMMUNITION TRAILER M23 USED AS SEMITRAILER WITH HEAVY CARRIAGE LIMBER M5

HEAVY WRECKING TRUCKS M1—LIMITED STANDARD; M1A1—STANDARD

HEAVY WRECKING TRUCK M1A1 WITH OPEN CAB, SHOWING CRANE IN TRAVELING POSITION

These vehicles are used for towing, salvaging, and recovering operations, as well as for numerous repair operations away from base repair shops, where heavy hoist and winch equipment is needed.

Heavy Wrecking Truck M1, standardized in July 1937, is now classified as Limited Standard.

Heavy Wrecking Truck M1A1, standardized in March 1944, is generally similar to the M1, but has an open cab, an improved crane assembly, and other improvements. It will tow vehicles weighing up to 60,000 pounds.

It consists of a 6x6 truck, with a payload of 8,000 pounds, on which is mounted a heavy crane assembly, rear winch assembly, and other equipment. The winches are operated by power through power take-offs mounted on the transfer case and the transmission. Body jacks, telescoping boom jacks, outriggers, and ground spades are provided to take the strain off the truck and the crane when heavy loads are lifted.

The crane can be used at the rear or at the side of the truck. Its capacity varies according to the elevation of the boom and the position of the boom hook line. It has a maximum capacity of 16,000 pounds on the inner sheave only when used with boom jacks at a jack height of 10 feet, 10 inches.

The rear winch is used for straight recovery, heavy recovery, and angle recovery operations, using a one-, two-, three-, or four-part line as required. Using one cable, it has a maximum direct pull of 37,500 pounds.

The front winch, used primarily for recovering the wrecker itself if mired or for anchoring it for rear-winch operations, has a direct-pull capacity of 20,000 pounds with one cable.

The vehicle carries welding and cutting equipment, an 8-ton and a 30-ton jack, tow chains, a towbar and a whiffletree assembly, and other necessary equipment.

Compressed-air brakes are provided, with trailer air connections at both the front and rear. A double check valve permits operation of the wrecker brakes from a vehicle ahead of the wrecker.

Provision is made for stowing two cal. .30 carbines.

Bows and paulins for camouflage are furnished. These give the wrecker the appearance of a cargo vehicle and make it a less conspicuous target from the air. Two floodlights on top of the crane A-frame furnish light for night work.

The vehicles are manufactured by the Ward La France Truck Division and the Kenworth Motor Truck Corp.

REFERENCES—TM 9-796; OCM 17983, 18100, 18153, 18371, 18806, 19036, 19107, 20442, 20511, 21812, 21954, 22853, 23130, 23146, 23504; MCM 25; SNL G-116.

TYPICAL CHARACTERISTICS

Crew 2

Physical Characteristics
Weight (gross)—M1 . . . . 38,500 lb.
   M1A1 . . . . 40,500 lb.
Length . . . . 23 ft., 5 in.
Width . . . . 8 ft., 4¾ in.
Height . . . . 10 ft.
Ground clearance . . . . 11 in.
Tread (center to center, rear) . . . . 88¾ in.
Wheelbase . . . . 181 in.
Tire equipment . . . . 11.00 x 20, 12-ply,
                                 mud and snow

Provision for:
  2 cal. .30 carbines

Ammunition, Stowage
Cal. .30 (carbine) . . . . 640 rounds

Performance
Maximum speed on level . . . . 45 m.p.h.
Maximum grade ability 65%
Fording depth (slowest forward speed) . . . . 48 in.
Angle of approach . . . . 55½°
Angle of departure . . . . 55°
Turning radius . . . . 38 ft.
Fuel capacity . . . . 100 gal.
Cruising range (approx.) . . . . 250 miles
Payload . . . . 8,000 lb.

Communication—Flag Set M238 1

Battery, Voltage, total 12

Fire Protection and Decontamination
Fire Extinguisher, CO.-2 lb. (hand) 3
   CCL.-1 qt. 1
Decontaminating Apparatus M2, 1½ qts. 2

Engine, Make and model . . . . Continental, 22R
Type . . . . In-line, valve-in-head
No. of cylinders 6
Fuel (gasoline) . . . . 70 octane
Displacement . . . . 501 cu. in.
Max. governed speed . . . . 2,400 r.p.m.
Net hp . . . . 133 at 2,400 r.p.m.
Max. torque . . . 365 lb.-ft. at 1,200 r.p.m.
Width . . . . 34 in.
Height . . . . 52 in.
Weight . . . . 1,650 lb.

Transmission, Gear ratios
First speed 7.07:1
Second speed 3.50:1
Third speed 1.72:1
Fourth speed 1.00:1
Fifth speed 0.776:1
Reverse 7.11:1

Transfer Case
Gear ratio 1.00:1, 2.55:1
Steering Ratio 25:1
Rear Axle, Gear ratio 8.27:1
Brakes, Service, Type . . . . Compressed air
Brakes, Parking, Type . Ventilated, disk, 4-shoe

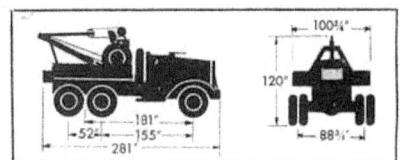

ORDNANCE MAINTENANCE TRUCKS, 2½-TON, 6x6 (4DT)

Artillery Repair M9A1

Automotive Repair M8A1

Electrical Repair M18A2

Instrument Repair M10A1, Load A

Instrument Bench M23

Machine Shop M16A2, Load A

Machine Shop M16A1, Loads B, B1, B2

Signal Corps General Repair M31

Signal Corps Repair M30

Small Arms Repair M7A2

Tire Repair M32

ORDNANCE MAINTENANCE TRUCK WITH ST-6 BODY, SHOWN ASSEMBLED

SAME TRUCK, WITH BODY COLLAPSED FOR SHIPMENT OVERSEAS

These are Mobile Shop Trucks, used for Ordnance maintenance, mounted on 2½-ton, 6x6 (4dt) truck chassis of 164-in. wheelbase. Bodies are all metal, completely inclosed. The same body is used for all the various models. They differ only in the various tools and equipment mounted or carried within them.

The present production model of the body is known as Model ST-6. This body incorporates a collapsible feature which permits the rear doors, front and rear belt panels, windows and other allied equipment to be removed and the top lowered approximately 24 inches. The mounted equipment remains intact and the disassembled parts can then be packed inside the collapsed body so as to form a compact item for shipping and thereby conserve shipping space.

The ST-6 Body is 148 inches long, 96 inches wide, and 81⅝ inches high, outside dimensions. Six windows are provided on each side, as well as a small window in the front and two windows in the doors. They are all protected by heavy brush guards and screen wire, so as to break up light reflection. Side windows can all be opened and all windows are provided with blackout curtains. A heating and ventilating unit is provided so that the truck can be used under all climatic conditions.

Standard equipment for the various models of the trucks includes a safety ladder for access to the rear of the unit and an electric light system having a blackout arrangement which automatically turns off the lights when the doors are opened. The equipment and tools furnished in the various loads are interchangeable to a great extent and are also to be found in common items for shop use.

Earlier models of Mobile Shop Trucks used a Model ST-5 Body, which lacked the collapsible feature. They were classified as Limited Standard by Ordnance Committee action in November 1942 and February 1943. They were:

Artillery Repair M9; Automotive Repair M8, Loads A and B; Electrical Repair M18; Instrument Repair M10, Loads A and B; Machine Shop Repair M16, Loads A, B, C, D, and F; Small Arms Repair M7; Spare Parts M14, Loads A and B; Tool and Bench M13; Welding Repair M12.

REFERENCES—TM 9-801; OCM 16017, 17890, 18115, 18392, 19230, 19392, 19722, 20249, 20513, 21555, 21876, 22195, 22213, 23486, 23999.

TYPICAL CHARACTERISTICS

Crew (for transport) 2
Physical Characteristics
  Weight (without load) . . . . 12,270 lb.
  Length . . . . 21 ft., 3 in.
  Width . . . . 8 ft.
  Height . . . . 9 ft., 9½ in.
  Ground clearance . . . . 10 in.
  Tread (center to center, rear) . . . . 67¾ in.
  Wheelbase . . . . 164 in.
  Tire equipment . . . . 7.50 x 20, 8-ply
Performance
  Maximum speed on level . . . . 45 m.p.h.
  Maximum grade ability 65%
  Angle of approach . . . . 54°
  Angle of departure . . . . 36°
  Turning radius . . . . 35 ft.
  Fuel capacity . . . . 40 gal.
  Cruising range (approx.) . . . . 240 miles
Battery, Voltage, total 6
Engine, Make and model . . . . G.M.C. 270
  Type . . . . In-line
  Number of cylinders 6
  Displacement . . . . 269.5 cu. in.
  Fuel (gasoline) . . . . .70 octane
Radiator, Type . . . . Fin and tube
  Capacity . . . . 19 qt.
Brakes, Type . . . . Hydraulic
  Other characteristics same as for 2½-ton, 6 x 6 (4DT) Truck.

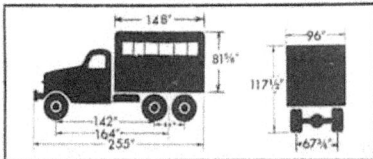

ARTILLERY REPAIR TRUCK M9A1, STANDARD, is intended for maintenance of various artillery items by the Heavy Maintenance Companies.

Each truck carries a workbench with drawers, as well as tackle blocks, rope, chain hoists, a 1-ton collapsible tripod, electrical cords and connections, portable electric drill, a vise, and allied equipment. Special artillery tools are added by the using organizations according to their assignments. The artillery mechanic's tool kits that are furnished include such items as chisels, drifts, files, hammers, punches, screwdrivers, sharpening stones, and wrenches.

Electric power is not available within this truck itself but is obtained from another unit within the company.

A similar set of equipment, known as "Ordnance Maintenance Set F," is furnished to Medium Maintenance Companies. This unit is carried in a standard 2½-ton, l.w.b. cargo truck.

REFERENCES—SNL G-140; OCM 15100, 18115, 19722, 21555, 21892.

AUTOMOTIVE REPAIR TRUCK M8A1, LOAD A, STANDARD, contains tools and equipment needed for general automotive repair work. It is used primarily by the Air Force for airfield vehicle maintenance.

The load consists of such items as general automotive tools, including a hydraulic portable press, drill sets, extractor sets, hammers, pliers, sledge, vises, test sets (both high and low tension and compression), pneumatic nut runner set, pneumatic chisel set, tube vulcanizer, socket wrench sets of various sizes, and automotive mechanic's tool kits with the individual mechanic's chisels, files, hammers, screwdrivers, etc.

Electric power for this unit is furnished from a combination air compressor and generator engine-driven set. The air compressor has a 60-cu.-ft. capacity. The generator can furnish 5-k.w., 110-v., alternating current.

REFERENCES—SNL G-139, Vol. 1; OCM 15100, 18115, 19722, 22362, 22569.

ELECTRICAL REPAIR TRUCK M18A2, STANDARD, is intended for use as a test and repair station for various automotive types of electrical equipment.

Its major items of equipment and its tools are an electrical test bench, magneto test stand, magnet charger, and other similar electrical test equipment. Repair tools and equipment include such items as

ARTILLERY REPAIR TRUCK M9A1, INTERIOR VIEW

INSTRUMENT REPAIR TRUCK M10A1, SHOWING INTERIOR

standard tools, a vise, hammers, chisels, pliers, wrenches, and automotive mechanic's tool kits.

A portable gasoline-engine-driven battery-charging generator is furnished, along with allied test and repair equipment. The unit has its own source of power in a 10-k.w., 115/230-v., a.c., engine-driven generator set.

REFERENCES—SNL G-149; OCM 18115; 18392, 19722, 23486, 23999.

INSTRUMENT BENCH TRUCK M23, STANDARD, is primarily intended to maintain and repair special fire-control equipment, such as antiaircraft directors and range and height finders. The truck body is ideally suited for this type of work in that the heater ventilation system is 97% efficient in removing all dust and foreign particles from the air.

Essential equipment consists of one bench across the front of the truck and two collapsible tables, which can be used within the truck or set up on the ground. In this manner, considerable space is made available for the setting up of the instruments to be worked upon. A special tripod is furnished for the Directors M5 and M6. Special harnesses are furnished for strapping down the directors should it be necessary to move a truck with the directors inside.

Small tools are furnished, as well as Instrument Repairmen's Kits. A set of outrigger jacks is provided to help stabilize the truck.

This unit has no power of its own, but connections are furnished so that it can obtain power from the generator normally used with the directors or from one of the other mobile shop trucks.

REFERENCES—SNL G-178; OCM 19230, 19392.

INSTRUMENT REPAIR TRUCK M10A1, LOAD A, STANDARD, is intended for repair and maintenance of optical instruments and equipment.

For major repair work, a standard 10-in. precision bench lathe, a ¼-in. precision drill press, a ½-ton arbor press, and an electric bench grinder are furnished.

Standard tools and equipment include surface plates with leveling screws, mandrel sets, drill sets, drifts, clamps, chisels, files, stud extractors, gages, hammers, pliers, reamers, rules, sharpening stones, threading sets (both U. S. standard and metric), vises, and wrenches.

Each truck is furnished with several Instrument Repairmen's Kits. These are equipped with forceps, gravers, hammers, watchmaker's loups, oilers, adjusting

pins, punches, scrapers, scribers, special wrenches, etc.

A Leatherworker's Kit is included for repair of the leather cases normally found with optical instruments. This kit has such items as awls, saddler's carriage, leather creaser, leather knives, needles, sailmaker's palm, punches, rivet set, and saddler's tools.

Special tools, fixtures, etc. are furnished to the using organizations for this truck in relation to the work assigned.

Outrigger jacks are provided to stabilize the truck for the delicate repair operations.

Normally this truck obtains its electric power from another truck or a commercial source. However, it has a 2-k.w., 115-v., a.c., engine-driven generator (portable) that can be set up on the ground so as not to cause vibrations within the truck.

REFERENCES—SNL G-141, Vol. 1; OCM 18115, 19722.

MACHINE SHOP TRUCK M16A1, M16A2, STANDARD. These units are intended for basic machine-shop work and are equipped for almost any general kind of machine-shop work encountered in the field. They are all equipped with an engine-driven, 10-k.w., 115/230-v., a.c., single-phase generator set.

MACHINE SHOP TRUCK M16A2, LEFT SIDE INTERIOR

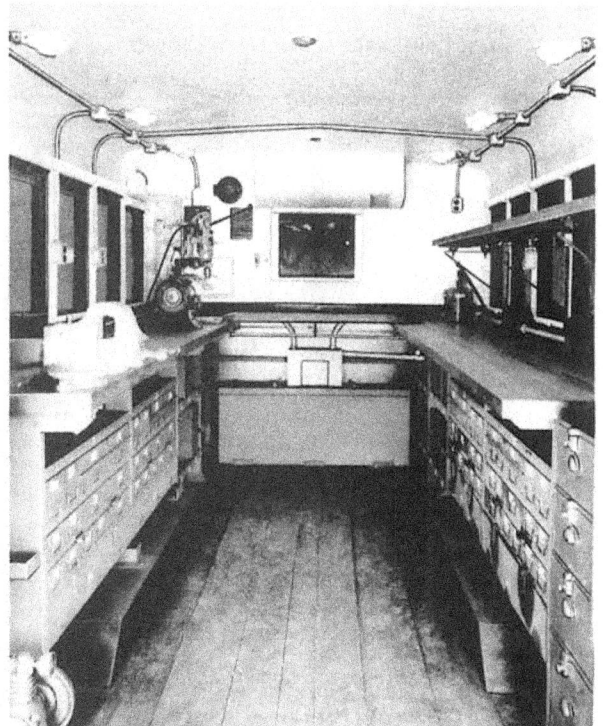

SIGNAL REPAIR TRUCK M30, INTERIOR VIEW

ORDNANCE MAINTENANCE TRUCKS, 2½-TON, 6 x 6 (4DT) (Continued)

M16A2, LOAD A—This unit is built around a standard 10-in. bench lathe with complete set of tools and accessories, electric bench grinder, a 7-in. bench shaper, a 10-ton hydraulic press, a milling head attachment for the lathe, and a special ½-in. drill press that is very much like a radial drill. A complete set of hand tools, gages, calipers, extractors, drill sets, threading sets (U. S. standard as well as metric), etc., are furnished to complement the basic machine tools.

M16A1, LOAD B—This is basically a heavy lathe truck. Load B is equipped with a 14–21-in. gap lathe, as well as a 1¼-in. portable electric drill with stand and a drill grinder. A few hand tools and drill sets are furnished with this load to supplement the Load A and to make the lathe as useful as possible.

M16A1, LOAD B1—This unit is much the same as the Load B, except that it has a 16-in.-swing lathe and a milling head attachment.

M16A1, LOAD B2—This unit is essentially the same as the Load B, except that it has an extension-gap lathe of 14–29-in. swing capacity. The gap can be extended to 19 inches.

REFERENCES—SNL G-146, Vols. 1 and 2; OCM 15053, 16017, 18115, 19722, 22195, 22536, 23486, 23999.

SIGNAL CORPS GENERAL REPAIR TRUCK M31, STANDARD. This unit is a redesignation of the former Small Arms Repair Truck M7 (Signal Corps). It is used by the Signal Corps for various repair functions of radio, wireless, etc. Its basic equipment includes two long benches, a bench grinder, a portable drill, drill sets, extension cords, spare parts boxes, and other similar equipment.

It obtains its power from an outside source.

REFERENCES—SNL G-138, Vol. 2; OCM 15100, 16017, 18115, 19722, 23486, 23999.

SIGNAL CORPS REPAIR TRUCK M30, STANDARD. This unit is equipped with a basic set of equipment for issuance to the Signal Corps for their use in repairing various radio, wire, and radar equipment. It is essentially the same as the Signal Corps General Repair Truck M31, except that it has additional equipment, such as a shockproof shelf for carrying the delicate test equipment, a small air compressor for cleaning purposes, a 12-volt battery, a battery charger, and special 6-, 12-, and 24-volt d.c. circuit. Many additional convenience outlets are furnished in order to permit testing and repairing of numerous pieces of equipment at the same time.

The unit obtains its electric power from an outside source.

REFERENCES—SNL G-138, Vol. 2; OCM 15100, 16017, 18115, 19722, 23486, 23999.

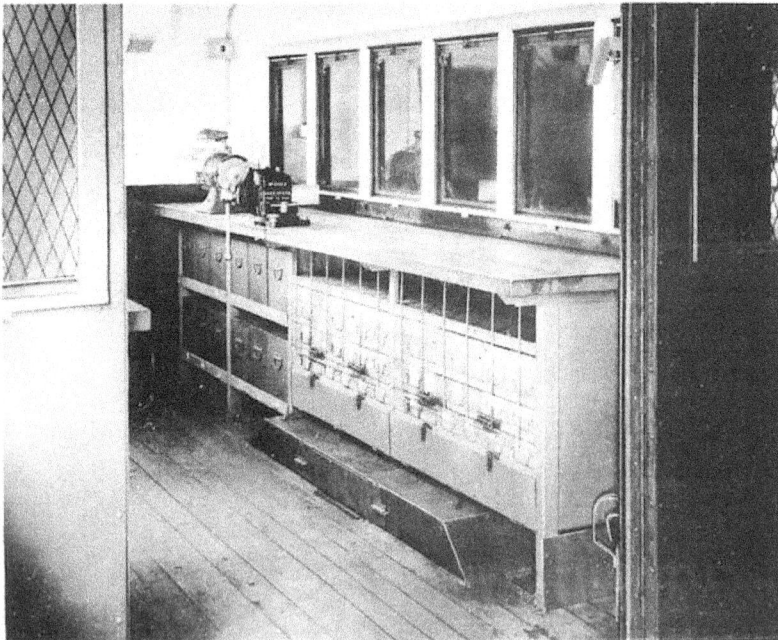

SMALL ARMS REPAIR TRUCK M7A2, SHOWING RIGHT SIDE INTERIOR

SMALL ARMS REPAIR TRUCK M7A2, STANDARD, is intended for inspection, maintenance, and repair of small arms.

The benches furnished provide space for the tools and the armorer's tool kits, and also for kits carrying spare parts for the individual weapons. Common tools, such as a ⅜-in. portable electric drill with stand, electric bench grinder, vises, drill sets, hack saws, hammers, reamers, cleaning rods, gasoline torches, trigger weights, are supplied. The armorer's tool kits are equipped with common hand tools and also special tools needed in small-arms repair work, such as cartridge extractors and oil stones.

A portable rifle rack is furnished for storing rifles under examination or repair. A portable table is also furnished to give additional work space outside the vehicle.

Electric power normally is furnished from one of the other mobile shop trucks, but the truck can get its own power from a portable, gasoline-engine-driven generator of 2-k.w. capacity.

REFERENCES—SNL G-138, Vol. 1; OCM 15100, 16017, 18115, 19722, 23486, 23999.

TIRE REPAIR TRUCKS M32, STANDARD. This unit consists of two trucks, Load A and Load B, and two 1-Ton, 2-Wheel, Tire Repair Trailers M25, Load A and Load B. The complete unit is used for sectional tire repair and tube work.

LOAD A—This unit carries all of the electric mold equipment, including an electric steam generator, some of the air bags, molds, matrices, and repair equipment.

LOAD B—This unit is primarily an inspection and work unit. Its equipment consists of a bench with tire mandrel and electrically driven air compressor, tire spreaders of three different sizes and types, tube inspection tank, some matrices, bead plates, air bags, and repair supplies and equipment.

TRAILER, LOAD A—The trailer loads are carried in the standard 1-ton cargo trailers. This load consists only of a 25-k.w., 115/230-v., a.c., 3-phase, engine-driven generator set. It furnishes all power needed for the complete unit.

TRAILER, LOAD B—This trailer carries additional equipment and accessories needed for the operation of the complete unit. Some of these items are buffing machines, additional matrices, bead plates, air bags, extra gasoline and water cans, supplies, and company equipment.

REFERENCES — OCM 18803, 23041, 23282, 24302.

5 PASSENGER LIGHT SEDANS (4x2)

Passenger cars for Army use are purchased from the regular stocks of the manufacturers, and differ from privately owned passenger cars of the same manufacturers principally in the fact that they are painted with U. S. Army standard dull-finish paint and equipped with blackout light equipment. This is done to reduce reflection of light to the minimum practicable.

Military characteristics for light sedans are described in MCM 17. Military equipment includes sturdy bumpers at the front and rear, and approved combat-zone safety lighting. All wheels are interchangeable at the hub. One spare wheel and tire assembly is mounted in the luggage compartment. Suitable motor vehicle tool equipment is provided. Equipment includes an oil-bath type air-cleaner, an oil filter with a minimum efficiency life of 120 hours and shock absorbers on both axles.

Military service requirements call for a brake mechanism so designed as to per-

CHEVROLET, 5 PASSENGER, LIGHT SEDAN

FORD, 5 PASSENGER, LIGHT SEDAN

CHEVROLET

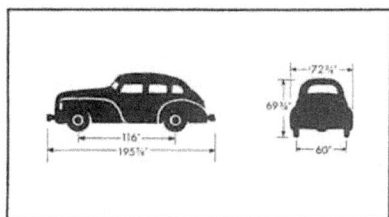

FORD

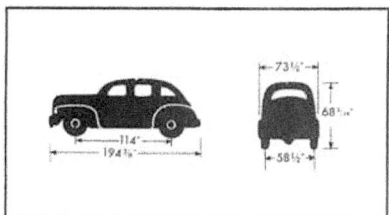

PLYMOUTH

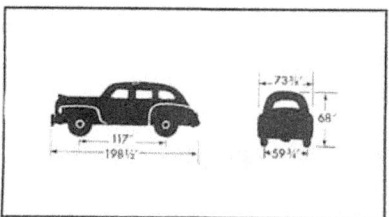

PLYMOUTH, 5 PASSENGER, LIGHT SEDAN

5 PASSENGER LIGHT SEDANS (4X2) (Continued)

mit ready external adjustment. Headlights are "sealed beam" construction, properly positioned. Ignition is suppressed to prevent radio interference, but vehicles are not otherwise equipped for radio transmitter installation.

Body is the manufacturer's standard commercial four-door, seven-window sedan.

The cars are required to be able to operate over unimproved roads, trails and open, rolling and hilly cross country, and must be able to attain a speed not less than 50 m.p.h. on smooth concrete highway.

Cars acceptable under this classification are: Chevrolet, 1,500 and 2,000 series, 1942; Ford, Model 2 GA–73B, 1942; and Plymouth, Model P–11, 1941.

REFERENCES—OCM 19107; MCM 17.

CHARACTERISTICS, LIGHT SEDAN

Physical Characteristics	CHEVROLET	FORD	PLYMOUTH
Weight (gross)	4,075 lb.	4,100 lb.	3,190 lb.
Length	16 ft., 3⅞ ins.	16 ft., 2⅜ ins.	16 ft., 6½ ins.
Width	6 ft., ¾ in.	6 ft., 1½ ins.	6 ft., 1⅜ ins.
Height	5 ft., 9⅜ ins.	5 ft., 8³⁄₁₆ ins.	5 ft., 8 ins.
Ground clearance	8½ ins.	7⅝ ins.	7⅛ ins.
Wheelbase	116 ins.	114 ins.	117 ins.
Tread (center to center)	60 ins.	58½ ins.	59¾ ins.
Tire equipment	6.00x16, 6 ply, Highway tread	6.00x16, 6 ply, Highway tread	6.00x16, 6 ply, Highway tread
Performance			
Maximum speed on level	80 m.p.h.	80 m.p.h.	70 m.p.h.
Maximum grade ability	38.3%	35%	30%
Fording depth	16½ ins.	18 ins.	18 ins.
Fuel capacity	16 gals.	17 gals.	17 gals.
Cruising range	224 miles	240 miles	238 miles
Payload	800 lb.	800 lb.	800 lb.
Angle of approach	25°	21°	28.5°
Angle of departure	15°	23°	15.5°
Turning radius	20½ ft.	21 ft.	20½ ft.
Engine, Make and Model	Chevrolet 2AA or BA	Ford, 2GA	Plymouth
Type	In line	In line	In line
No. of cylinders	6	6	6
Cycle	4	4	4
Displacement	216.5 cu. ins.	226 cu. ins.	201.3 cu. ins.
Fuel (gasoline)	70 octane	70 octane	70 octane
Cooling System, Type	Liquid	Liquid	Liquid
Capacity	15 qts.	17½ qts.	14 qts.
Battery, Voltage	6	6	6
Brakes, Type	Hydraulic	Hydraulic	Hydraulic

5 PASSENGER MEDIUM SEDAN (4x2)

This car, which is larger and roomier than the light sedans, and which has a higher speed and greater cruising range, is provided for the transportation of staff officers.

Military characteristics, as given in MCM 18, provide for a minimum weight of 4,000 pounds, and for a vehicle with not less than 8 cylinders. Military equipment and military service requirements are the same as for the light sedans.

The car selected under this classification is the Packard, Model 2001, 1942. The manufacturer's standard commercial four-door, seven-window sedan is used. The vehicle is painted with U. S. Army standard dull-finish paint.

The car is equipped with an overdrive feature, which permits greater speed and fuel economy. Normal maximum speed is 90 m.p.h. At 40 m.p.h., the vehicle will average about 18.4 miles per gallon, with a cruising range of approximately 312 miles. With the overdrive, maximum speed may be increased to 95 m.p.h. At 40 m.p.h., mileage is increased to 20.9 miles per gallon, with a cruising range of approximately 355 miles.

REFERENCES—OCM 19107; MCM 18.

PACKARD, 5 PASSENGER, MEDIUM SEDAN

CHARACTERISTICS, MEDIUM SEDAN, PACKARD

Physical Characteristics
Weight (gross)	4,400 lb.
Length	17 ft., 4½ ins.
Width	6 ft., 4⅛ ins.
Height	5 ft., 3½ ins.
Ground clearance	6¹¹⁄₁₆ ins.
Wheelbase	120 ins.
Tread (center to center)	60½ ins.
Tire equipment	6.50x15, 4 ply, Highway tread

Performance
Top speed, without overdrive	90 m.p.h.
with overdrive	95 m.p.h.
Maximum grade ability	25%
Fording depth	18¾ ins.
Fuel capacity	17 gals.
Cruising range, with overdrive	355 miles*
without overdrive	312 miles*
Payload	800 lb.
Angle of approach	15°
Angle of departure	16°
Turning radius	21 ft.

*At 40 m.p.h.

Engine, Make and Model . . . . . . Packard, 2001
Type	In line
No. of cylinders	8
Cycle	4
Displacement	282 cu. ins.
Fuel (gasoline)	70 octane
Cooling System	Liquid
Capacity	17 qts.
Battery, Voltage	9
Brakes, Type	Hydraulic

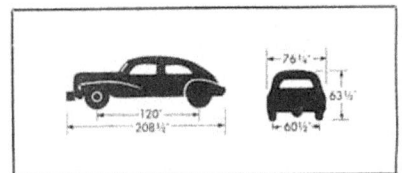

CHAIN DRIVE SOLO MOTORCYCLE—STANDARD
EXTRA LIGHT SOLO MOTORCYCLE M1—STANDARD

TYPICAL CHARACTERISTICS

Physical Characteristics	Solo	Extra Light Solo
Weight (with gas, oil and accessories)	576 lb.	241 lb.
Length	7 ft., 4 in.	6 ft., 5½ in.
Width	3 ft., ¼ in.	2 ft., 4 in.
Height	3 ft., 5 in.	3 ft., ¼ in.
Ground clearance (amidships)	4 in.	5½ in.
Wheelbase	59½ in.	50 in.
Tire equipment	4.00x18, 4-ply	3.00x18, 4-ply
Desert	5.50x16, 4-ply	

Performance		
Maximum allowable speed	65 m.p.h.	45 m.p.h.
Maximum grade ability	30%	25%
Fording depth	12 in.	12 in.
Turning diameter	15 ft.	10 ft., 8 in.
Fuel capacity	3⅜ gal.	2½ gal.
Cruising range (approx.)	125 miles	250 miles

Engine, Make and model	Harley-Davidson, WLA	Indian, Model 144
Type	L-head, V, A.C.	L-head, A.C.
No. of cylinders	2	1
Cycle	4	4
Displacement	45.12 cu. in.	13.50 cu. in.
Bore and stroke	2¾x3 13⁄16 in.	2½x2¾ in.
Gross horsepower	23	6.2 at 4,700 r.p.m.
Max. torque	28 lb.-ft. at 3,000 r.p.m.	8.1 lb.-ft. at 3,600 r.p.m.

Sprockets, No. of teeth		
Engine	30	15
Clutch	59	38
Countershaft	17	17
Rear wheel	41	43

Transmission, Type	Constant mesh	Constant mesh
Gear ratios		
First speed	11.71:1	18.2:1
Second speed	7.45:1	10.4:1
Third Speed	4.74:1	6.4:1

CHAIN DRIVE SOLO MOTORCYCLE, SUPPLIED TO ALL ARMS AND SERVICES

EXTRA LIGHT SOLO MOTORCYCLE M1, DEVELOPED FOR AIRBORNE USE

CHAIN DRIVE SOLO MOTORCYCLE—STANDARD—Except for special military equipment, the standard solo motorcycle is similar to the familiar 2-cylinder motorcycles used by police and civilians. It is used by the Army for reconnaissance, messenger service, and police operations, and can be supplied to all arms and services. In addition to conventional equipment, it has a box for submachine gun ammunition, a bracket for carrying a submachine gun, and combat zone safety lighting.

For special operations, 5.50x16 desert tires can be provided in place of the standard 4.00x18 tires, in which case the rear wheel is fitted with a beadlock to prevent creeping of the tire at the low inflation needed on soft terrain.

The manufacturer is the Harley-Davidson Motor Co. A somewhat similar machine made by the Indian Motorcycle Co. also meets the specifications for the Chain Drive Solo Motorcycle.

REFERENCES—TM 9-879, MC 9c; OCM 19107, 20341, 21016, 21221, 21809, 22019.

EXTRA LIGHT SOLO MOTORCYCLE M1—STANDARD—This motorcycle was developed especially for airborne troops, but it can be used by other services requiring lightweight motorcycle equipment. It was standardized in December 1944.

Although its weight is only 241 lb., less than half that of the standard heavy motorcycle, tests have shown that it is a

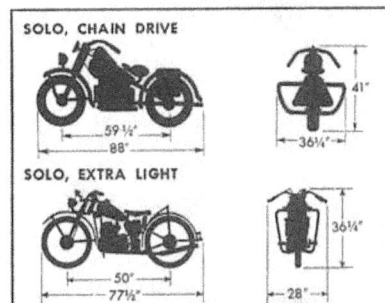

rugged and versatile vehicle. It can operate successfully off the road, in mud or sand, or in water a foot deep. In tests, its operation was not affected when it was dropped 800 feet by parachute from an airplane traveling at a ground speed of 100 m.p.h. Because the engine has magneto ignition, the generator, battery, and the lights can be removed. The weight can thus be reduced to 224 lb.

The motorcycle is of clean design and free of projections and snares that might entange parachute or rigging. It has a non-spillable, 10-ampere-hour storage battery, a non-spillable, oil-bath air cleaner, and rings for attaching a parachute and a paracrate into which the wheels fit for protection when the motorcycle is dropped by parachute. There is a pintle hook at the rear for towing a lightweight utility cart.

The machine is manufactured by the Indian Motorcycle Co.

REFERENCES — OCM 24145, 24276, 25611, 26057.

MEN'S AND WOMEN'S BICYCLES—STANDARD

MEN'S BICYCLE, DESIGNED FOR ALL ARMS AND SERVICES

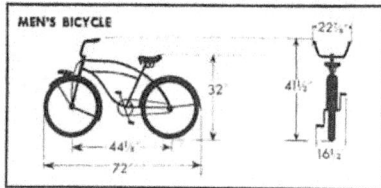

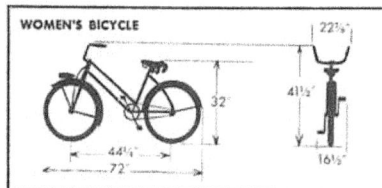

WOMEN'S BICYCLE, DESIGNED FOR THE WOMEN'S ARMY CORPS

MEN'S BICYCLES, although previously in Army use for administrative purposes, were not standardized until October 1942. The standard bicycle is designed for all arms and services.

The machine has a men's type of frame and leather seat, and a sprocket ratio of 26 to 10. Tires are size 2⅛x26, 2-ply, balloon, with heavy duty inner tubes, mounted on drop-center rims that are integral with the wheel.

Equipment includes a tool bag and tools, tire pump, bell, an electric headlight operated by dry cells, a reflector tail light, coaster brake, front and rear fenders, chain guard, and kick stand. The finish is non-reflecting paint.

The men's bicycles are made by the Huffman Manufacturing Co. and the Westfield Manufacturing Co.

REFERENCES—MCM 32; OCM 18948, 19039, 20395, 20734.

WOMEN'S BICYCLES, developed at the request of the Women's Army Corps after that organization had been set up, were standardized in February 1943.

The women's bicycle has the typical open frame and a lower sprocket ratio than the men's. Except for the frame, chain, front sprocket, and seat, all parts for both men's and women's bicycles are interchangeable, and the equipment and finish are the same.

Women's bicycles are also made by the Huffman Manufacturing Co. and the Westfield Manufacturing Co.

REFERENCES—MCM 32; OCM 19423, 19548, 19770, 20395, 20734.

TYPICAL CHARACTERISTICS

Physical Characteristics

Weight (net)	55 lb.
Length, overall	6 ft.
Width, over handle bars	1 ft., 10⅞ in.
Over pedals	1 ft., 4½ in.
Height, top of handle bars	3 ft., 5½ in.
Less handle bars	2 ft., 8 in.
Wheelbase	44¼ in.
Tire equipment	2⅛x26, 2-ply, balloon
Sprocket ratio	
Men's	26:10 (for 1-in. pitch chain)
Women's	22:10 (for 1-in. pitch chain)

Performance

Payload	200 lb.

MOTOR SCOOTERS AND MOTOR-DRIVEN BICYCLES

STANDARD 3-WHEEL MOTOR SCOOTER WITH SIDE CAR

2-WHEEL MOTOR SCOOTER PROCURED FOR AIRBORNE USE

3-WHEEL MOTOR SCOOTER WITH SIDE CAR—STANDARD
—Standardized in November, 1943, this vehicle is used principally for messenger use. It has a payload of 375 pounds.

Power is supplied by a one-cylinder, four-cycle gasoline engine of 4 hp. A kick starter and an A.C. type generator are provided. A spring type, imitation leather, driver's seat; a headlight and tail light, tools, a gasoline filter, and an air cleaner are furnished.

The vehicle is manufactured by the Cushman Motor Works.

REFERENCES—MCM 109; OCM 20313, 21805, 21517, 21673, 22018.

2-WHEEL AIRBORNE MOTOR SCOOTER—STANDARD—
This vehicle was standardized in March, 1944.

It has two speeds, with a maximum speed of approximately 40 m.p.h. Parachute-attaching rings are mounted at two balanced points. A small pintle hook is mounted on the rear. Payload is 250 pounds, including the driver.

Military equipment includes a motorcycle type leather driver's seat, tools, a gasoline filter, and an air cleaner.

The vehicle is manufactured by the Cushman Motor Works.

REFERENCES—MCM 41; OCM 21934, 22139, 23182.

MOTOR-DRIVEN BICYCLE—Limited procurement of these vehicles, was authorized in April, 1943.

Power is carried to the rear wheel through two V-belts. High and low ratio are obtained by actuating a foot lever, which, in turn, tightens, or loosens the V-belt in the pulley, causing the

MOTOR-DRIVEN BICYCLE PROCURED FOR AIRBORNE USE

belts to move higher or lower in their pulleys. The machine is started by pushing. It has a maximum speed of 30 m.p.h.

Fuel is fed by gravity to a carburetor, and from there through a rotary valve carrying mixed oil and gasoline into the crankcase.

Equipment includes a spring type leather driver's saddle; a headlight, combat zone lighting, a tool bag and tools, a gasoline filter and an air cleaner, front and rear fenders, a luggage carrier, a jiffy stand, and a speedometer.

The vehicles are manufactured by the Simplex Mfg. Co.

REFERENCES—MCM 35; OCM 20250, 21421, 21674, 21893.

TYPICAL CHARACTERISTICS

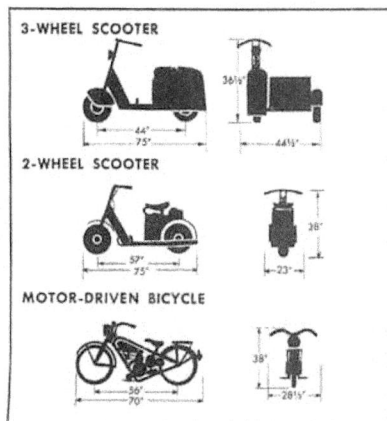

Physical Characteristics	3-Wheel Scooter	2-Wheel Scooter	Motor-Driven Bicycle
Weight (gross)	735 lb.	499 lb.	365 lb.
Length	6 ft., 3 ins.	6 ft., 3 ins.	5 ft., 10 ins.
Width	3 ft., 8½ ins.	1 ft., 11 ins.	2 ft., 4½ ins.
Height	3 ft., ½ in.	3 ft., 2 ins.	3 ft., 2 ins.
Ground clearance	4 ins.	6¾ ins.	5½ ins.
Wheelbase	44 ins.	57 ins.	56 ins.
Tire equipment	4.00 x 8, 4 ply	6.00 x 6, 4 ply	2.25 x 26, 2 ply
Performance			
Maximum speed	25 m.p.h.	40 m.p.h.	30 m.p.h.
Maximum grade ability	5%	30%	15%
Fording depth	10 ins.	12 ins.	12 ins.
Fuel capacity	1¼ gals.	2 gals.	2½ gals.
Cruising range	50 miles	100 miles	
Payload (incl. driver)	375 lb.	250 lb.	200 lb.
Engine			
Make and Model	Cushman	Cushman	Servi-Cycle
No. of cylinders	1	1	1
Cycle	4	4	2
Fuel (gasoline)	70 octane	70 octane	70 octane
Brake hp.	4 at 3,500 r.p.m.	4 at 3,500 r.p.m.	1.6 at 2,000 r.p.m.

¼-TON, 4X4, TRUCK—STANDARD

This vehicle, popularly called the "jeep," is one of the outstanding automotive developments of this war. Developed by the Quartermaster Corps, it and other motor transport vehicles were transferred to the Ordnance Department in August, 1942.

It has been found useful in a variety of ways, and despite its light weight has been able to function under rigorous conditions. Operated by a crew of two, it has a space for equipment or additional personnel.

The truck is capable of operation over unimproved roads, trails, and open, rolling, and hilly cross country. It will climb a 60% grade, and will operate at a speed of 65 m.p.h. on level highways. It can ford a stream 18 inches deep, while fully equipped and loaded. It has a cruising range of approximately 300 miles on 15 gallons of gasoline.

Towing a 37 mm antitank gun, it will climb a 7% grade, and can achieve a speed of 20 m.p.h. on a level highway.

Power is supplied by a four-cylinder L head gasoline engine equipped with a counter-balanced crankshaft. The clutch is a single-plate, dry-disk type. The transmission is of the three-speed, syncromesh type, which, through a transfer case, provides six speeds forward and two reverse.

The vehicle has internal-expanding, hydraulic four-wheel brakes and a mechanical handbrake.

A base plate is provided for a pedestal mount for a cal. .30 or a cal. .50 machine gun. The infantry uses the Cal. .30 Machine Gun Mount, M48, on the dash, and other arms use the Pedestal Truck Mount, M31.

Provision is made for a lighting socket connection for a trailer, and for a radio outlet. The windshield may be folded down over the hood when desired. A removable canvas top is provided.

Desert equipment includes a radiator surge tank, a power-driven air compressor, a low-pressure tire gage, a 3-inch copper fin radiator, and a fuel filter, relocated to minimize vapor lock.

A tandem hitch makes it possible to use two of these vehicles for emergency towing of a 155 mm howitzer. When used in this way, speed is limited to 30 m.p.h. on level highway, and 10 m.p.h. down hill.

The vehicles are produced, to identical specifications, by the Willys-Overland Motors, Inc., and the Ford Motor Co.

REFERENCES—MCM 8e; TM 10–1207, 10–1349; OCM 19107, 19549, 21179, 21221, 21590, 21788.

THE POPULAR "JEEP" TRANSPORTS PERSONNEL AND CARGO; TOWS GUNS OR ¼-TON TRAILER

TYPICAL CHARACTERISTICS

Crew 2
Physical Characteristics
  Weight (gross) . . . . 3,253 lb.
  Length . . . . 11 ft., ¼ in.
  Width . . . . 5 ft., 2 ins.
  Height—top of cowl . . . . 3 ft., 4 ins.
    top of steering wheel . . . . . . 4 ft., 4 ins.
    with top up . . . . 5 ft., 9¾ ins.
  Ground clearance . . . . 8¾ ins.
  Wheelbase . . . . 80 ins.
  Tread (center to center of tires) . . . . . 49 ins.
  Ground pressure . . . . 20.8 lb./sq. in.
  Tire equipment 6.00x16, 6 ply (mud and snow)
Armament
  Provision for one cal. .30 or cal. .50 machine gun
Performance
  Maximum speed on level . . . . 65 m.p.h.
    with towed load . . . . 20 m.p.h.
  Maximum grade ability 60%
    with towed load 45%
  Angle of approach . . . . 45°
  Angle of departure . . . . 35°
  Fording depth . . . . 18 ins.
  Fuel capacity . . . . 15 gals.
  Cruising range (approx.) . . . . 300 miles
    with towed load . . . . 260 miles
  Normal towed load (37 mm gun carriage
    or ¼-ton, 2-wheel, cargo trailer) . . . 1,000 lb.
  Payload (including driver and assistant) . 800 lb.
  Turning radius . . . . 17½ ft.
Communication . . . . Radio outlet
Battery, Voltage 6-12
Engine, Type . . . . "L" head
  No. of cylinders 4

Cycle 4
Fuel (gasoline) . . . . 68 octane
Bore and stroke . . . . 3⅛ x 4⅜ ins.
Displacement . . . . 134.2 cu. ins.
Compression ratio 6.48:1
Net h.p. . . . . 54 at 4,000 r.p.m.
Max. torque . . . . . 105 lb.-ft. at 2,000 r.p.m.
Crankshaft rotation . . . . C'Clockwise
  Length . . . . 27 ins.
  Width . . . . 22½ ins.
  Height . . . . 26¾ ins.
Ignition . . . . Battery
Weight . . . . 355 lb.

Master Clutch, Type . . . . Dry, single plate
Radiator, Type . . . . Fin and tube
  Capacity of system . . . . 11 qts.
Transmission, Gear ratios
  First speed 2.67:1
  Second speed 1.56:1
  Third speed 1.00:1
  Reverse 3.55:1
Transfer case, Gear ratio, Low 1.97:1
  High 1.00:1
Differential, Gear ratio 4.88:1
  Type of drive . . . . Hypoid bevel
Steering ratio 14, 12, 14:1
Suspension, Type . . . . Semi-elliptic
  Wheel construction . . . . Divided
Brakes, Type . . . . Internal Hydraulic
Brakes, Parking, Type . . . . External Contracting
Front Axle, Type . . . . Full floating
Rear Axle, Gear ratio 4.88:1

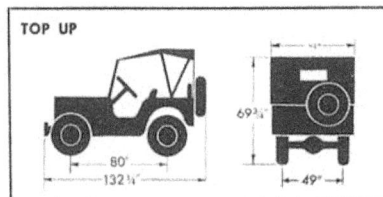

TOP UP

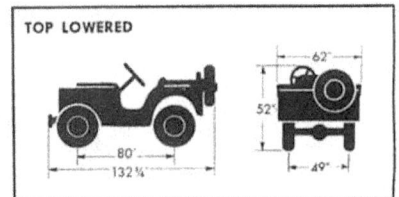

TOP LOWERED

¼-TON AMPHIBIAN TRUCK—STANDARD

This is a modification of the ¼-Ton, 4 x 4 Truck, designed for use on water as well as on land. It was standardized in February, 1943.

Power plant, transmission and many other components are the same as on the non-amphibious truck. The body is in the form of a waterproof hull, with special equipment required for operation on water.

Military characteristics, as given in MCM 26, provide for a vehicle with a payload of 800 pounds and a towing capacity of 1,000 pounds.

The vehicle has a grade ability of 45% without towed load, in transmission lowest forward gear and transfer case low range. It is capable of operation over unimproved roads, trails, and open, rolling and hilly cross country, and on water.

Maximum speed on land is 55 miles per hour, and on water is 5½ miles per hour.

Tires are 6.00 x 16, 6 ply, mud and snow tread, with heavy-duty type inner tubes. Wheels are standard divided type, single front and rear. One spare wheel and tire assembly is furnished.

Military equipment includes a towing eye at the front, a brush guard and a rear pintle. Sealed beam type headlights are supplemented by combat-zone safety lighting. A trailer lighting socket and a radio terminal box are provided.

A power take-off aperture at the rear of the transfer case is designed to supply power with the vehicle moving or at a standstill. A folding windshield is provided. An engine-operated power capstan of 3,500 pounds direct pull is installed at the bow centerline.

The vehicle has a marine rudder and controls, and a propeller. Five chocks and four lifting eyes are provided. Five life preservers are carried.

A 12 volt electrical system for radio is used. The vehicle will tow a ¼-Ton Trailer, which also will float with its rated payload.

The truck is manufactured by the Ford Motor Car Co.

REFERENCES—MCM 26; OCM 19107, 19487, 19771, 20771, 21010.

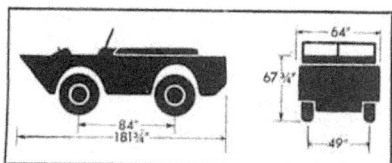

THE ¼-TON, 4 x 4, AMPHIBIAN TRUCK, TRAVELS ON LAND AT 55 M.P.H.

WATERPROOF HULL, PROPELLER AND RUDDER PERMIT TRAVEL IN WATER

TYPICAL CHARACTERISTICS

Crew 4

Physical Characteristics

Weight (gross)	4,300 lb.
Length	15 ft., 1¾ ins.
Width	5 ft., 4 ins.
Height, w/o top	5 ft., 7¾ ins.
Height of pintle	28¼ ins.
Ground clearance	8 ins.
Freeboard, loaded—front	17 ins.
—rear	9½ ins.
Draft, loaded, to underside of tires	33½ ins.
Ground clearance	8 ins.
Tread (center to center)	49 ins.
Wheelbase	84 ins.
Tire equipment 6.00 x 16, 6 ply (mud and snow)	

Performance

Maximum speed on land	55 m.p.h.
—with towed load	35 m.p.h.
Maximum speed in water	5½ m.p.h.
Maximum grade ability	45%
Angle of approach	39°
Angle of departure	37°
Turning radius	18 ft.
Fuel capacity	15 gals.
Cruising range—land	250 miles
—with towed load	200 miles
—in water	35 miles

Normal towed load	1,000 lb.
Payload (including personnel)	800 lb.
Battery, Voltage, total	12
Fire Protection, Fire Extinguisher	1
Life Preservers	5
Engine, Type	L head
No. of cylinders	4
Cycle	4
Bore and Stroke	3⅛ x 4⅜ ins.
Fuel (gasoline)	68 octane
Displacement	134.2 cu. ins.
Weight	355 lb.
Compression	111 at 185 r.p.m.
Net hp.	54 at 4,000 r.p.m.
Max. torque	105 lb.-ft. at 2,000 r.p.m.
Crankshaft rotation	C'Clockwise
Transmission, Gear ratios	
First speed	2.675:1
Second speed	1.564:1
Third speed	1.00:1
Reverse	3.55:1
Transfer Case, Gear ratios	1.97:1; 1.00:1
Front Axle, Type	Full floating
Rear Axle, Gear ratio	4.88:1
Brakes, Type	Hydraulic
Brakes, Parking, Type	External Contracting

¾-TON, 4 x 4, TRUCKS AND AMBULANCE—STANDARD

Standard vehicles in the ¾-ton, 4 x 4, class are the Weapons Carrier and Telephone Installation Trucks, and the Ambulance. The ¾-ton Carryall Truck and ¾-ton Command and Reconnaissance Truck are Limited Standard.

The vehicles have top governed speeds of 54 miles per hour. They are capable of operation over unimproved roads, trails and open, rolling and hilly cross country with a towed load. Wheels are equipped with 9.00 x 16, 8-ply tires.

The engine is of the liquid-cooled, 6-cylinder, L-head type, and clutch is of the single dry-plate type. Power is transmitted from the four-speed selective gear transmission through a short propeller shaft to the transfer case, and thence to both front and rear axles. The vehicles may be driven with all four wheels, or with the rear wheels only.

A power take-off is provided on vehicles equipped with a winch.

Service brakes are hydraulic, internal-expanding, and handbrakes are mechanical, external-contracting. Wheel and tire assemblies are interchangeable, front and rear.

Desert equipment includes a radiator surge tank of at least four quart capacity; a power driven air compressor with sufficient hose to inflate all tires; a radiator with shroud ring for those vehicles not already equipped; and a low pressure tire gage.

Pioneer tools, two five-gallon liquid containers and a fire extinguisher are furnished with each truck.

These vehicles are manufactured by the Fargo Motor Corporation.

REFERENCES—MCM12B; OCM 18758, 18986, 19060, 19107, 20486, 20735, 21011, 21221, 21853, 22504, 23100; TM 9-808.

GENERAL CHARACTERISTICS

Performance

Maximum speed on level	54 m.p.h.
Maximum grade ability—Weapons Carrier and Telephone	60%
—Ambulance	55%
—with towed load—Weapons Carrier and Telephone	50%
—Ambulance	48%
Fording depth (slowest forward speed)	34 ins.
Angle of approach, without winch	53°
—with winch	36½°
Angle of departure—Weapons Carrier	31°
—Telephone	29°
—Ambulance	24°
Turning radius—Weapons Carrier and Ambulance	22 ft.
—Telephone	27 ft.
Fuel capacity	30 gals.
Cruising range	240 miles
—with towed load	210 miles
Normal towed load	1,000 lb.
Payload (including personnel)—Weapons Carrier and Ambulance	1,800 lb.
—Telephone	1,300 lb.
Winch capacity	5,000 lb.

Battery, Voltage, total—Weapons Carrier . . 12
—Telephone and Ambulance 6

Engine, Make and Model . . . . . Dodge T-214
Type . . . . In line, liquid cooled

No. of cylinders	6
Cycle	4
Fuel (gasoline)	70 octane
Bore and stroke	3¼ x 4⅝ ins.
Displacement	230.2 cu. ins.
Compression, ratio	6.7:1
Net hp.	76 at 3,200 r.p.m.
Max. torque	176 lb.-ft. at 1,000 r.p.m.
Crankshaft rotation	C'Clockwise
Length	37½ ins.
Width	24 ins.
Height	30 ins.
Weight, dry	603 lb.

Transmission, Gear ratios

First speed	6.40:1
Second speed	3.09:1
Third speed	1.69:1
Fourth speed	1.00:1
Reverse	7.82:1

Transfer Case, Gear ratio	1.00:1
Suspension, Type	Semi-elliptic
Master Clutch, Type	Single dry plate
Radiator, Type	Fin and tube
Capacity of system	17 qts.
Brakes, Type	Internal hydraulic
Brakes, Parking, Type	External contracting
Front Axle, Type	Full floating
Rear Axle, Gear ratio	5.83:1

¾-TON, 4 x 4, COMMAND AND RECONNAISSANCE TRUCK—This vehicle, used to provide transportation for staff officers in the field, is classified Limited Standard. The body is the U. S. Army standard phaeton type with folding windshield. The vehicle is adapted for radio installation, including a 12-volt electrical system and U. S. Army standard 55-ampere output generator. Provisions are made for an antenna mount. The truck is available with or without a winch.

¾-TON, 4 x 4, WEAPONS CARRIER TRUCK—This truck, designed for all arms and services, is used to transport weapons, tools and equipment. The body is of the commercial pickup type, with a removable canvas top mounted on three bows. Troop seats are provided within the body. Inside body dimensions are 72 x 48¼ inches. In lieu of a driver's cab, the vehicle has a seat box on which are mounted two bucket seats. A removable canvas top and a folding windshield are provided. The truck is available with or without a winch. It has a 12-volt electrical system.

Physical Characteristics

Weight—without winch	7,050 lb.
—with winch	7,350 lb.
Length—without winch	13 ft., 10⅞ ins.
—with winch	14 ft., 8½ ins.
Width	6 ft., 10¾ ins.
Height	6 ft., 9⅞ ins.
—with top lowered	5 ft., 2¼ ins.
Ground clearance	10⅝ ins.
Tread (center to center, rear)	64¾ ins.
Wheelbase	98 ins.
Ground pressure	33.8 lb./sq. in.
Ground contact	208 sq. ins.
Tire equipment (mud and snow type)	9.00 x 16, 8 ply

¾-TON, 4 x 4, WEAPONS CARRIER TRUCK, WITH WINCH, SHOWING TOP RAISED

¾-TON, 4 x 4, TRUCKS AND AMBULANCE (Continued)

¾-TON, 4 x 4, TELEPHONE INSTAL-LATION AND MAINTENANCE TRUCK, K-50—This vehicle, designed for the Signal Corps, has an open cab, with a folding windshield and a folding canvas top, and a steel body containing trays, drawers and various shaped storage spaces for tools and equipment used in maintaining communications systems. The body has two doors at the right side and two doors at the rear. A 24 foot extension ladder is mounted on the left side of the body.

¾-TON, 4 x 4, AMBULANCE, KD—Designed for the Medical Corps, this vehicle is used for the transportation of sick and wounded personnel. Present standard body is of knock-down wood and steel construction and is equipped to carry four litter patients or eight seated patients, with attendant. It is insulated, with provisions for heating and ventilating. It has an open cab. A special spring and shock absorber design provides improved riding characteristics.

The body is painted conspicuously with the Red Cross and the insignia of the Medical Corps. No winch is supplied with this model. The vehicle has a 6-volt electrical system and a U.S. Army standard 40-ampere output generator.

¾-TON, 4 x 4, TELEPHONE INSTALLATION AND MAINTENANCE TRUCK, K-50

Physical Characteristics

Weight	6,700 lb.
Length	15 ft., 11½ ins.
Width	6 ft., 5¾ ins.
Height	6 ft., 8¾ ins.
Ground clearance	10⅝ ins.
Tread (center to center, rear)	64¾ ins.
Wheelbase	121 ins.
Ground contact	208 sq. ins.
Ground pressure	31.7 lb./sq. in.
Tire equipment (mud and snow type)	9.00 x 16, 8 ply

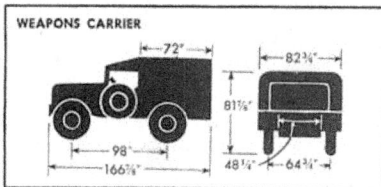

¾-TON, 4 x 4, AMBULANCE, WITH OPEN CAB. EARLIER MODEL HAD CLOSED CAB

Physical Characteristics

Weight	8,046 lb.
Length	15 ft., 11¹³⁄₁₆ ins.
Width	6 ft., 10½ ins.
Height	7 ft., 8⁵⁄₁₆ ins.
Ground clearance	10⅝ ins.
Tread (center to center, rear)	64¾ ins.
Wheelbase	121 ins.
Ground contact	208 sq. ins.
Ground pressure	38.6 lb./sq. in.
Tire equipment (mud and snow type)	9.00 x 16, 8 ply

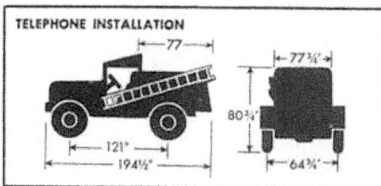

WEAPONS CARRIER

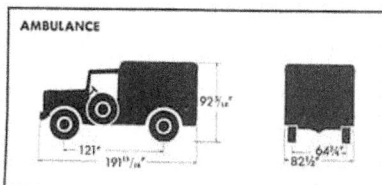

TELEPHONE INSTALLATION

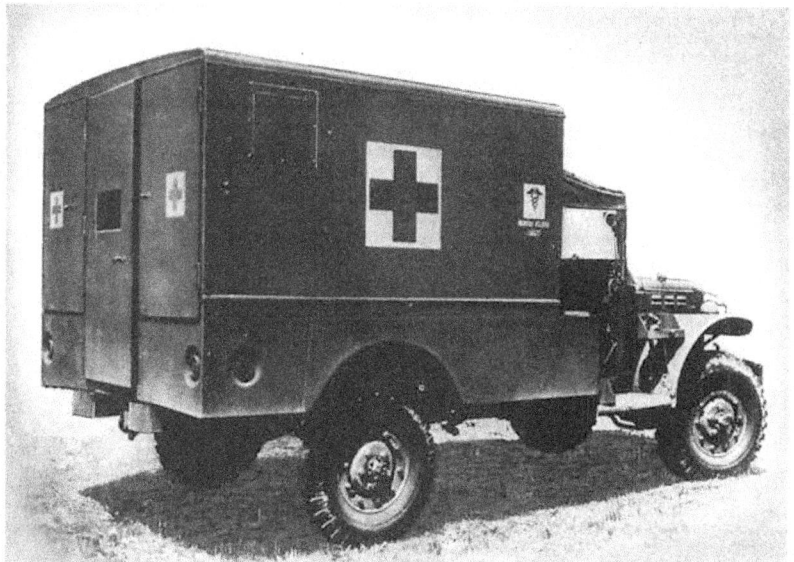

AMBULANCE

1½-TON, 4x4 (2DT) TRUCKS—STANDARD

These trucks have payloads of 3,000 pounds each, and will tow a load of 4,000 pounds. The truck tractor has a payload of 4,500 pounds and will tow a semi-trailer weighing 12,000 pounds gross.

The trucks are available in several standard body styles or a chassis upon which may be placed special bodies required by the various services. Wheelbase is 145 inches or 175 inches.

The vehicle has a maximum grade ability of 65% and is capable of operation over unimproved roads, trails and open, rolling and hilly cross country. It has a top governed speed of 48 miles per hour. Cruising range is approximately 270 miles.

The truck has four wheels, including two dual-tire wheels, using 7.50 x 20, 8 ply tires. Power is supplied to all four wheels, with a declutching control for the front axle.

The engine is a six-cylinder valve-in-head type, equipped with a counterbalanced crankshaft. A single plate dry disk type clutch is used. The four-speed transmission is a heavy-duty type of sturdy construction. A two-speed transfer case connects the transmission with the front and rear axles.

Wheels are interchangeable front and rear. Dual wheels can be installed on the front wheels, as well as on the rear wheels, without changing the wheel mounting.

The braking system combines hydraulically operated service brakes, a hydrovac booster system, a mechanically operated parking brake, and an electric controller for trailer brakes.

A power-operated winch, with a 10,000 pound capacity, is mounted on the front end of some of the cargo trucks.

Military characteristics call for open cabs. At present, however, only closed cab models are being produced.

Desertization equipment includes size 11.00 x 18, 10 ply, tires, with heavy duty tubes; army combat wheels with beadlock, size 8.00CV x 18, single front and rear, and one spare tire and wheel assembly with carrier. A radiator surge tank of at least 4 quart capacity, a power driven air compressor with hose to permit inflation of all tires, a low pressure-tire gage, tire chains for driving wheels, a speedometer correction adapter and a six bladed fan are also included. Winterization kits are supplied for those trucks whose use will require them.

The vehicles are manufactured by the Chevrolet Motor Div., General Motors Corp.

REFERENCES— MCM2c and 23; OCM 19107, 21221.

1½-TON, 4x4 CHASSIS IS USED FOR VARIETY OF SPECIAL PURPOSE VEHICLES

TRUCK, 1½-TON, 4x4 (4DT) CHASSIS— STANDARD—This is the basic chassis for all 1½ ton, 4x4 Army trucks, including not only the standard body styles shown herewith, but also a number of vehicles for special purposes. Among these are the Signal Corps Telephone Maintenance Truck, K–43; the Signal Corps Earth Borer and Pole Setter Truck, K–44; and the Air Corps Field Lighting truck.

REFERENCE—MCM 2c.

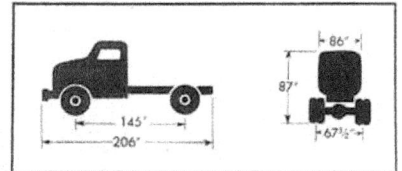

TYPICAL CHARACTERISTICS

Physical Characteristics
Weight (dry chassis)..............4,500 lb.
Length......................17 ft., 2 ins.
Width.......................7 ft., 2 ins.
Height......................7 ft., 3 ins.
Ground clearance................9⅞ ins.
Tread (center to center, rear)......67½ ins.
Wheelbase...............145 or 175 ins.
Ground contact............243.6 sq. ins.
Ground pressure.........18.4 lb./sq. in.
Tire equipment 7.50 x 20, 8 ply (mud and snow)
   desert.............11.00 x 18, 10 ply

Performance
Maximum speed on level..........48 m.p.h.
Maximum grade ability..............65%
Fording depth (slowest forward speed)..32 ins.
Angle of approach, with winch..........39°
   without winch...................45°
Angle of departure.................30°
Turning radius.....................30 ft.
Fuel capacity....................30 gals.
Cruising range..................270 miles
   with towed load...............195 miles
Maximum drawbar pull.........10,000 lb.

Normal towed load...............4,000 lb.
Winch capacity................10,000 lb.

Battery, Voltage, total................6

Fire Protection—Fire Extinguisher

Engine, Make and
Model............Chevrolet BV-1001 UP
Type.................Valve-in-head
No. of cylinders....................6
Cycle.............................4
Fuel (gasoline)...............70 octane
Bore and stroke....3⁹⁄₁₆ x 3¹⁵⁄₁₆ ins.
Displacement............235.5 cu. ins.
Compression........110 at 210-220
Max. governed speed........3,100 r.p.m.
Net hp...........83.5 at 3,000 r.p.m.
Max. torque....189 lb.-ft. at 1,600 r.p.m.
Crankshaft rotation.........C'Clockwise
Length..........................40 ins.
Width...........................22 ins.
Height..........................28 ins.
Ignition......................Battery
Weight, dry...................574 lb.

Transmission—Gear ratios
First speed....................7.06:1
Second speed...................3.48:1
Third speed....................1.71:1
Fourth speed...................1.00:1
Reverse.......................6.98:1

Transfer Case, Gear ratios....1.94:1; 1.00:1

Differential, Type...............Hypoid
Gear ratio....................6.67:1

Suspension, Type..........Semi-elliptic
Wheel size....................20 x 7
Wheel construction.........Pierced disk

Master Clutch, Type....Single dry plate

Radiator, Type.........Fin and tube
Capacity of system..........17¼ qts.

Steering Ratio................23.6:1

Brakes, Type..........Internal Hydraulic

Brakes, Parking, Type....External Band

Front Axle, Type........Full floating

Rear Axle, Gear ratio..........6.67:1

1½-TON, 4x4 (2DT) CARGO TRUCK STANDARD—This truck, designed for use by all arms and services, has the U. S. Army standard cargo body, with troop seats with lazy backs. A detachable canvas top is supported by five bows, and is provided with roll-up straps arranged to permit ventilation in the body. The top is equipped with front and rear curtains with window flaps. Inside dimensions are approximately 70 x 108 inches. It has a payload of 2,320 lb. Wheelbase is 145 inches.

Present military characteristics call for the U. S. Army standard open type cab with collapsible top and folding windshield.

The vehicle is available with or without a winch, of 10,000 pounds capacity.

REFERENCES—TM 10-1127, 10-1438.

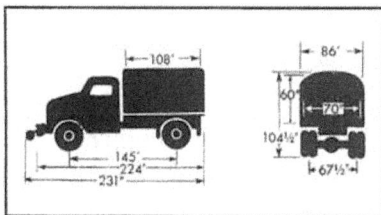

CARGO TRUCK, WITH TOP UP. TROOP SEATS ARE PROVIDED IN THE BODY

Physical Characteristics

Weight, without winch	10,865 lb.	Ground clearance	9⅞ ins.
with winch	11,535 lb.	Wheelbase	145 ins.
Length, without winch	18 ft., 8 ins.	Tread (center to center, rear)	67½ ins.
with winch	19 ft., 3 ins.	Tire equipment	
Width	7 ft., 2 ins.	7.50 x 20, 8 ply (mud and snow)	
Height	8 ft., 8½ ins.	Ground contact	243.6 ins.
with bows removed	7 ft., 3 ins.	Ground pressure per sq. in.	43.4 lb.

1½-TON, 4x4 (2DT) STAKE AND PLATFORM TRUCK—STANDARD—This truck, designed for the Signal Corps, has a body of the commercial stake and platform type. It is used to transport general cargo. The outside dimensions are approximately 96 x 192 inches, with 42 inch stakes. It has a payload of 2,300 lb.

Present military characteristics call for the U. S. Army standard Cab-over-Engine open type cab with collapsible top and folding windshield.

No winch is furnished with this vehicle.

REFERENCES—TM 10-1130, 10-1131.

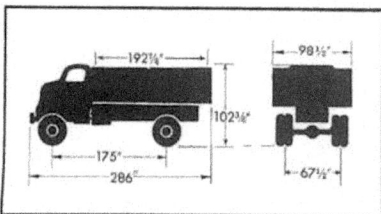

1½-TON, 4x4, STAKE AND PLATFORM TRUCK IS USED BY THE SIGNAL CORPS

Physical Characteristics

Weight (gross)	11,570 lb.	Wheelbase	175 ins.
Length	23 ft., 10 ins.	Tread (center to center, rear)	67½ ins.
Width	8 ft., 2½ ins.	Tire equipment 7.50 x 20, 8 ply (mud and snow)	
Height	8 ft., 6⅜ ins.	Ground contact	243.6 sq. ins.
Ground clearance	10 ins.	Ground pressure per sq. in.	47.4 lb.

PANEL DELIVERY TRUCK HAS CLOSED CAB INTEGRAL WITH THE BODY

1½-TON, 4x4 (2DT) PANEL DELIVERY TRUCK—STANDARD—This vehicle, designed for all arms and services, has the U. S. Army standard panel delivery body, and a cab that is integral with the body. The truck is used to transport light general cargo, and also to transport Signal Corps radio equipment. It has a payload of 3,320 pounds. Two rear doors facilitate loading and unloading.

No winch is furnished with this model.

REFERENCES—TM 10–1127, 10–1438, 10–1461.

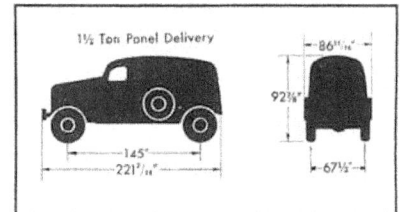

Physical Characteristics

Weight (gross)	10,080 lb.	Wheelbase	145 ins.
Length	18 ft., 5³⁄₁₆ ins.	Tread (center to center, rear)	67½ ins.
Width	7 ft., 2¹¹⁄₁₆ ins.	Tire equipment 7.50 x 20, 8 ply (mud and snow)	
Height	7 ft., 6⅞ ins.	Ground contact	243.6 sq. ins.
Ground clearance	9⅞ ins.	Ground pressure per sq. in.	40 lb.

1½-TON 4x4 TRACTOR TRUCK WILL TOW SEMI-TRAILERS TO 6 TONS

1½-TON, 4x4 (2DT) TRACTOR TRUCK—STANDARD—This truck, designed for all arms and services, is used for towing semi-trailers with a gross weight up to 12,000 pounds. It has a payload of 4,820 pounds, consisting of the weight imposed by the semi-trailer on the fifth wheel and the weight of the lower half of the fifth wheel, but exclusive of the driver.

The fifth wheel is of the U. S. Army standard universal type. An electric-brake hand controller on the truck steering column permits independent operation of the semi-trailer brakes.

No winch is provided with this model and rear bumperettes are omitted.

Present military characteristics call for the U. S. Army standard open type cab with collapsible top and folding windshield.

REFERENCE—MCM 23.

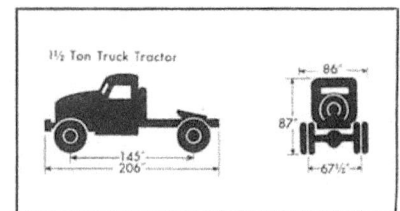

Physical Characteristics

Weight (gross)	10,885 lb.	Wheelbase	145 ins.
Length	17 ft., 2 ins.	Tread (center to center, rear)	67½ ins.
Width	7 ft., 2 ins.	Tire equipment 7.50 x 20, 8 ply (mud and snow)	
Height	7 ft., 3 ins.	Ground contact	243.6 sq. ins.
Ground clearance	9⅞ ins.	Ground pressure per sq. in.	43.4 lb.

1½-TON, 6x6, CARGO TRUCK—STANDARD

TYPICAL CHARACTERISTICS

Physical Characteristics
Weight (gross) without winch . . . . . . 10,225 lb.
   with winch . . . . 10,525 lb.
Length, without winch . . . . 17 ft., 10⅞ ins.
   with winch . . . . 18 ft., 8½ ins.
Width . . . . 6 ft., 10¾ ins.
Height, without Truck Mount . . . . . 7 ft., ¾ in.
   —with Truck Mount . . . . 7 ft., 5¾ ins.
Ground clearance . . . . 10⅝ ins.
Tread (center to center, rear) . . . . 64¾ ins.
Wheelbase . . . . 125 ins.
Ground contact . . . . 312 sq. ins.
Ground pressure . . . . 32.7 lb./sq. in.
Tire equipment . 9.00x16, 8 ply (mud and snow)

Armament
Truck Mount, M50, or Pedestal Mount, M24A2,
   for cal. .50 Machine Gun, M2, HB (flex.)
   (On one vehicle in each four)

Performance
Maximum speed on level . . . . 50 m.p.h.
Maximum grade ability 60%
   —with towed load 44%
Fording depth (slowest forward speed) . 34 ins.
Angle of approach, without winch . . . . . . 54°
   with winch . . . . 37°
Angle of departure . . . . 33°
Turning radius . . . . 26½ ft.
Fuel capacity . . . . 30 gals.
Cruising range . . . . 240 miles
   —with towed load . . . . 210 miles
Normal towed load . . . . 3,500 lb.
Payload (including personnel) . . . . . . 3,300 lb.
Winch capacity . . . . 7,500 lb.

Battery, Voltage, total 6

Fire Protection—Fire Extinguisher

Engine, Make and Model . . . . Dodge T-214
Type . . . . In-line, liquid-cooled
No. of cylinders 6
Cycle 4
Fuel (gasoline) . . . . 70 octane
Bore and stroke . . . . 3¼ x 4⅝ ins.
Displacement . . . . 230.2 cu. ins.
Compression . . . . 108–118 at c.s.
Net hp. . . . . 76 at 3,200 r.p.m.
Max. torque . . . . 184 lb.-ft. at 1,400 r.p.m.
Crankshaft rotation . . . . C'Clockwise
Length . . . . 37½ ins.
Width . . . . 24 ins.
Height . . . . 30 ins.
Ignition . . . . Battery
Weight, dry . . . . 603 lb.

Transmission—Gear ratios
First speed 6.40:1
Second speed 3.09:1
Third speed 1.69:1
Fourth speed 1.00:1
Reverse 7.82:1

Transfer Case—Gear ratios . . 1.50:1; 1.00:1

Steering Ratio 23.2:1

Suspension, Type . . . . Semi-elliptic
Wheel construction . . . . Divided rim

Master Clutch, Type . . . . Single dry plate

Radiator, Type . . . . Fin and tube
Capacity of system . . . . 17 qts.

Brakes, Type . . . . Internal hydraulic

Brakes, Parking, Type . . . External contracting

Rear Axle, Type . . . . Full floating

Front Axle, Gear Ratio 5.83:1

1½-TON, 6x6, CARGO TRUCK, SHOWING TRUCK MOUNT, M50, FOR CAL. .50 MACHINE GUN

This truck was designed as a substitute in certain instances for the 2½-Ton, 6x6, Truck, in which size a heavy production demand exists.

It is manufactured by using, as far as possible, those units found in the standard ¾-ton, 4x4, Truck. The principal changes are the addition of the extra bogie axle and lengthening of the frame and body, thus raising the load capacity to 3,000 pounds.

Military characteristics, as given in MCM No. 28a, call for a minimum dry chassis weight of 4,500 pounds and a towed load ability of 3,500 pounds. Wheelbase is 125 inches.

It is capable of operation over unimproved roads, trails, and open, rolling, and hilly cross country. It has a top governed speed of 54 miles per hour. Cruising range is approximately 240 miles.

The truck has six wheels, using 9.00 x 16, 8-ply tires. Power is supplied to all six wheels. The power to the front axle can be disengaged in the driver's compartment by a control.

Power is supplied by a liquid-cooled, L-head type, 6-cylinder gasoline engine. It is transmitted from the four-speed sliding-gear type transmission through a short propeller shaft to the transfer case, and thence to both front and rear axles. The vehicle may be driven with power on all six wheels or with the four rear wheels only.

Foot brakes are of the hydraulic internal-expanding four-wheel type. Hand brakes are mechanical, external-contracting.

Wheel and tire assemblies are interchangeable, front and rear.

The body is of the U. S. Army standard cargo type, with troop seats with lazy backs. A detachable canvas top is supported by five bows, and is provided with roll-up straps arranged to permit ventilation in the body. The top is equipped with front and rear curtains with window flaps. Inside dimensions are approximately 89 x 120 inches. There are two rows of seat boxes, with a space 48 inches wide between. The seat boxes are 14 inches deep.

The vehicle has an open cab. A Truck Mount, M50, or a Pedestal Mount, M24A2, is supplied on some vehicles.

The truck is supplied with or without a winch, of 7,500 pound capacity.

Desertization equipment includes a 4-pound pressure cap for the radiator surge tank, a power-driven air compressor with hose to permit inflation of all tires, and a low-pressure tire gage.

The vehicle is manufactured by the Fargo Motor Corporation.

REFERENCES—MCM 28a; TM 9-810A; OCM 18785, 19049, 19181, 19701, 19877, 19924, 20147, 20251, 20440, 20521, 20728, 20804, 21221, 21990.

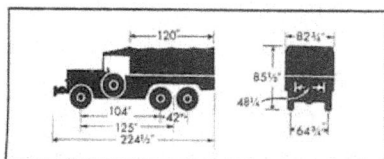

2½-TON, 6x6 (4DT) TRUCKS—STANDARD

With its payload of 5,350 pounds, and with a towing capacity of 4,500 pounds, the 2½-ton, 6 x 6 (4DT) Truck has become one of the most versatile of Army vehicles.

It is available in a number of standard body styles and as a standard chassis upon which may be placed special bodies required by the various services. Wheelbase is 164 inches or 145 inches.

The truck has six wheels including four dual-tire wheels, using 7.50 x 20, 8 ply tires. Power is supplied to all six wheels with driver control for declutching the front axle.

Power is supplied by a G.M.C. six-cylinder, valve-in-head type gasoline engine. The clutch is a single-plate dry disk type. The selective, sliding gear transmission has five speeds forward and one reverse. Transmission is direct drive in the fourth speed, and over-drive in the fifth speed. The transfer case is essentially a two-speed auxiliary unit with three power take-off shafts, one for front axle and two for rear axles.

The brakes are hydraulic, supplemented by a Hydrovac unit which utilizes atmosphere and engine manifold vacuum to assist the driver in the application of the brakes.

The axles may be "split" or "banjo" type. The type of axles used determines the type of transfer case and propeller shaft arrangement.

A 10,000 pound capacity winch, supplied on some models, is power driven by a drive shaft connected between the winch and the power take-off on the transmission. It has two speeds forward and a reverse. Winch operation is controlled by a manual shift lever in the cab and a jaw clutch at the winch.

Early production vehicles had closed cabs. Provision was made to supply a Truck Mount, M32, for a cal. .50 machine gun, long wheelbase, and a Truck Mount, M37, with one in each four trucks, short wheelbase. Present production calls for U. S. Army standard open type cabs, with collapsible tops and folding windshields. One vehicle in each four is provided with a Truck Mount, M36 or M37A3, for a cal. .50, HB, machine gun for antiaircraft protection.

Desertization equipment includes size 11.00 x 18, 10 ply, tires with heavy-duty tubes; army combat wheels with beadlock, size 8.00 CV x 18, single front and rear, and one spare tire and wheel assembly with carrier. A radiator surge tank of at least four-quart capacity, a power-driven air compressor with hose to permit inflation of all tires, a low-pressure gage, a speedometer correction adapter, and a five-bladed fan are also included. Winterization kits are supplied for those trucks whose use will require them.

REFERENCES—MC3C; OCM 19107, 19303, 19304, 19427, 19547, 19817, 19923, 20099, 20100, 20152, 20606, 20938, 20964, 21221, 21933, 22141, 22883, 22920.

2½-TON, 6x6 (4DT) TRUCK CHASSIS —This rugged chassis is used for all 2½-ton, 6 x 6, G.M.C. trucks, including not only the standard body styles shown herewith, and the standard ordnance maintenance trucks shown elsewhere in these pages, but also a number of vehicles for special purposes. Among these are Chemical Service Truck, M1; Van, K-57; an air compressor truck, a decontamination truck, an engineer shop truck, and a water purification truck.

CHASSIS OF 2½-TON, 6x6 (4DT) TRUCK, SHOWING PRESENT PRODUCTION STYLE OPEN CAB

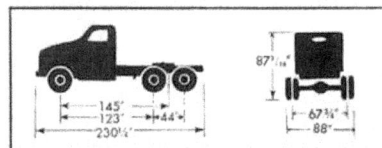

Physical Characteristics
Weight (curb)	6,000 lb.
Length, long wheelbase	21 ft., 3 ins.
short wheelbase	19 ft., 2¼ ins.
Width	7 ft., 4 ins.
Height	7 ft., 3³⁄₁₆ ins.
Ground clearance	10 ins.
Tread (center to center, rear)	67¾ ins.
Wheelbase, long wheelbase	164 ins.
short wheelbase	145 ins.
Ground contact	406 sq. ins.
Ground pressure	14.7 lb./sq. in.
Tire equipment	7.50 x 20, 8 ply
desert	11.00 x 18, 10 ply

Armament
Truck Mount, M32, M36, M37, or M37A3, for cal. .50 Machine Gun, M2, HB (Supplied with one vehicle in four)

Performance
Maximum speed on level	45 m.p.h.
Maximum grade ability	65%
Vertical obstacle ability	10 ins.
Angle of approach—w/o winch	54°
cab-over-engine model	45°
Angle of approach—with winch	31°
Angle of departure	
long wheelbase models	36°
short wheelbase models	44°
cab-over-engine model	32½°
Turning radius	32 ft.
Fuel capacity	40 gals.
Cruising range (approx.)	220 miles
with towed load	190 miles
Maximum drawbar pull	13,063 lb.
Normal towed load	4,500 lb.
Payload (including personnel)	5,350 lb.
Winch capacity	10,000 lb.

Battery, Voltage, total ... 6

Fire Protection ... Fire Extinguisher

Engine, Make and Model ... G.M.C. 270
Type	In-line, liquid-cooled
No. of cylinders	6
Cycle	4
Fuel (gasoline)	70 octane
Bore and stroke	3 25/32 x 4 ins.
Displacement	269.52 cu. ins.
Compression	130 lb. at C.S.
Max. governed speed	2,750 r.p.m.
Net hp.	94 at 3,000 r.p.m.
Max. torque	217 lb.-ft. at 1,600 r.p.m.
Crankshaft rotation	C'Clockwise
Length	41¼ ins.
Width	22½ ins.
Height	32 ins.

Ignition	Battery
Weight, dry (less accessories)	535 lb.

Transmission, Gear ratios
First speed	6.06:1
Second speed	3.50:1
Third speed	1.80:1
Fourth speed	1.00:1
Fifth speed	0.799:1
Reverse	6.00:1

Transfer Case, Gear ratios
(G.M.C. model)	1.16:1; 2.63:1
(Timken model)	1.16:1; 2.61:1

Differential, Type ... Spiral bevel
Gear ratio	6.6:1
Steering ratio	23.6:1

Suspension, Type ... Semi-elliptic
Wheel size	20 x 7
Wheel construction	Disk

Master Clutch, Type ... Dry, single plate

Radiator, Type ... Fin and tube
Capacity of system	19 qts.

Brakes, Type ... Internal hydraulic

Brakes, Parking, Type ... Band

Front Axle, Type ... Banjo or split

Rear Axle, Gear ratio ... 6.6:1

$2\frac{1}{2}$-TON, 6x6 (4DT) TRUCKS (Continued)

$2\frac{1}{2}$-TON, 6x6 (4DT) CARGO TRUCK—STANDARD—Designed for all arms and services, this 164 inch wheelbase truck has the U. S. Army standard cargo body, with troop seats with lazy backs. The seats may be folded up out of the way when desired, in order to provide additional cargo space. A detachable canvas top is supported by five bows, and is provided with roll-up straps arranged to permit ventilation in the body. The top is equipped with front and rear curtains with window flaps. Inside dimensions are approximately 80 inches by 144 inches. The truck has a payload of 5,000 pounds. A spare tire rack is mounted underneath the body.

The vehicle is available with or without a winch.

REFERENCE—TM 9-801.

164 INCH WHEELBASE CARGO TRUCK HAS SPARE TIRE BRACKET BENEATH THE BODY

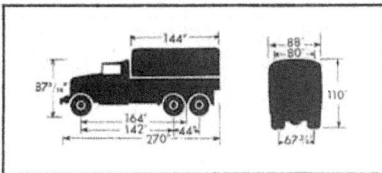

Physical Characteristics

Weight, without winch	15,450 lb.
with winch	16,450 lb.
Length, without winch	21 ft., 4 ins.
with winch	22 ft., 6 ins.
Width	7 ft., 4 ins.
Height, over bows	9 ft., 2 ins.
over cab	7 ft., 3 3/16 ins.
reducible to	6 ft., 2¼ ins.
Ground clearance	10 ins.
Tread (center to center, rear)	67¾ ins.
Wheelbase	164 ins.
Ground contact	406 sq. ins.
Ground pressure	38 lb./sq. in.

$2\frac{1}{2}$-TON, 6x6 (4DT) SHORT WHEELBASE CARGO TRUCK—STANDARD—This is similar to the preceding model, but is built on a chassis with 145 inch wheelbase, and is designed for use as a prime mover. The body is the same in style, but has inside dimensions approximately 80 inches by 108 inches. The vehicle has a payload of 5,350 pounds. It is supplied with or without a winch. Brackets for two spare tires are mounted in back of the cab.

Limited procurement of kits to modify this truck for airborne transportation was authorized by Ordnance Committee action in February, 1944. The truck is split into two sections, each carried in a separate plane, and is reassembled at the destination.

REFERENCE—TM 9-801.

SHORT WHEELBASE CARGO TRUCK HAS SPARE TIRE BRACKETS IN BACK OF CAB

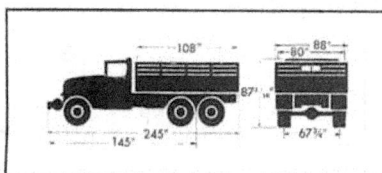

Physical Characteristics

Weight, without winch	15,350 lb.
with winch	16,350 lb.
Length, without winch	19 ft., 3 ins.
with winch	20 ft., 5 ins.
Width	7 ft., 4 ins.
Height, over bows	9 ft., 2 ins.
over cab	7 ft., 3 3/16 ins.
reducible to	6 ft., 2¼ ins.
Ground clearance	10 ins.
Tread (center to center, rear)	67¾ ins.
Wheelbase	145 ins.
Ground contact	406 sq. ins.
Ground pressure	37.8 lb./sq. in.

2½-TON, 6x6 (4DT) TRUCKS (Continued)

15 FOOT CARGO TRUCK IS CAB-OVER-ENGINE TYPE, HAS LARGEST CARGO SPACE

2½-TON, 6x6 (4DT) 15 FT. CARGO TRUCK—STANDARD—This is a 164 inch wheelbase truck, which, because of its cab-over-engine design, provides more cargo space than the vehicle with engine in front. It has inside body dimensions of approximately 80 inches by 180 inches, and is equipped with cargo racks. The vehicle has a payload of 3,950 pounds, including personnel. Intended primarily for hauling general cargo, ammunition, and equipment, it may also be used as a prime mover for guns and trailers.

A detachable canvas top is supported by six bows, and is provided with roll-up straps to permit ventilation in the body. The top is equipped with front and rear curtains with window flaps.

No winch is supplied with this model.

REFERENCE—TM 9–809.

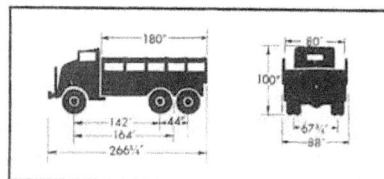

Physical Characteristics

Weight (gross)	14,760 lb.	Ground clearance	10 ins.
Length	22 ft., 2¼ ins.	Tread (center to center, rear)	67¾ ins.
Width	7 ft., 4 ins.	Wheelbase	164 ins.
Height, over bows	8 ft., 10 ins.	Ground contact	406 sq. ins.
over cab	8 ft., 4 ins.	Ground pressure	36.3 lb./sq. in.

2½-TON DUMP TRUCK MAY ALSO BE USED AS CARGO AND PERSONNEL CARRIER

2½-TON, 6x6 (4DT) DUMP TRUCK—STANDARD—Designed for the Corps of Engineers, this vehicle is a combination cargo and dump truck. The body is equipped with troop seats, removable front rack, an adjustable cab protector, and bows and tarpaulins, and when so equipped resembles other cargo trucks.

For use as a dump truck, this equipment is removed. A hinged partition, which is in a horizontal position as a part of the cargo floor, can be raised and backed in a vertical position to provide a dump body of approximately 2½ yards capacity. The body is attached to a hoist subframe by means of two hinges and can be elevated by an underbody hydraulic arm type hoist.

The double-acting tail gate may be hinged at either the bottom, for use as a cargo truck, or at the top, to serve as a spreader when used as a dump truck.

REFERENCE—TM 9–801.

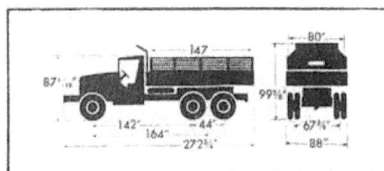

Physical Characteristics

Weight (gross)	16,850 lb.	Ground clearance	10 ins.
Length	22 ft., 8¾ ins.	Tread (center to center, rear)	67¾ ins.
Width	7 ft., 4 ins.	Wheelbase	164 ins.
Height, over bows	9 ft., 2 ins.	Ground contact	406 sq. ins.
over apron	8 ft., 3⅝ ins.	Ground pressure	41.5 lb./sq. in.
over cab	7 ft., 3 3/16 ins.		

2½-TON, 6x6 (4DT) GASOLINE TANK TRUCK, 750 GALLON — STANDARD —

Designed for all arms and services, this vehicle consists of a 164 inch wheelbase chassis on which are mounted two U.S. Army standard elliptical gasoline tanks of 375 gallons each. Each section is 61 inches long by 54½ inches wide by 34 inches high. Manholes, flanges, piping, valves, running-boards, and equipment compartments are provided.

Bows and tarpaulins are furnished for camouflage, giving the vehicle the appearance of a cargo truck, and thus making it a less distinctive target from the air.

No winch is supplied with this model.

REFERENCE—TM 9–801.

750 GALLON GASOLINE TANK MAY BE CAMOUFLAGED TO RESEMBLE CARGO BODY

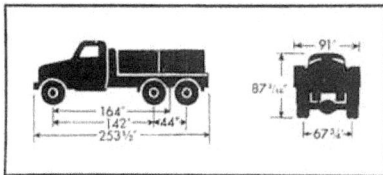

Physical Characteristics

Weight (gross)	15,450 lb.	Ground clearance	10 ins.
Length	21 ft., 1½ ins.	Tread (center to center, rear)	67¾ ins.
Width	7 ft., 7 ins.	Wheelbase	164 ins.
Height, over bows	9 ft., 2 ins.	Ground contact	406 sq. ins.
over cab	7 ft., 3 3/16 ins.	Ground pressure	38 lb./sq. in.

2½-TON, 6x6 (4DT) WATER TANK TRUCK, 700 GALLON—STANDARD—

This vehicle, designed for all arms and services, consists of a 164 inch wheelbase truck on which is mounted a U. S. Army standard elliptical tank of 700 gallon capacity. The tank is 136½ inches long, 52 inches wide, and 34 inches high. It is complete with manholes, flanges, a heater aperture, piping, valves, running-boards, equipment compartments, an auxiliary gasoline engine driven pump, and a hose.

Like the gasoline truck, it is provided with bows and tarpaulins for camouflage, giving it the appearance of a cargo truck, and making it a less conspicuous target for enemy planes.

REFERENCE—TM 9–801.

700 GALLON WATER TANK ALSO IS CAMOUFLAGED IN COMBAT ZONES

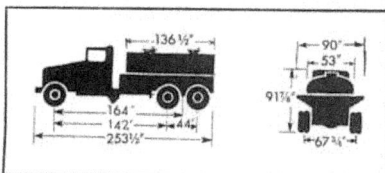

Physical Characteristics

Weight (gross)	17,690 lb.	Ground clearance	10 ins.
Length	21 ft., 1½ ins.	Tread (center to center, rear)	67¾ ins.
Width	7 ft., 6 ins.	Wheelbase	164 ins.
Height, over bows	9 ft., 2 ins.	Ground contact	406 sq. ins.
over body	7 ft., 7⅞ ins.	Ground pressure	43.5 lb./sq. in.

2½-TON, 6X6, AMPHIBIAN TRUCK—STANDARD

2½-TON, 6x6, AMPHIBIAN TRUCK, "THE DUCK," IS USEFUL IN LANDINGS ON ENEMY BEACHES. TRUCK MOUNT, M36, IS PROVIDED ON ONE VEHICLE IN FOUR.

Standardized in October, 1942, this vehicle has proved its usefulness in operations against enemy beaches, and is at home on water as well as on land. It is nicknamed "the Duck," from its official nomenclature as DUKW-353.

The vehicle was developed for the military service by the National Defense Research Committee in accordance with a directive issued by the Commanding General, Services of Supply, through the Quartermaster General.

Based on the standard 2½-ton, 6x6, Truck, it is equipped with an integral watertight hull designed in such a manner that truck chassis and drive units are attached to and in the body of the hull.

For land operation, the vehicle utilizes its six driving wheels and conventional steering-gear assembly. In water, it is propelled with a water propeller, and is steered by the combined use of the front wheels and a rudder which is interconnected to and operated by the steering-gear column.

Springs and driving axles are attached to the bottom of the hull and suspend in water when the vehicle is in use as a boat. The welded steel hull is decked forward of the driver's compartment, to the rear of the rear wheels, and along both sides. A crash rail is installed all around the hull at deck height.

The driver's compartment is of the open type, with removable canvas top and open back, and removable side curtains. The windshield may be folded forward, or tilted upward and outward. One vehicle in each four is provided with a Truck Mount, M36, for an antiaircraft machine gun.

The cargo compartment will accommodate approximately 25 men and equipment or approximately 5,000 pounds payload for land operation. Hatches in the rear deck and floor provide access to tool and storage holds and to the rudder-operating mechanism and rear winch shaft. Two hatches in the bow facilitate access to the engine, accessories, and forward compartment.

A two-speed transfer case permits drive of both front and rear axles, or only the rear axle, as required. The water propeller transfer case, mounted in drive line between transmission and transfer case, permits engagement or disengagement of the water propeller.

A 10,000 pound capacity winch is mounted at the rear. Cable guides are provided to permit operation at either the front or the rear.

A marine rudder and controls and a propeller are provided for use in water. An anchor with shackle is furnished. One ring type life preserver and three life preserver jackets are supplied. Mooring eyes, suitable davit eyes and fender eyes for rope fenders are provided.

A 60 gallon per minute rotary pump and a 260 gallon per minute centrifugal pump are used to pump water out of the hull. A 50 gallon per minute hand pump is furnished for emergency use.

The vehicles are manufactured by the Yellow Truck and Coach Manufacturing Co.

REFERENCES—MCM 27; TM 9-802; OCM 18950, 19059, 19817, 19876, 19923, 20100, 20514, 20633, 21166, 21419, 22074, 22196.

CHARACTERISTICS

Crew (operating) 1

Physical Characteristics

Weight	19,570 lb.
Length	31 ft.
Width	8 ft., 2⅞ ins.
Height (top up)	8 ft., 9½ ins.
(top down)	7 ft., 1⅜ ins.
Ground clearance	10½ ins.
Tread (center to center)	63⅝ ins.
Wheelbase	164 ins.
Loaded freeboard—to deck—front	24 ins.
to deck—rear	16 ins.
to coaming—front and rear	29 ins.
Loaded draft—to under side of tires	51 ins.
Tire equipment	11.00 x 18, 10 ply (desert)

Armament

Truck Mount, M36, for cal. .50 Machine Gun
(On one vehicle in each four)

Performance

Maximum speed on land	45 m.p.h.
Maximum speed in water	6.3 m.p.h.
Maximum grade ability	60%
Vertical obstacle ability	18 ins.
Angle of approach	38°
Angle of departure	26½°
Turning radius—land	36 ft.
water	20 ft.
Fuel capacity	40 gals.
Cruising range—land	220 miles
water	50 miles
Payload	5,350 lb.
Winch capacity	10,000 lb.

Battery, Voltage, total 6
(Other characteristics same as for 2½-Ton, 6x6, Cargo Truck.)

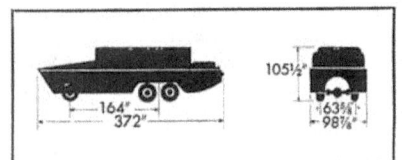

4-TON, 6x6 (4DT) TRUCKS—STANDARD

These vehicles have payloads of 8,000 pounds each and will tow a 12,000 pound trailer. Body styles are cargo, cargo long wheelbase, wrecker, and dump. In addition, the chassis is supplied to the Corps of Engineers for use with various special bodies.

The vehicles are capable of operations over unimproved roads, trails and open, rolling hilly cross country at gross weight with towed load. Maximum speed at gross weight with towed load on smooth concrete roadway is 40 miles per hour. Maximum grade ability is 65%.

Wheelbase is in two sizes, 151 and 172 inches. Tires are 9.00 x 20, 10 ply, mud and snow tread.

Military equipment includes towing hooks on the two front corners, brush guards, a sturdy front bumper and U. S. Army standard rear bumperettes. Sealed beam type headlights are used, as well as U. S. Army standard combat-zone safety lighting. A trailer light socket is provided. Brakes are air operated and have a foot valve and hand controller for independent operation of the airbrakes on the trailer

load. Four air connections for towed vehicles are provided.

The vehicle is powered with a 131.5 horsepower gasoline engine of L-head design. The clutch is a single plate dry disk type. The transmission has five forward speeds, with fifth speed overdrive and one reverse. Constant mesh helical gears are used in the three top speeds for quiet operation. The first, second, and reverse speed gears are spur cut.

Power is delivered to the front and rear axles through the transfer case, which is offset to permit the forward propeller shaft to clear the engine crankcase. A speed reduction, independent of the transmission, is provided in the transfer case. A control lever in the cab permits disengagement of the front axle if desired.

The wrecker transfer case is equipped with a power take-off which operates the wrecker winches. This take-off is mounted at the rear end of the transfer case drive shaft and transmits its power to the winches through a chain drive.

Steering gear is of the cam and twin-lever type which automatically provides

a variable gear ratio for ease of steering.

Present production calls for open cabs, with folding canvas tops. One vehicle in four is provided with a Truck Mount, M36, for an antiaircraft machine gun. Earlier production models have closed cabs, and one vehicle in four is provided with a Truck Mount, M56.

Desertization equipment includes size 14.00 x 20, 12 ply tires with heavy-duty tubes; army combat wheels with bead-lock, size 10CW x 20, single front and rear, and one spare tire and wheel assembly with carrier. A low-pressure tire gage, tire chains for driving wheels, a speedometer correction adapter, a packless type water pump, and front wheel stops and rear axle stops are also included.

The vehicles are manufactured by the Diamond T Motor Car Co.

REFERENCES—TM 10–1533; MCM 4d; OCM 18888, 19107, 19436, 19676, 20100, 20340, 20512, 20580, 21221, 21872, 22212, 22332, 23565; SNL G–509.

GENERAL CHARACTERISTICS

Performance
Maximum speed on level	40 m.p.h.
Maximum grade ability	65%
with towed load	57%
Vertical obstacle ability	12 ins.
Fording depth (slowest forward speed)	24 ins.
Angle of approach	35°
Angle of departure	From 35° to 45°
Turning radius	36 ft.
Fuel capacity	60 gals.
Cruising range (approx.)	175 miles
with towed load	150 miles
Maximum drawbar pull	21,550 lb.
Normal towed load	11,000 lb.
Payload	8,000 lb.
Winch capacity	15,000 lb.

Battery, Voltage, total	6–12
Fire Protection	Fire Extinguisher
Engine, Make and Model	Hercules RXC
Type	L-head
No. of cylinders	6
Cycle	4
Fuel (gasoline)	70 octane
Bore and stroke	4⅝ x 5¼ ins.
Displacement	529 cu. ins.
Compression	110 lb. at C.S.
Net hp.	119 at 2,200 r.p.m.
Max. torque	395 lb.-ft. at 1,000 r.p.m.
Crankshaft rotation	C'Clockwise
Length	50½ ins.
Width	32 ins.
Height	44½ ins.
Ignition	Battery
Weight, dry	1,395 lb.

Transmission, Gear ratios	
First speed	7.08:1
Second speed	3.82:1
Third speed	1.85:1
Fourth speed	1.00:1
Fifth speed	0.768:1
Reverse	7.08:1
Transfer Case, Gear ratios	1.72:1, 1.00:1
Steering Ratio	22, 18, 22:1
Suspension, Type	Semi-elliptic
Wheel size	20 x 8
Master Clutch, Type	Single plate dry disk
Radiator, Type	Fin and tube
Capacity of system	48 qts.
Brakes, Type	Air
Brakes, Parking, Type	Disk
Front Axle, Type	Double reduction
Rear Axle, Gear ratio	8.435:1

4-TON, 6x6 (4DT) TRUCK CHASSIS—STANDARD—This chassis is supplied to the Corps of Engineers for use for various special purpose vehicles, including a bituminous supply truck, water distributor truck, and bituminous distributor truck. No winch is supplied. The vehicle is provided with or without a rear mounted pintle, depending on its intended use.

REFERENCES—OCM 18888, 19463.

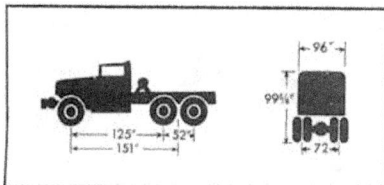

CHASSIS IS USED AS A BASIS OF SPECIAL VEHICLES FOR CORPS OF ENGINEERS

Physical Characteristics
Weight (dry chassis)	11,500 lb.
Ground clearance	11 ins.
Tread (center to center, rear)	72 ins.
Wheelbase	151 ins.

Ground contact	496 sq. ins.
Ground pressure	23.1 lb./sq. in.
Tire equipment	9.00 x 20, 10 ply
	(mud and snow)

CARGO BODY, WITH WINCH, SHOWING PAULINS OVER BOWS, ON OPEN CAB VEHICLE

4-TON, 6x6 (4DT) CARGO TRUCK—STANDARD—This vehicle, designed for all arms and services, for hauling general cargo and personnel, has the U. S. Army standard cargo body with troop seats with lazy backs. It has a detachable canvas top, with roll-up straps to permit ventilation in the body, and front and rear curtains with window flaps. The inside dimensions are approximately 88 x 132 inches.

An open cab, with folding windshield, is provided.

The vehicle has a payload of 8,300 pounds. It is equipped with a winch.

REFERENCES—TM 10-1600 with supplement, 10-1607, 9-1811A.

Physical Characteristics

Weight (gross)	26,400 lb.	Tread (center to center, rear)	72 ins.
Length	22 ft., 4½ ins.	Wheelbase	151 ins.
Width	8 ft.	Ground contact	496 sq. ins.
Height	9 ft., 10¼ ins.	Ground pressure	53.2 lb./sq. in.
reducible to	8 ft., 3⅝ ins.	Tire equipment	9.00 x 20, 10 ply
Ground clearance	11 ins.		(mud and snow)

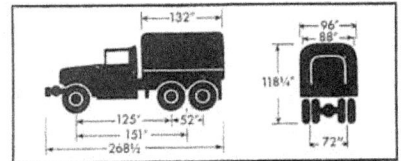

THIS LONG WHEELBASE CARGO TRUCK TRANSPORTS PONTON BRIDGE EQUIPMENT

4-TON, 6x6 (4DT) CARGO TRUCK, LWB — STANDARD — Designed for the Corps of Engineers, for transporting ponton bridge equipment, this truck has a U. S. Army standard cargo body. Inside dimensions are approximately 88 x 147 inches. It has a payload of 8,300 pounds.

It has a detachable canvas top, with roll-up straps to permit ventilation in the body, and front and rear curtains with window flaps. An open cab, with folding windshield, is furnished. A front-mounted winch is provided.

REFERENCES—TM 10-1532, 10-1533, 10-1604 with supplement, 10-1605, 10-1606 with supplement, 10-1607, 9-1811A.

Physical Characteristics

Weight (gross)	26,800 lb.	Tread (center to center, rear)	72 ins.
Length	24 ft., 8⅝ ins.	Wheelbase	172 ins.
Width	8 ft.	Ground contact	496 sq. ins.
Height	9 ft., 8 3/16 ins.	Ground pressure	54 lb./sq. in.
reducible to	8 ft., 3⅝ ins.	Tire equipment	9.00 x 20, 10 ply
Ground clearance	11 ins.		(mud and snow)

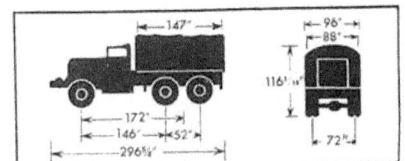

4-TON, 6x6 (4DT) TRUCKS (Continued)

4-TON, 6x6 (4DT) DUMP TRUCK—STANDARD—This vehicle is supplied to the Corps of Engineers to haul and dump earth, sand, gravel, etc. It has the U. S. Army standard dump type body with a hydraulic hoist. The inside body dimensions are approximately 80 x 120 inches. An open cab, with folding windshield, is provided. A winch is provided with present production models.

This vehicle has a steel shield over the driver's cab for protection from heavy objects.

REFERENCES—TM 9-811A, 9-1811A.

DUMP TRUCK, SHOWING STEEL SHIELD TO PROTECT DRIVER'S COMPARTMENT

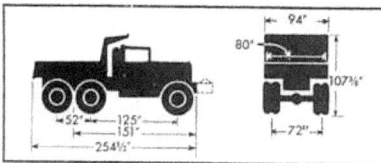

Physical Characteristics

Weight (gross)	26,400 lb.
Length	21 ft., 2½ ins.
Width	7 ft., 10 ins.
Height	8 ft., 11⅜ ins.
Ground clearance	11 ins.
Tread (center to center, rear)	72 ins.
Wheelbase	151 ins.
Ground contact	496 sq. ins.
Ground pressure	53.2 lb./sq. in.
Tire equipment	9.00 x 20, 10 ply (mud and snow)

4-TON, 6x6 (4DT) WRECKER TRUCK—STANDARD—Designed for all arms and services, this wrecker is used primarily for light recovery operations of wheeled vehicles. A frame just behind the cab supports two manually operated booms, one at each corner, each equipped with a winch and arranged to swing in a 90° arc over its respective side of the vehicle. Each winch may be used separately or in conjunction with the other. An additional winch is mounted on the front of the truck, for use as an anchor or for recovering the wrecker itself.

Bows and paulins for camouflage, giving the appearance of a cargo vehicle, are provided, in order that the wrecker will present a less conspicuous target to observers from the air.

REFERENCES—TM 10-1606, 10-1607; OCM 21872, 22140.

THIS WRECKER TRUCK MAY BE CAMOUFLAGED TO RESEMBLE CARGO VEHICLE

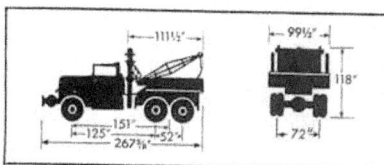

Physical Characteristics

Weight (gross)	21,700 lb.
Length	22 ft., 3⅜ ins.
Width	8 ft., 3½ ins.
Height	9 ft., 10 ins.
reducible to	8 ft.
Ground clearance	11 ins.
Tread (center to center, rear)	72 ins.
Wheelbase	151 ins.
Ground contact	496 sq. ins.
Ground pressure	43.8 lb./sq. in.
Tire equipment	9.00 x 20, 10 ply (mud and snow)

4-5 TON, 4X4 (2DT), TRACTOR TRUCK—STANDARD

This vehicle is furnished to the Air Corps for towing its Fuel Servicing Semi-trailer, and to the Quartermaster Corps for towing 6 ton cargo semi-trailers. It is of the cab-over-engine type.

No body is required. A tread plate platform is provided across the top of the frame, extending from the rear of the cab to a line representing the front edge of the lower fifth wheel.

Two spare wheel and tire assemblies are mounted on a split type carrier behind the cab. A hand control valve is provided for independent operation of the semi-trailer brakes. Three trailer air-hose assemblies and four trailer air connections are furnished.

When furnished to the Air Corps, the vehicle is finish painted in Army yellow, dull and lusterless, if specified. For the Quartermaster Corps, the finish is Army olive drab, dull and lusterless.

Single wheels are used at the front and dual wheels at the rear. Tires are 9.00 x 20, 10 ply, balloon, mud and snow tread, with heavy-duty tubes.

Military equipment includes towing hooks on the two front corners, a brush guard, a front bumper, a rear bumper when specified and a military type pintle. Approved combat-zone lighting is used.

Desertization equipment includes size 14.00 x 20, 12 ply tires with heavy-duty tubes; army combat wheels with bead-lock, size 10.00CW x 20, single front and rear, and one spare tire and wheel assembly with carrier. A special radiator with built-in overflow return, a low-pressure tire gage, tire chains for driving wheels, a packless type water pump, and a speedometer correction adapter are also included.

Power is supplied by a Hercules RXC in-line, liquid-cooled gasoline engine. The clutch, of the single disk type, is designed for non-shock loading and automatic compensation for loss of spring pressure.

The transmission has five speeds forward and one reverse, and is equipped with silent helical gears running in constant mesh in third speed and overdrive. Fourth speed is direct drive and fifth speed is overdrive.

Power is supplied to all four wheels through a two-speed transfer case. A lever in the driver's cab permits de-clutching of the front wheels when not required. The vehicle has air-brakes, with connections for braking the trailer.

Present production calls for open cabs. One vehicle in four is provided with a Truck Mount, M36, for a cal. .50, HB, machine gun. Earlier production vehicles have closed cabs, with provision for use of a Truck Mount, M60 or M61, on one in each four.

The vehicles are manufactured by Autocar Co. and Federal Motor Truck Co.

REFERENCES—TM 10-1116, 10-1117, 10-1458, 10-1459; MCM 14a; OCM 19107, 20100, 21221, 22212; SNL G-510, G-513, G-691.

4-5 TON, 4x4, TRACTOR TRUCK, SHOWING OPEN CAB AND TRUCK MOUNT FOR MACHINE GUN

TYPICAL CHARACTERISTICS

Crew...2
Physical Characteristics
Weight (gross)......................21,010 lb.
Length......................16 ft., 11½ ins.
Width.........................7 ft., 11 ins.
Height.........................9 ft., 4¾ ins.
  reducible to................7 ft., 11½ ins.
Ground clearance................11¾ ins.
Tread (center to center, rear).......72 ins.
Wheelbase.......................134½ ins.
Tire equipment
  9.00 x 20, 10 ply (mud and snow)

Armament
Truck Mount, M36, M60, or M61, for cal. .50 Machine Gun, M2, HB

Performance
Maximum speed on level.........41 m.p.h.
Maximum grade ability................65%
  with towed load..................57½%
Trench crossing ability.............20 ins.
Fording depth (slowest forward speed) 24½ ins.
Angle of approach....................54°
Angle of departure...................50°
Turning radius......................30 ft.
Fuel capacity.......................60 gals.
Cruising range (approx.)...........180 miles
Payload..........................9,350 lb.
Normal towed load...............20,000 lb.
Battery, Voltage, total.............6-12
Fire Protection..........Fire extinguisher

Engine, Make and Model......Hercules RXC
Type...............In-line, liquid-cooled
No. of cylinders........................6
Cycle..................................4
Fuel (gasoline)................68 octane
Bore and stroke.........4⅝ x 5¼ ins.
Displacement................529 cu. ins.
Compression ratio............110 at C.S.
Net hp.............112 at 2,200 r.p.m.
Max. torque....395 lb.-ft. at 1,000 r.p.m.
Crankshaft rotation........C'Clockwise
Length......................50½ ins.
Width........................32 ins.
Height.......................44½ ins.

Transmission, Gear ratios
First speed......................5.90:1
Second speed.....................3.60:1
Third speed......................1.84:1
Fourth speed.....................1.00:1
Fifth speed.......................75:1
Reverse..........................7.37:1
Transfer Case, Gear ratios....1.72:1; 1.00:1
Steering Ratio............22, 18, 22:1
Suspension, Type..........Semi-elliptic
  Wheel construction...............Disk
Master Clutch, Type.........Single disk
Radiator, Type............Fin and tube
  Capacity of system..............38 qts.
Brakes, Type.............Internal, air
Brakes, Parking, Type............Disk
Front Axle, Type......Double reduction
Rear Axle, Gear ratio..........8.43:1

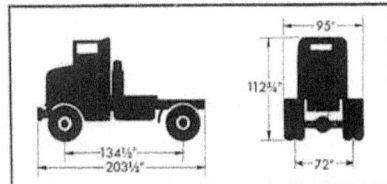

5-6 TON, 4x4 (2DT) TRACTOR AND VAN TRUCKS—STANDARD

5-6 TON, 4x4 (2DT) TRACTOR TRUCK, USED BY CORPS OF ENGINEERS

5-6 TON, 4x4 (2DT) VAN TRUCK, HAULS SIGNAL CORPS EQUIPMENT

These cab-over-engine vehicles are similar in many respects to the 4-5 Ton, 4x4, Tractor Truck.

Present production calls for open cabs, with folding windshields. One vehicle in four is provided with a Truck Mount, M36, for a machine gun.

Tires are 12.00 x 20, 14 ply, mud and snow tread, with heavy-duty tubes. Dual rear wheels are provided.

Desertization equipment includes size 14.00 x 20, 12 ply tires with heavy-duty tubes; army combat wheels with beadlock, size 10.00 CW x 20, single front and rear, and one spare tire and wheel assembly with carrier. A special radiator with built-in overflow return, a low-pressure tire gage, tire chains for driving wheels, a packless type water pump, and a speedometer correction adapter are also included.

REFERENCES—TM 9-817; MCM 10b; OCM 18889, 19107, 20100; SNL G-511.

5-6 TON, 4x4 (2DT) TRACTOR, PONTON TRUCK—STANDARD—This vehicle, supplied to the Corps of Engineers, is used to tow a semi-trailer with ponton bridge equipment. A 48-inch tool chest is mounted on the off-road side. A tread plate platform is provided across the top of the frame.

A winch of 15,000-pound capacity is mounted at the front of the vehicle. It is supported between the two side-frame rails. Power for operating the winch is transmitted from the main transmission through the power take-off unit and drive-shaft unit to the worm shaft of the winch. It is controlled by a power take-off shift lever in the cab.

5-6 TON, 4x4 (2DT), VAN TRUCK—STANDARD—This vehicle, supplied to the Signal Corps, is used to house and transport Signal Corps field installations. No winch is furnished with this model.

TYPICAL CHARACTERISTICS OF TRACTOR

Physical Characteristics
Weight (gross)...................27,120 lb.
Length....................20 ft., 6½ ins.
Width.....................8 ft., 1½ ins.
Height....................9 ft., 6½ ins.
   reducible to...............8 ft., 1 in.
Ground clearance..............10¾ ins.
Tread (center to center).......72¼ ins.
Wheelbase...................163½ ins.
Tire equipment.......12.00 x 20, 14 ply
                        (mud and snow)
   desert............: 4.00 x 20, 12 ply

Armament
Truck Mount, M36 or M61, for cal. .50
   Machine Gun, M2, HB
(On one vehicle in each four)

Performance
Maximum speed on level........47 m.p.h.
Maximum grade ability............65%
   with towed load.............40%
Trench crossing ability....1 ft., 10 ins.
Fording depth (slowest forward speed) 35½ ins.
Angle of approach..............32½°
Angle of departure...............54°
Turning radius...................35 ft.
Fuel capacity.................90 gals.

Cruising range (approx.)........270 miles
Maximum drawbar pull.........14,360 lb.
Normal towed load............20,000 lb.
Payload.....................10,910 lb.
Winch capacity..............15,000 lb.
Battery, Voltage, total...........6-12
Fire Protection...........Fire Extinguisher
Engine, Make and Model......Hercules RXC
                        (See page 108.)
Transmission, Gear ratios
First speed...................5.90:1
Second speed.................3.60:1
Third speed..................1.84:1
Fourth speed.................1.00:1
Fifth speed....................75:1
Reverse.....................7.08:1
Transfer Case, Gear ratios..1.72:1; 1.00:1
Steering Ratio........27, 23, 27:1
Suspension, Type.........Semi-elliptic
   Wheel construction.............Disk
Radiator, Type.........Fin and tube
   Capacity of system..........38 qts.
Brakes, Type.........Internal, Air
Brakes, Parking, Type............Disk
Front Axle, Type......Double reduction
Rear Axle, Gear ratio..........8.15:1

TYPICAL CHARACTERISTICS OF VAN

Physical Characteristics
Weight (gross)...................28,330 lb.
Length....................24 ft., 8¾ ins.
Width.....................8 ft., 1½ ins.
Height...................10 ft., 10¾ ins.
   reducible to............8 ft., 13/16 in.
Ground clearance..............10¾ ins.
Tread (center to center).......72¼ ins.
Wheelbase...................163½ ins.
Tire equipment.......12.00 x 20, 14 ply
                        (mud and snow)

Performance
Maximum speed on level..........47 m.p.h.
Maximum grade ability...........60%
Fording depth (slowest forward speed) 35½ ins.
Angle of approach...............57°
Angle of departure...............17°
Turning radius...................35 ft.
Fuel capacity.................90 gals.
Cruising range (approx.)........270 miles
Payload.....................11,150 lb.
(Other characteristics same as for 5-6 Ton,
   4x4 Tractor Truck.)

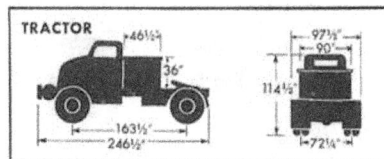

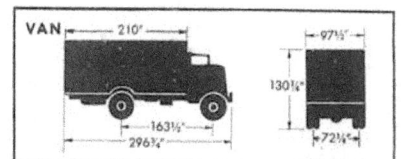

6-TON, 6x6 (4DT) TRUCK—STANDARD

6-TON, 6x6, PRIME MOVER TRUCK WILL TOW HEAVY ARTILLERY AND CARRY PERSONNEL

These trucks have a payload without towed load of 12,350 pounds, including personnel, or of 7,000 pounds with a towed load. The prime mover will pull a trailer with a gross weight of 16,500 pounds.

Military mud and snow tread tires and heavy-duty tubes are used. Wheels are of the U. S. Army standard type, single at the front and dual at the rear. One spare wheel and tire assembly is carried.

The engine is of a four-cycle, six-cylinder, in-line, liquid-cooled type. The single disk type clutch has non-shock loading and has an automatic adjustment for loss of spring pressure caused by wear.

Transmission is of selective gear type, with four speeds forward and one reverse. First and reverse gears are of spur gear type. Second, third, and fourth speeds have constant mesh helical gears, and are

engined by sliding clutches. Provision is made for power take-off on both sides.

A two-speed transfer case is used to transfer power to the front and rear axles and the winch. Levers in the driver's cab permit selection of direct or low transfer case speed, and also permit declutching the front wheels when advisable.

The truck is equipped with air-controlled service brakes on all six wheels, and has hose connections at both front and rear for towing purposes.

Present production calls for open cabs, with folding windshields and canvas, folding-type tops with side curtains. One vehicle in each four is provided with a Truck Mount, M36, for a cal. .50 Machine Gun, M2, HB. Earlier production models had closed cabs, with provision for Truck Mount, M57, M58, or M59, for one vehicle in each four.

Desertization equipment includes size 14.00 x 20, 12 ply tires with heavy-duty tubes; army combat wheels with bead-lock, size 10.00 CW x 20, single front and rear, and one spare tire and wheel assembly with carrier. Military equipment also includes a low-pressure tire gage, tire chains for driving wheels, a packless water pump and a speedometer correction adapter.

REFERENCES—TM 10-1220, 10-1221, 10-1528, 10-1529; MCM 5e; OCM 17600, 18748, 18916, 19002, 19107, 19180, 19277, 20100, 20511, 20578, 20733, 21221, 22212, 22695, 23332, 23565.

6-TON, 6x6 (4DT) TRUCK, PRIME MOVER (AA)—STANDARD—Designed for the Coast Artillery, this vehicle is used to transport heavy artillery and general cargo or personnel. It has the Army flat-bed cargo type body, with troop seats and lazy backs, and will accommodate 16 men with full field packs.

A detachable canvas top is mounted on removable bows, and is provided with roll-up straps to permit ventilation in the body, and with front and rear curtains with window flaps. The inside body dimensions are approximately 88 by 132 by 37 inches.

The wheelbase is approximately 185 inches. Tires are 10.00 x 22, 12 ply.

A winch is mounted midship. Two U. S. Army standard pintles are mounted, one on the front and one on the rear, with provisions for mounting a Universal joint type on the rear pintle mounting bracket.

The vehicle is manufactured by the White Motor Co., the Mack Mfg. Corp., and the Corbitt Company.

REFERENCES—TM 10-1220, 10-1221; MCM 5e; SNL G-512, G-526, G-535.

TYPICAL CHARACTERISTICS OF PRIME MOVER

Crew................................5

Physical Characteristics
Weight (gross), closed cab........35,250 lb.
Length........................24 ft., 1 in.
Width..............................8 ft.
Height..........................9 ft., 6 ins.
  reducible to..................7 ft., 5 ins.
Ground clearance...............10¾ ins.
Tread (center to center, rear)....72¼ ins.
Wheelbase.......................185 ins.
Tire equipment..........10.00 x 22, 12 ply
                          (mud and snow)
Armament
Truck Mount, M36, M57, M58, for cal.
  .50 Machine Gun, M2, HB
(On one vehicle in each four)

Performance
Maximum speed on level........35 m.p.h.
Maximum grade ability.............65%
Fording depth (slowest forward speed)..24 ins.
Angle of approach..................59°
Angle of departure.................47°
Turning radius......................41 ft.
Fuel capacity.....................80 gals.

Cruising range (approx.)..........300 miles
  with towed load...............250 miles
Normal towed load.............16,500 lb.
Winch capacity................25,000 lb.
Battery, Voltage, total............6-12
Fire Protection..........Fire Extinguisher
Engine, Make and Model.....Hercules HXD
Type...............In-line, liquid-cooled
No. of cylinders.....................6
Cycle................................4
Fuel (gasoline)................70 octane
Bore and stroke..........5¼ x 6 ins.
Displacement................779 cu. ins.
Compression ratio..............5.69:1

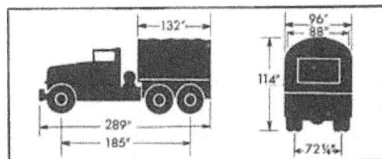

Net hp..............180 at 2,150 r.p.m.
Max. torque......556 lb.-ft., at 1,000 r.p.m.
Crankshaft rotation...........C'Clockwise
Length.......................55½ ins.
Width........................26½ ins.
Height..........................39 ins.
Weight, dry..................2,465 lb.

Transmission, Gear ratios
First speed.....................6.54:1
Second speed....................3.27:1
Third speed.....................1.76:1
Fourth speed....................1.00:1
Reverse.........................7.24:1

Transfer Case, Gear ratios.....2.55:1; 1.00:1
Suspension, Type............Semi-elliptic
  Wheel construction.................Disk
Master Clutch, Type........Single plate
Radiator, Type.........Fin and tube
  Capacity of system..............80 qts.
Brakes, Type..............Internal, air
Brakes, Parking, Type................Disk
Front Axle, Type........Double reduction
Rear Axle, Gear ratio............7.33:1

6-TON, 6x6 (4DT) TRUCK CHASSIS, SIGNAL CORPS — STANDARD — This chassis is supplied to the Signal Corps, and is used for mounting the Communication Van body, K-56. The chassis is the same as that used for the Truck, 6-ton, 6x6 Prime Mover. Wheelbase is 185 inches. Tires are 10.00 x 22, 12 ply. No winch is required. A pintle is mounted at the rear.

The chassis is manufactured by the White Motor Co., the Mack Mfg. Corp., and the Corbitt Company.

REFERENCES—TM 10-1220, 10-1221; MCM 5e.

6-TON, 6x6 TRUCK CHASSIS, CORPS OF ENGINEERS — STANDARD — This chassis is supplied to the Corps of Engineers and is used for mounting its Bridge-Erecting body. The completed vehicle is provided with a rear-mounted derrick operated by hydraulic hoists. Metal bridge sections can be quickly moved into position directly from the truck by use of the derrick.

The chassis has a wheelbase of 220 inches, and has a winch mounted at the front and a pintle at the rear. Tires are 12.00 x 20, 14 ply. Two air compressors are provided, one for the airbrakes and the other for ponton inflation.

Because the completed vehicle is so conspicuous from the air, bows and tarpaulins are provided for camouflage, and give it an appearance similar to that of a cargo truck.

The vehicle is manufactured by the Brockway Co.

REFERENCES—TM 10-1528, 10-1529; MCM 5e; OCM 20511.

CHASSIS AS SUPPLIED TO SIGNAL CORPS, SHOWN WITH OPEN CAB AND TRUCK MOUNT

CHASSIS, SIGNAL CORPS

Physical Characteristics

Length	23 ft.
Width	8 ft.
Height	9 ft., 6 ins.
reducible to	7 ft., 5 ins.
Ground clearance	10¾ ins.
Tread (center to center, rear)	72¼ ins.
Wheelbase	185 ins.

TRUCK, CORPS OF ENGINEERS

Physical Characteristics (including body)

Weight	38,850 lb.
Length (overall)	30 ft., 10 ins.
Width	8 ft., 4 ins.
Height	9 ft.
reducible to	8 ft., 8½ ins.
Ground clearance	10¾ ins.
Tread (center to center, rear)	74 ins.
Wheelbase	220 ins.

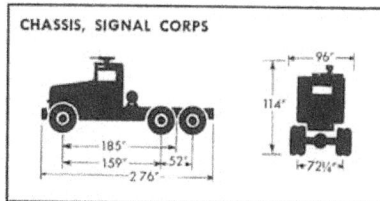

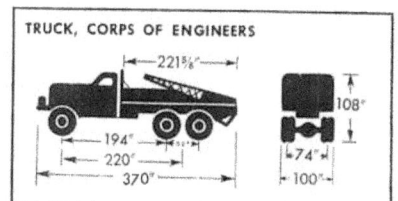

ORDNANCE DEPARTMENT SUPPLIES CHASSIS FOR ENGINEERS' BRIDGE-ERECTING TRUCK, CARRYING BRIDGE SECTIONS AND DERRICK FOR LIFTING THEM

7½-TON, 6x6 (4DT) PRIME MOVER TRUCK—STANDARD

This vehicle is used as a prime mover for heavy artillery and as a cargo and personnel carrier.

It has a payload of 15,450 pounds without towed load, and of 5,000 pounds with a towed load.

It will tow the 8 inch Howitzer, M1,
with a traveling weight of 32,000 pounds, or the 155 mm Gun, M1, with a traveling weight of 31,000 pounds.

It has a maximum grade ability of 65% without towed load. The vehicle is capable of operation over unimproved roads, trails and open, rolling and hilly cross country

with its towed load. It has a maximum speed of 31½ miles an hour with a towed load on a smooth concrete highway.

Body is of the U. S. Army standard cargo type, with inside body dimensions approximately 94 x 140 inches. Present production calls for an open type cab, with removable top and removable windshield. The left half of the windshield is hinged to swing out and fold over the right half. A Truck Mount, M36, for a cal. .30 or cal. .50 machine gun is provided with one vehicle in each four.

Tires are 12.00 x 24, 14 ply, mud and snow tread, and use heavy-duty type inner tubes. Wheels are U. S. Army standard type. Dual wheels are used at the rear. Two spare wheels and tire assemblies are provided.

Military equipment includes towing shackles on the two front corners, a brush guard and a sturdy front bumper. An Ordnance pintle, Model M–5, is furnished, together with special coupling attachments for the 8 inch Howitzer, M1, and the 155 mm Gun, M1. A special superstructure and chain fall is provided for raising and lowering gun trails to and from the coupling.

The vehicle has sealed beam type headlights and U. S. Army standard combat-zone safety lighting, together with a lighting socket for the towed load.

The front-mounted winch has a line pull capacity of 40,000 pounds.

Power is supplied by a six-cylinder, in-line, gasoline engine. A single dry disk clutch is used. The transmission has five speeds forward and one reverse, in which fifth speed is direct drive. Helical gears are used for the constant mesh, intermediate and high gears. The lower speeds employ spur gears.

A two-speed transfer case receives power from the transmission and divides it between the front and two rear axle driving units. Levers in the driver's compartment permit change of the transfer case gear ratio, and also permit declutching of the front wheels when advisable.

The vehicle has airbrakes, with a hand air-controller for the trailer brakes.

The truck is manufactured by the Mack Manufacturing Corp.

REFERENCES—TM 10-1478, 10-1479; MCM No. 19; OCM 19107, 20100.

THIS 7½-TON PRIME MOVER IS USED TO TOW HEAVY ARTILLERY AND CARRY CARGO OR PERSONNEL

TYPICAL CHARACTERISTICS

Crew...............................2

Physical Characteristics
Weight (gross)................43,570 lb.
Length..................24 ft., 8⅝ ins.
Width....................8 ft., 5¾ ins.
Height..................10 ft., 3 ins.
    reducible to............7 ft., 10 ins.
Ground clearance............13½ ins.
Tread (center to center)........76¼ ins.
Wheelbase...................156 ins.
Tire equipment........12.00 x 24, 14 ply
                        (mud and snow)

Armament
Truck Mount, M32 or M36, for cal. .50
    Machine Gun, M2, HB
(On one vehicle in each four)

Performance
Maximum speed on level........31½ m.p.h.
Maximum grade ability..............65%
Angle of approach...................35°
Angle of departure..................45°
Turning radius......................34 ft.
Fuel capacity...................160 gals.
Cruising range (approx.)........400 miles
    with towed load.............240 miles
Maximum drawbar pull.........43,200 lb.
Normal towed load............32,000 lb.
Payload......................15,450 lb.
Winch capacity...............40,000 lb.

Battery, Voltage, total............6–12

Engine, Make and Model.........Mack, EY

Type...........................In-line
No. of cylinders....................6
Cycle...............................4
Fuel (gasoline)................70 octane
Displacement..............707 cu. ins.
Bore and stroke............5 x 6 ins.
Compression.............106 at C.S.
Net hp..........156 at 2,100 r.p.m.
Max. torque....550 lb.-ft. at 750 r.p.m.
Crankshaft rotation........C'Clockwise
Length..........................53 ins.
Width.........................29½ ins.
Height.........................46 ins.

Transmission, Gear ratios
First speed....................8.05:1
Second speed..................4.57:1
Third speed...................2.61:1
Fourth speed..................1.45:1
Fifth speed...................1.00:1
Reverse.......................8.13:1

Transfer Case, Gear ratios.....2.50:1; 1.00:1

Steering Ratio.............27, 23, 27:1

Suspension, Type...........Semi-elliptic
    Wheel size.................24 x 11

Brakes, Type............Internal, air

Brakes, Parking, Type............Disk

Front Axle, Type............Front drive

Rear Axle, Gear ratio...........9.02:1

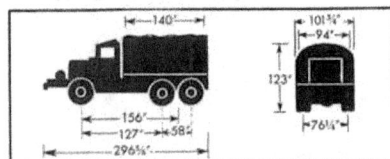

¼-TON, 2-WHEEL, AMPHIBIAN CARGO TRAILER—STANDARD

This is an all-steel, flat-bed cargo type trailer, designed to be towed by the ¼-ton, ½-ton and ¾-ton trucks, including the ¼-ton amphibian truck.

It has a gross weight of 1,050 pounds and a payload of 500 pounds. At gross weight, the trailer is capable of being towed behind a motor truck for indefinite periods, under all conditions of terrain and speeds encountered in military operations. The body is water-tight, and the trailer, with 500 pound load, will float with 6 inches freeboard.

Tires, tubes, rims and wheels are identical with those on the ¼-ton, 4x4, Truck. Approved combat-zone safety lighting is provided, current being furnished from the towing vehicle by a lighting plug connection with cable assembly.

A military type lunette, mounted at the front, is used to attach the trailer to the pintle on the towing vehicle.

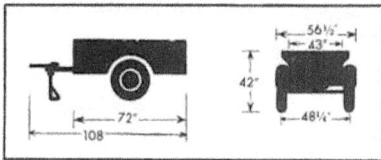

THE ¼-TON CARGO TRAILER WILL FLOAT IN WATER WITH 500 LB. LOAD

The drawbar and support assembly is adjustable in the support bracket to three positions, namely, horizontal when fully retracted, vertical when the trailer is detached, and intermediate (45°) when the angle is used as a skid. A tarpaulin cover is furnished. The trailer has a hand brake.

These trailers are manufactured by the Willys Overland Motors Co. and the American Bantam Car Co.

REFERENCES—MCM 24a; TM 10–1230; OCM 18947, 19307.

Physical Characteristics
Weight (gross)......................1,050 lb.
Length (overall) ....9 ft.
Length (inside body) ....6 ft.
Width (overall) ....4 ft., 8½ ins.
Width (inside body, top) ....3 ft., 10 ins.
Height (overall) ....3 ft., 6 ins.
Height (inside body) ....16 ins.
Ground clearance.................12½ ins.
Tread (center to center)...........48¼ ins.
Tire equipment............6.00 x 16, 6 ply

Performance
Payload...........................500 lb.
Angle of departure...................35°

2-WHEEL, 2-HORSE, VAN TRAILER—STANDARD

This is a van type, 2-wheel trailer, designed for the transportation of horses. The body, of wooden construction, is subdivided into three compartments, consisting of two longitudinal horse stalls at the rear, and a transverse groom and tack compartment at the front.

There is one door in the groom and tack compartment on the right side of the trailer, and one window in the front end of the trailer. The tail gate is designed to be usable as a ramp.

One spare wheel and tire assembly is mounted inside the body.

Electrically operated brakes are controlled from the towing vehicle.

U. S. Army standard combat-zone lighting is provided, with current supplied from the towing vehicle by means of a trailer lighting cable assembly.

The vehicles are manufactured by the Bartlett Trailer Co., the Schult Co., A. J. Miller Auto Cruiser Co., and the Porto Products Co.

REFERENCES—MCM 16a; OCM 19107.

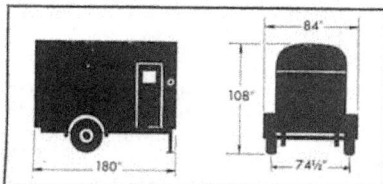

THIS TRAILER IS DESIGNED TO TRANSPORT TWO HORSES AND EQUIPMENT

Physical Characteristics
Weight (gross)....................4,700 lb.
Length (overall) ....15 ft.
Length (inside body) ....12 ft., 8 ins.
Width (overall) ....7 ft.
Width (inside body)...........4 ft., 10 ins.
Height (overall) ....9 ft.
Ground clearance.................13½ ins.
Tread (center to center)...........74½ ins.
Tire equipment.....7.50 x 16, 8 ply (highway)
Performance—Payload............2,400 lb.
Brakes, Parking, Type.............Electric

1-TON, 2-WHEEL TRAILERS—STANDARD

These trailers, with payloads of 2,000 pounds each, are capable of being towed over unimproved roads, trails, and open, rolling, and hilly cross country. They can be towed at speeds up to 18 miles per hour on average cross-country terrain, and to 50 miles per hour on smooth concrete roadway.

Tires are 7.50 x 20, mud and snow tread, using heavy-duty type tubes. Wheels are single, U. S. Army standard type, with integral rims.

A parking brake, operated by a hand-lever, is located on the right side of the trailer. U. S. Army standard combat-zone safety lighting is used.

The trailer has a standard type lunette for attaching it to the pintle of the towing vehicle. It has a detachable "A" type drawbar frame, and a standard retractable landing-wheel assembly, with a steel wheel. Fenders are provided.

Desertization equipment includes size 11.00 x 18, 10 ply tires with heavy-duty tubes, and army combat wheels with beadlocks, size 8.00 CV x 18. No fenders are required.

THIS 1-TON, 2 WHEEL, CARGO TRAILER HAS ALL WOOD BODY

THE WATER TANK MAY BE CAMOUFLAGED AS A CARGO TRAILER

1-TON, 2-WHEEL, CARGO TRAILER —STANDARD—Present production vehicles have flat-bed cargo type bodies of all-wood construction, with wooden side and end stakes. Bows and paulins are provided for covering the vehicles. Approximate inside dimensions are 45 x 96 inches, with 18 inch high wood sides and beds.

A hinged tail gate is provided at the rear of the vehicle.

These trailers are manufactured by the American Bantam Car Co., Ben Hur Mfg. Co., Century Boat Works, Checker Cab Mfg. Co., Dorsey Brothers, Gerstenlager Co., Henney Motor Co., Hercules Body Co., Highland Body Co., J. W.

Hobbs Corp., Mifflinburg Body Co., W. C. Nabors Co., Nash-Kelvinator Corp., Omaha Standard Body Corp., Pike Trailer Co., Queen City Mfg. Co., Redman Trailer Co., Steel Products Co. Inc., Strick Co., Transportation Equipment Co., Truck Engineering Corp., Willys-Overland Motors Co., Winter-Weiss Co.

REFERENCES—TM 9-883; MCM 6c; OCM 19745, 19921, 20148, 20850, 21141, 21711, 21906, 22214, 22584.

1-TON, 2-WHEEL, WATER TANK TRAILER, 250-GALLON—STANDARD —The body of this trailer consists of a standard elliptical steel tank of 250 gallon capacity. It is complete with manhole, inlet and outlet plugs, a pump, a suction hose 25 feet long, a suction hose strainer, one large and two small self-closing faucets on each side, faucet protection boxes, and necessary piping. The pump has a capacity to permit filling the tank in 20 minutes, and is of such construction that nonuse will not affect its serviceability. Bows and paulins for camouflage are provided, to give the appearance of a cargo vehicle.

The vehicles are manufactured by the Ben Hur Mfg. Co., the Checker Cab Co., and the Springfield Auto Works.

REFERENCES—TM 10-1464; MCM 6d; OCM 20252, 21463, 21588, 21754, 22382, 22702.

TYPICAL CHARACTERISTICS
1-TON CARGO TRAILER
Physical Characteristics

Weight (gross)	3,460 lb.
Length, overall	12 ft., 1½ ins.
Length, inside body	8 ft.
Width, overall	5 ft., 11⅛ ins.
Width, inside body	3 ft., 10¼ ins.
Height, overall, top up	6 ft., 1 in.
Height, inside body, top up	3 ft., 7 ins.
Ground clearance	16¼ ins.
Tread (center to center)	59 ins.
Tire equipment	7.50 x 20, 8 ply (mud and snow)
desert	11.00 x 18, 10 ply

Performance

Payload	2,000 lb.
Angle of departure	50°

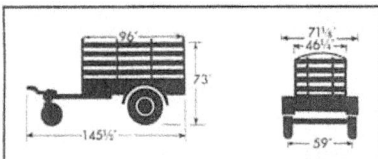

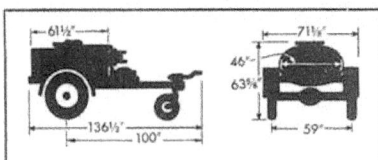

Brakes, Parking, Type | Hand

1-TON WATER TANK TRAILER
Physical Characteristics

Weight (gross)	3,390 lb.
Length, overall	11 ft., 4½ ins.
Length, inside body	5 ft., 1½ ins.
Width, overall	5 ft., 11⅛ ins.
Width, inside body	3 ft., 10 ins.
Height	5 ft., 3⅝ ins.
Ground clearance	16¼ ins.
Tread (center to center, rear)	59 ins.
Tire equipment	7.50 x 20, 8 ply (mud and snow)
desert	11.00 x 18, 10 ply

Performance

Payload	2,000 lb.
Angle of departure	50°

3- AND 3½-TON, 2-WHEEL (2DT) SEMI-TRAILERS—STANDARD

Military characteristics for the 3-and 3½-Ton, 2-Wheel (2dt) Semi-trailers call for minimum chassis weights of 2,400 pounds, and maximum fifth wheel loads, with the trailers loaded, of 4,500 pounds each.

The trailers, fully equipped and loaded, are capable of being towed over hard-surfaced roads at speeds up to 45 miles per hour. They are designed so that in any position, loaded or empty, the tractor-truck may assume a 90° angle to the semi-trailer without interference.

Tires are 7.50 x 20, truck and bus balloon, with heavy-duty tubes. Ventilated disk dual wheels are used, and are interchangeable with the wheels of the tractor-truck. Standard commercial rims are used. One spare wheel and tire assembly is carried on a bracket beneath the body.

The electrically operated brakes are controlled from the towing vehicle, and are provided with safety controls which automatically apply the brakes if the trailer is accidentally disconnected from the towing vehicle.

Current for the lights is obtained from the towing vehicle, by means of a U. S. Army standard trailer lighting cable assembly. A lower fifth wheel is supplied when specified. Support legs of either the hinge or vertical type are required. A sturdy rear bumper is provided.

REFERENCES — MCM 104b; OCM 19107, 21341, 21519.

3½-TON, 2-WHEEL STAKE AND PLATFORM SEMI-TRAILER — STANDARD— This semi-trailer, designed for all arms and services, has a stake and platform type body with removable sides and ends, mounted on a steel frame. Inside body dimensions are 79½ x 190 inches. Payload is 7,000 pounds.

Semi-trailers, conforming generally to these characteristics, are manufactured by the Black Diamond Trailer Co., Dorsey Bros., Highway Trailer Co., Hobbs Mfg. Co., Kingham Trailer Co., Strick Co., Utility Trailer Mfg. Co., Truck Engineering Corp., Winter-Weiss Co.

REFERENCES—TM 9–866A; TM 10–1391; MCM 104b.

3-TON, 2-WHEEL (2DT) VAN SEMI-TRAILER — STANDARD — Designed for all arms and services, this semi-trailer has a van type body, and has a payload of 6,000 pounds. Minimum inside dimensions are: width, 78 inches; height, 76 inches; length, 216 inches.

The vehicles are manufactured by the Black Diamond Trailer Co., Carolina Trailer Co., Checker Cab Mfg. Co., Highway Trailer Co., Kingham Trailer Co., A. J. Miller Auto Cruiser Trailer Co., Steel Products Co., Strick Co., Truck Engineering Corp.

REFERENCE—MCM 104b.

3½-TON, 2-WHEEL, STAKE AND PLATFORM SEMI-TRAILER HAS REMOVABLE SIDES

3-TON, 2-WHEEL VAN SEMI-TRAILER ON FOLDING FRONT SUPPORT LEGS

TYPICAL CHARACTERISTICS

STAKE AND PLATFORM		VAN	
Physical Characteristics		**Physical Characteristics**	
Weight (gross)	11,440 lb.	Weight (gross)	11,810 lb.
Length	16 ft., 7 ins.	Length	18 ft., 4 ins.
Width	7 ft., 3 ins.	Width	6 ft., 11½ ins.
Height	8 ft.	Height	10 ft., 7¼ ins.
Ground clearance	15½ ins.	Ground clearance	15½ ins.
Tread (center to center)	65¼ ins.	Tread (center to center)	65¼ ins.
Wheelbase—fifth wheel to rear axle	145 ins.	Wheelbase—fifth wheel to rear axle	162¾ ins.
Tire equipment	7.50 x 20, 8 ply (highway)	Tire equipment	7.50 x 20, 8 ply (highway)
Performance		**Performance**	
Maximum towing speed	45 m.p.h.	Maximum towing speed	45 m.p.h.
Payload	7,000 lb.	Payload	6,000 lb.
Brakes, Type	Electric	**Brakes,** Type	Electric

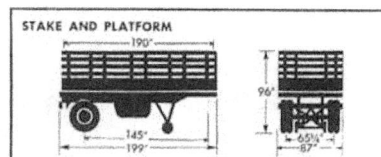

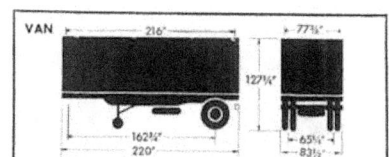

6-TON, 2-WHEEL (2DT), SEMI-TRAILERS—STANDARD

THIS VAN TYPE BODY CAN BE DISASSEMBLED FOR SHIPPING

THIS 6-TON SEMI-TRAILER CARRIES MOBILE RECORDS UNITS

These semi-trailers have payloads of 12,000 pounds each, and gross weights of approximately 20,000 pounds.

They are capable of being towed over unimproved roads, trails, and open, rolling, and hilly cross country, and can be towed on smooth concrete roadway at speeds up to 50 miles per hour.

They are so designed that when in the level and loaded position, the tractor-truck may assume a 90° angle to the semi-trailer without interference.

Tires are 9.00 x 20, 10 ply, U. S. Army standard mud and snow tread. Heavy-duty type tubes are furnished. The vehicle uses Army standard dual wheels. Rims are an integral portion of the wheels.

Compressed air operated brakes are controlled from the towing vehicle. They are provided with safety controls which will automatically apply the brakes if the trailer is accidentally disconnected from the towing vehicle.

The fifth wheel is of the semi-automatic type. Screw type support legs with hinged wheel supports and steel wheels are provided.

Desertization equipment includes size 14.00 x 20, 12 ply tires with heavy-duty tubes, and army combat wheels with beadlocks, size 10.00 CW x 20.

REFERENCES — OCM 18985, 19107, 19136, 21221, 21722; MCM 11c.

6-TON, 2-WHEEL (2DT), VAN SEMI-TRAILER — STANDARD — Designed for the Quartermaster Corps, this semi-trailer

TYPICAL CHARACTERISTICS

Physical Characteristics	Van	Mobile Records	Animal & Cargo
Weight (gross)	19,450 lb.	21,000 lb.	20,820 lb.
Length	20 ft., 8¾ ins.	22 ft., 6 ins.	24 ft., 1³⁄₁₆ ins.
Width	8 ft.	8 ft.	8 ft.
Height	10 ft., 9¾ ins.	11 ft., 3 ins.	10 ft., 6 ins.
Ground clearance	14 ins.	16½ ins.	14 ins.
Tread (center to center)	72 ins.	69 ins.	72 ins.
Wheelbase—fifth wheel to axle	193½ ins.	197 ins.	193½ ins.
Tire equipment	9.00 x 20, 10 ply (mud and snow)	9.00 x 20, 10 ply (mud and snow)	9.00 x 20, 10 ply (mud and snow)
Performance			
Angle of departure	45°	50°	50°
Payload	12,000 lb.	12,000 lb.	12,000 lb.

is used to transport general cargo. It has a van type body, with inside body dimensions of: length, 240 inches; width, 89 inches; height, 78 inches. One spare wheel and tire assembly is provided. The vehicle is equipped with a sturdy rear bumper.

These semi-trailers are manufactured by the American Body and Trailer Co., Dorsey Brothers, Gramm Truck and Trailer Corp., Highway Trailer Co., Kentucky Mfg. Co., Olson Mfg. Co., Strick Co., Timpte Brothers, Trailer Company of America, Carter Mfg. Co., and Utility Trailer Mfg. Co.

REFERENCES — TM 10-1169; MCM 11b; OCM 19107, 21722.

6-TON, 2-WHEEL (2DT), COMBINATION ANIMAL AND CARGO CARRIER —STANDARD—This semi-trailer is designed to transport eight men and eight horses, with equipment for both, including rifle and saddle racks. It is for all arms and services. Inside body dimen-

sions are: length, 281 inches; width, 90 inches; height, 88 inches.

The vehicle is manufactured by the Highway Trailer Co. and Gramm Motor Truck and Trailer Corp.

REFERENCES—MCM 21a; TM 10-1372; OCM 19107.

6-TON, 2-WHEEL (2DT), MOBILE RECORDS SEMI-TRAILER—STANDARD —This is a modification of the 6-Ton, 2-Wheel Van, Semi-trailer. It was designed for the Adjutant General's Office for mounting machine record units to be used in the theater of operations for tabulating military records. It has a van type body with minimum inside dimensions: length, 264 inches; width, 90 inches; height, 78 inches. The payload is 12,000 pounds. No spare wheel or tire is furnished.

The vehicle is manufactured by the Lufkin Foundry & Machine Co. and the Watson Automotive Equipment Co.

REFERENCES—MCM 11b; OCM 18985, 19107, 19136, 21221, 21722.

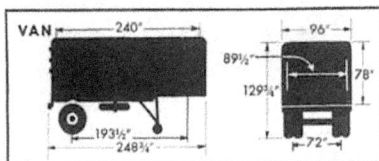

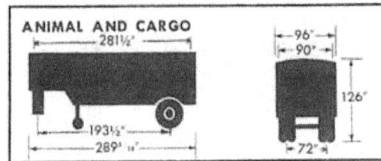

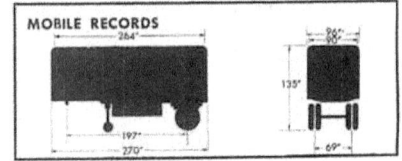

FORDING EQUIPMENT FOR VEHICLES

Successful use of fording kits for Medium Tank M4A1 and Light Tank M5 during the North African invasion prompted the development of similar kits for other vehicles normally used in landings upon enemy beaches.

By the use of these kits, the vehicles can be waterproofed to operate satisfactorily in water deeper than otherwise would be possible, permitting them to wade in from landing craft at greater distances offshore. Special attachments permit rapid jettisoning of any waterproofing equipment which interferes with satisfactory operation of the vehicles on shore.

Tanks and Tank-Like Vehicles

In sealing tanks and tank-like vehicles, all unvented openings are sealed with tape and sealing compound to render the hull watertight, after which all vented openings are extended by use of stacks and adapters.

TANK FORDING KIT T-O—This is a universal kit, containing all common materials, such as tape, paint, sealing compound, brushes, welding rod, etc., for sealing holes and cracks. It is used in connection with specialized adapter and stack fording kits.

ADAPTER AND STACK FORDING KITS LT-3 AND LT-5—These kits consist of metal adapters and stacks as required for sealing of the exhaust system and engine compartment, and canvas for sealing the air intake of particular vehicles. Kit LT-3 is used for Light Tank M3A1, and Kit LT-5 for Light Tank M5A1 and 75-mm Howitzer Motor Carriage M8. They are used in connection with the Tank Fording Kit T-O.

STACK FORDING KIT MT-S contains standard stacks and stack covers suitable for use on all M4 series medium tanks and other vehicles built on similar chassis. They are used in connection with the Tank Fording Kit T-O and an adapter fording kit or an adapter and stack fording kit.

ADAPTER FORDING KITS MT-1, MT-2, MT-3, MT-4 contain special metal adapters for attaching stacks to engine compartments of Medium Tanks M4A1, M4A2, M4A3, and M4A4 respectively.

ADAPTER AND STACK FORDING KITS SPA-7, SPA-10, AND SPA-70 contain metal adapters for attaching stacks to the engine compartments of 105-mm Howitzer Motor Carriage M7, 3-In. Gun Motor Carriage M10, and 76-mm Gun Motor Carriage M18 (T70), respectively.

Wheeled and Half-Track Vehicles; Tractors

Wheeled and half-track vehicles and tractors are prepared for fording by seal-

MEDIUM TANK WITH OPENINGS SEALED AND STACKS INSTALLED FOR FORDING

EXHAUST PIPE IN ¾-TON, 4 x 4, TRUCK

EXHAUST PIPE INSTALLED ON HALF TRACK

ing the individual components and extending air and exhaust vents above the water level.

FORDING KIT WV-6—This is a universal kit for ¼-ton to 2½-ton trucks. It contains all necessary materials such as tape, paint, flexible tubing, sealing compound, air intake hose, etc.

FORDING KIT WV-7 is a universal kit for 4-ton to 10-ton trucks.

FORDING KIT HT-1 is a universal kit for all half-track vehicles, scout cars, Light Armored Car M8, and Armored Utility Car M20.

FORDING KIT T-AC-M4 is for use on High-Speed Tractor M4.

FORDING KIT T-IHC-M5 is for use on High-Speed Tractor M5.

FORDING KIT T-AC-M6 is for use on High-Speed Tractor M6.

FORDING KIT TRV-1 contains special metal adapter and attaching parts for attaching stacks to engine exhaust system on Tank Recovery Vehicles M32 and M32B1. This kit is used in connection with T-O Fording Kit and TRV-S Fording Kit.

FORDING KIT TRV-3 contains special metal adapter and attaching parts for attaching stacks to engine exhaust system on Tank Recovery Vehicle M32B3. It is used in connection with Fording Kits T-O and TRV-S.

FORDING KIT TRV-S contains standard exhaust stacks suitable for use on Tank Recovery Vehicles M32, M32B1 and M32B3. This kit is used in connection with T-O Fording Kit and TRV-1 and TRV-3 Adapter Kits.

REFERENCES — TM 9-2853; OCM 20150, 20977, 21814, 21955, 23290, 23515.

KITS FOR AIRBORNE PREPARATION OF TRUCKS—STANDARD

1½-TON, 4x4, BOMB SERVICE TRUCK M6 COMPLETELY DISASSEMBLED AND READY FOR STOWING IN CARGO PLANE

REASSEMBLED BOMB SERVICE TRUCK, SHOWING SPLICE ON FRAME

CHASSIS OF 1½-TON, 6x6, TRUCK LOADED IN CARGO COMPARTMENT

Kits to permit the ready disassembly and reassembly of certain trucks for air transportation in C-47A airplanes to advanced bases were standardized in October 1944 following the completion of a development program based on a procedure first employed in the South Pacific theaters of war.

When these kits are used, the chassis of trucks larger than the ¾-Ton Weapons Carrier are cut at a point behind the cab, and fishplates with bolting flanges are welded to the frame where the cut has been made. The chassis can then be loaded into cargo planes and reassembled at their destination. The wood or steel bodies are also cut and are spliced together later with material provided in the kits.

In the case of trucks with closed cabs, the upper part of the cab, including the windshield, must be removed to the belt line. The windshield is then reinstalled by means of flanges welded to the pillar posts. It can thus be removed for loading.

To load the ¾-Ton, 4x4, Weapons Carrier Truck, no cutting is required except for the removal of a triangular section of metal from the platform of the driver's seat. Removal of the rear assem-bly, body, running-boards, and right bumperette permits this vehicle to be loaded into one airplane. Two 1½-ton trucks require three airplanes: one airplane for each chassis and a third for the two bodies. The 2½-ton trucks are divided into two loads, each carried in a separate airplane.

In addition to the fishplates and splicing material, each kit contains a valve and coupling unit, consisting of two valves, one union, and the necessary nipples, to prevent loss of hydraulic fluid when the brake line is separated. Each kit likewise contains tubing to connect the fuel line of the engine with a standard 5-gallon gasoline can, which serves as an auxiliary tank when the front section of a truck is being maneuvered into a plane under its own power, and also a small, single-wheel dolly to support the rear of the front section when it is being loaded in this manner. No special equipment is required for disassembly of the drive-shaft.

KIT FOR ¾-TON, 4x4, WEAPONS CAR-RIER TRUCK contains a valve and coupling unit for sealing the brake line when the rear axle is removed and a single-wheel, pneumatic-tired loading dolly.

KIT FOR 1½-TON, 4x4, CARGO TRUCK OR BOMB SERVICE TRUCK M6 contains universal fishplates for reassembling the frame, splicing material for wood or steel bodies, a valve and coupling unit to seal the brake line, tubing to connect the engine fuel line with an auxiliary fuel supply, and a single-wheel loading dolly.

KIT FOR 1½-TON, 6x6, CARGO TRUCK contains fishplates with bolting flanges, body splicing material, a valve and coupling unit for sealing the brake line, rubber tubing for the fuel line, and a load-ing dolly.

KITS FOR 2½-TON, 6x6, TRUCKS, CARGO (LWB OR SWB) OR DUMP (LWB) contain universal fishplates with bolting flanges, body splicing material, a valve and coupling unit for the brake line, tubing for the fuel line, and a loading dolly. Each kit also contains a device for compressing the right front spring.

REFERENCES — OCM 21933, 22141, 22883, 23224, 23503, 25116, 25362.

www.ingramcontent.com/pod-product-compliance
Lightning Source LLC
Chambersburg PA
CBHW062104090426
42741CB00015B/3325